AN
AUTOBIOGRAPHY OF
BLACK
CHICAGO

AN
AUTOBIOGRAPHY OF
BLACK
CHICAGO

DEMPSEY **TRAVIS**

BOLDEN

AN AGATE IMPRINT

CHICAGO

Library of Congress Catalogue Card Number : 81-53024

First Agate Bolden edition, June 2013
978-1-932841-67-1 (trade paperback)
978-1-57284-707-1 (ebook)

Printed in the United States.

Some of the material in this book appeared in *Dollars & Sense* magazine in a different form.

13 14 15 16   10 9 8 7 6 5 4 3 2 1

Bolden Books is an imprint of Agate Publishing. Agate books are available in bulk at discount prices. For more information, go to agatepublishing.com.

My wife, Moselynne, to whom I have dedicated this book, has been both patient and supportive of my writing efforts. In addition to reading and criticizing my drafts, she has permitted the author to clutter one room of the house with more than 1,500 books and several thousand news clippings. I have promised her that I will straighten the library as soon as I have finished this project. Ha! That's the same thing I said after the last project.

Contents

INTRODUCTION TO THIS
FIRST REVISED EDITION

An Autobiography of Black Chicago

IN ORDER TO HAVE A FULL UNDERSTANDING OF HOW THE BLACK community fits into Chicago's urban mosaic, it's necessary to understand the intersection between race relations, politics, and business. *An Autobiography of Black Chicago* understands exactly that. Dempsey Travis clearly grasped how the history of those three elements contributed to making the Chicago of the 1980s what it was.

When this book was first published in 1981, it gave me and many others a bird's-eye view of the black Chicago that we'd only heard about from either our grandparents or an assortment of aunts and uncles who by that time had joined the ranks of community elders. Dempsey Travis put many of those stories into proper perspective by documenting actual events. His personal story and family history illustrate the kind of grit it took to make it in Chicago at the dawn of the twentieth century. In short, I concluded that this book was a well-researched, very interesting piece of literature that was also a great read.

I first met Dempsey Travis in the late seventies and I was a bit intimidated by his presence. He had a hearty laugh and a wicked sense of humor, but he was also a bare-knuckled brawler when it came to business and politics. I was very careful not to offend. Jazz music was where we found common ground. He was a former musician and self-styled jazz historian. I was a young disc jockey at the time and had the good fortune of occasionally filling in for famed jazz radio personality Daddy-O Daylie. He and Dempsey were good friends and that gave me credibility.

Each time I interviewed him on my own radio show, he talked about why he decided to write books about his own people. One of his most memorable quotes was, "If we don't tell our own story, we may look up one day in the distant future and Duke Ellington will be white." His view was that African Americans had to be very committed to telling their own story, and he believed this kind of information could be especially beneficial to black students. It would give them a sense of the enormity of the struggle that black Chicagoans faced and how they managed to survive and even thrive. It might even go a long way toward instilling a sense of pride and purpose in their lives.

I'm sure that's what Mr. Travis would want. He and I had a number of conversations that focused not only on the past, but also on his vision for the future. He knew that he was truly blessed to have attained substantial wealth, a loving wife of fifty years, and the fulfillment he got from having played a significant role in the civil rights movement of the sixties. He felt that by writing this book, he was contributing something meaningful, helpful, and lasting for Chicago's black community. By writing this history from an insider's point of view, he clearly met those objectives.

—Richard Steele

Chicago

2013

Richard Steele is an award-winning host and correspondent for WBEZ Chicago Public Media, where he contributes interviews and reports to Eight Forty-Eight, The Afternoon Shift, World View, Morning Edition, All Things Considered, wbez.org, vocalo.org, *and special programming. Since joining WBEZ in 1987, he has hosted a number of acclaimed programs. Before joining WBEZ, he hosted many successful radio programs on other Chicago stations, WVAZ, WGCI, WBMX, WVON, WJPC, and WGRT. He has served as a board member of the local American Federation of Television and Radio Artists and the Chicago Association of Black Journalists.*

FOREWORD

I BECAME AN ARDENT ADMIRER OF THE AUTHOR OF THIS IMPOR-
tant contribution to black autobiographical writing during the seventies
as I read his occasional articles in *The Black Scholar*. I was especially
impressed by a frank but forward-looking discussion in the February 1974
issue, "Can Black Builders and Bankers Survive?" Here was an "insider" talking without condescension to a public not familiar with the intricacies of
high finance and making complex matters plain while stating a strong case for
sympathy and understanding of industries that are often "scapegoated." At the
same time, he was telling his colleagues what they needed to do if they wanted
the confidence and support of the black masses. The article taught me things
about money and about black institutions seeking to control and channel
some of it, both for private profit and social development, that I should have
learned when Cayton and I were revising *Black Metropolis* in 1970 and didn't.
Of the fifty-two contributing and advisory editors of this journal of black
studies and research, Dempsey Travis has the distinction of being the only
businessman among them. That, in itself, makes him unique, a banker with
serious scholarly interests and a flair for lucid communication. Everything he
writes has relevance and is marked by clarity.

I had known of the author as a man of great talent and outstanding promise long before I began to read the *Black Scholar* articles, however, because he
is a graduate of Roosevelt University of Chicago, an institution where I taught
sociology and anthropology for over two decades. I knew he had gone on to
Northwestern for graduate work and had then become greatly concerned with

the problem of trying to make adequate housing available for black people in Chicago, in any area they wanted to live in, at prices that were not exorbitant. Before "Black Power" became a slogan he was seeking ways to achieve some of it, was succeeding and teaching others. I have tried to follow the careers of Roosevelt graduates who were making substantial contributions to black liberation and to the solutions of economic, political, educational, and cultural problems throughout the black world. They scatter across a wide spectrum from left to right. Some years ago, alumnus James Forman of SNCC fame wrote an autobiography, *The Making of Black Revolutionaries*. Now Dempsey Travis presents us with a book that might well have as a subtitle, *The Making of a Progressive Black Banker*. I consider it a privilege to have the opportunity of writing a foreword to it. If we are to "overcome" we need entrepreneurial skill of a high order combined with honesty and social concern within specific personalities as well as militant protest leadership—and every conceivable kind of professional, semi-professional, and artisan competence, too. I have always been influenced by a scriptural quotation my preacher-father liked to use, "Wisdom is justified of all her children." Hopefully, this book will make the author a role model for some young people seeking their place in the ongoing struggle for a piece of the action in this complex American milieu, and who will take to heart the quotation from Paul Robeson he uses to make his social commitment clear.

The making of this book was, for its author, a labor of love, inspired by his warm family relations, a host of loyal friendships, and his commitment to the welfare of black people of every clime and condition. The many hours of reading, interviewing, sifting and sorting of data, reflection, and writing that went into this chronicle of his own life in relation to the black community's life, are a testimony to unusual dedication and discipline. Always busy, as he was, with the affairs of Travis Realty Company, as well as the United Mortgage Bankers of America, Dempsey Travis managed to conserve enough time to design and complete this work whose "Notes and Documentation" and list of "Voices From the Past and Present" reveal the full dimensions of the task. He was determined to pay tribute to unsung pioneers and quiet heroes in black families and institutions, distinguished leaders and role models, some now passed away, and others still bearing the burden and the heat of the day. And he has not forgotten the few rare individuals of the other race who gave encouragement and support to black people, especially a former teacher, Mary Herrick. He can say proudly, "mission accomplished."

The author gives us a guided tour of Black Chicago through time and constantly expanding space, calling our attention to landmarks, human and physical; reminding us of crucial historical turning points; introducing us to makers of history, living and dead, letting them tell us their stories in their own words. His synthesis of data in the prologue, *Before My Time*, is a fascinating presentation distilled from a mass of historical detail that evokes the spirit of a past that should not be forgotten.

Dempsey Travis has intuitively mastered a technique of research and presentation that I had to be trained in by anthropologists at the University of Chicago, what we call "participant-observation." He has lived a full, creative, useful life, with his eyes wide open, his ears attuned, and ever-ready to listen as well as to ask questions. Acting constantly, but observing all the while, thinking all the while, reacting sensitively all the while. And then, withdrawing occasionally to think about it and write about it. Now he has shared some of that life with us, thereby enriching ours. We appreciate his decision to share what he has found out about our world with us.

—*St. Clair Drake*

PALO ALTO, CALIFORNIA

AUGUST 27, 1981

Dr. Drake is professor emeritus, department of anthropology, Stanford University, former chairman of the program in African and Afro-American Studies, and author (with Horace Cayton) of Black Metropolis: A Study of Negro Life in a Northern City *(1945, revised 1962, 1970) and* Race Relations in a Time of Rapid Social Change.

PUBLISHER'S NOTE TO THIS
AGATE BOLDEN EDITION

I FIRST BECAME AWARE OF DEMPSEY J. TRAVIS AND HIS REMARK-
able career—businessman, musician, activist, publisher, and author—
when I came to Chicago in the mid-eighties. I met the man once, in the
mid-2000s; I sought him out because of my interest in his work, and visited
with him briefly in his Chatham offices. After his death in 2009, the agent
Lynette McMillon, representing Travis's estate, contacted me about whether
Agate would be interested in republishing any of Travis's many books. This
revised edition of *An Autobiography of Black Chicago* is the first of his books
to return to print, and the first in Agate's new Bolden Lives series of memoirs,
autobiographies, and biographies by African Americans.

Travis had a remarkable life that afforded him an important perspective
on the lives of African Americans in general and black Chicagoans in particular. As someone whose family lived in Chicago before and through the
period of the Great Migration of African Americans from the South to the
major industrial cities of the North, he saw first-hand how this influx shaped
Chicago. As a jazz musician, he was deeply involved in this most significant
of American cultural movements, and was an active performer and band
leader during the period when "swing" jazz became America's most popular
music—as led principally by a new generation of white musicians and band
leaders. As a civil rights leader, he played a significant role in the rise of the
(Southern-based) civil rights movement in Chicago. And as a businessman—
in particular, a real estate professional—he had immediate knowledge of how
African Americans' fortunes were distorted by deep-dyed patterns of injustice

in the housing market. His personal testimony of his experiences is fresh and immediate, even thirty years later.

The book has been altered from its original form as published by Travis's own Urban Research Press in 1981. This is not a scholarly edition, or a re-evaluation of Travis, but an attempt to bring his important work back to light. Unfortunately, Agate and the Travis estate were unable to recover the many original drawings, photographs, and charts that illustrated this book's first edition. The book has also been abridged to focus it on Travis's own story and recounting of the history in which he and his family took part. There have also been a few slight changes to the editorial style and punctuation of the book as originally published. We at Agate are proud to bring this important work back into print.

—*Doug Seibold*
Chicago
2013

There can be no greater tragedy than to forget one's origin and finish despised and hated by the people among whom one grew up. To have that happen would be the sort of thing to make me rise from my grave.

—Paul Robeson, 1938

Before My Time

H E WAS EIGHTEEN YEARS OLD, A TALL, BROAD-SHOULDERED young man with a habitual half smile. The brightness of his eyes and the slightly defiant tilt to his black derby hat were the only signs he gave that he was embarking on the biggest adventure of his life.

Louis Travis was traveling from Georgia via Memphis, Tennessee, to Chicago. He would not be going back.

It was June 1, 1900, and Louis was only vaguely aware that he was participating in the beginning of the greatest mass migration in American history, as blacks fled the South to seek jobs and self-respect in the cities of the North. Some 1.5 million blacks have made the same journey to Chicago in the eighty years since Louis Travis's journey.

Louis's two older brothers had gone before him. From one of them he had had word that there was a job for him as a strikebreaker, working construction at the Mandel Brothers' department store in the Loop. More and more Chicago companies were beginning to bring in blacks as strikebreakers. For their part, blacks, like the Travis brothers, accepted the work because, since they were barred from most unions, it was the only opportunity they had for a better life.

This was the very first time the young man in the faded green box-back suit had ever ridden a train. It turned out to be a bad trip. The train's swaying motion as it rushed and clattered over the Tennessee farmland combined with the heat and Louis' excitement and produced a predictable result: he got sick. He started vomiting within a half hour after the train pulled out of the Memphis station.

The elderly black car porter became alarmed and went to get a white doctor from the train's Pullman section. The doctor took Louis' temperature and then pressed both sides of his stomach firmly with his huge hands while the young man stared at him gravely. He peered into his eyes and mouth and then handed him two giant yellow pills.

"This boy will be all right if he can lie down and get some sleep," the doctor said, turning to the porter.

The porter scratched his head. It wasn't going to be that simple. The only place for a colored person to lie down was in the aisle of the Jim Crow coach, but the "colored section" was so tightly packed that that was out of the question.

The porter finally went to ask "George," the Pullman porter, if Louis could sleep in his berth in the small smoking room of the white folks' Pullman coach. "George" wasn't really his name, of course: it was really a slave tag that indicated he was the "boy" of his employer, in this case George Mortimer Pullman. "George" was reluctant to give up his bed, but the older man was firm.

So Louis Travis spent a night of unheard-of comfort and privilege in the Pullman porter's bed. And he wasn't so sick that he didn't use that occasion to learn about another face of Jim Crow.

Jim Crow laws dictated what washrooms and drinking fountains blacks were supposed to use, but he never suspected that there was a mandatory requirement by the Pullman Company for black porters to sleep under old blankets and faded sheets that had been dyed blue in order to avoid integrating the colored linen with that was to be used "for white bodies only."

Louis Travis later learned that the president of the Pullman Company that published the "for white bodies only" linen instructions was Robert Todd Lincoln, the son of the martyred President Abraham Lincoln. The 12th Street Station where Travis began his urban odyssey was the same Chicago train station to which President Lincoln's body had been transported before being placed aboard Pullman's "Pioneer" coach for the final journey to Springfield, Illinois.

On the morning of June 2, 1900, Louis Travis was watching the hot, white steam gush from the black steam pipes of the engine of the New Orleans and Vestibule Limited as he clutched his few belongings and prepared to enter the city he had been dreaming of after months of planning.

Looking north from the 12th Street Station, he got a breathtaking view of row after row of three-story mansions, with hundreds of windows sparkling in the morning sun. The tallest building in the city was the seventeen-story Auditorium Hotel, presently the home of Roosevelt University.

But he was not heading north. Instead, he walked west to catch the southbound State Street cable car. As he walked, he began to notice the foul odor that was rolling in on a northeast wind from the Union Stockyards, about five and three-quarters miles southwest of the train terminal.

That was the direction Louis was heading: down to the "Black Belt" of Chicago, at 3715 Butterfield (Federal) Street.

But even as he noted the growing pervasiveness of the stockyards odor and the increasingly squalid appearance of the housing as the cable car headed south, he could feel his face breaking into a smile. It was a bright sunny day, and he was young. If he had met up with a shameful crust of impersonal discrimination on his trip to the North, he had also discovered friendship and concern. He had found some strength in himself as well. And he had folks waiting for him at the end of the journey.

Whatever challenges and opportunities Chicago had in store for the black man, Louis Travis was going to participate in them. It was his city now.

CHAPTER 1

Beginnings

WHEN MY FATHER, LOUIS TRAVIS, ARRIVED IN CHICAGO IN 1900, he found a city that had little experience with racial animosity. With only a small black population, Chicago was still fairly open in its dealings with blacks. All that, though, was beginning to change as the importation of Southern blacks into the city accelerated. Where blacks and Caucasians had been able to live and work together in relative harmony, white folks would begin to perceive blacks as a threat, and housing segregation by race and class would become rigid and cruel as the numbers increased.

In 1900, blacks lived in all thirty-five wards of the city. Their numbers were large enough to constitute a community in eight wards.

The Travis family lived in the south section of the 4th Ward. Its unsightly houses, dirty alleys, and pitted and littered streets emphasized a general shabbiness. A snowfall was the only cosmetic that ever alleviated this drabness.

Well-to-do and highly educated black people shared this environment with poorer folks. Attorney John G. Jones, the nephew of the late tailor John Jones, lived next door to my family at 3717 Butterfield (Federal) Street, and conducted his law practice from room number four at 194 South Clark Street. The Autumn Club, the "in" place for the literary and social set, met each month at 3623 Butterfield Street.

For myself, class mixing would later have great benefits because it would expose me to an educational and economic dimension that would lead to a higher intellectual life in the middle of a physically depressing environment. But my maternal grandmother had already long understood that such a thing was possible. She used to tell her children, "You can learn something on the hottest day in the cotton field if you open your mind, eyes, and ears."

My father had been in Chicago less than two months when he attended the First Bible class held at Rev. Reverdy C. Ransom's newly opened Institutional Church and Social Settlement House at 3825 South Dearborn Street. It was July 24, 1900. The large brick building had been known as the Railroad Chapel when the area was occupied by white Irish Catholics who came into Chicago as railroad employees.

The settlement house could seat more than 1,200 in its main auditorium. It also had eight community rooms, a dining room, a kitchen, and a gymnasium. The well-equipped gym in the basement offered the first structured, racially integrated physical education programs in Chicago outside of the public school system. The settlement house got encouragement and support from Jane Addams of Hull House, the Rev. Graham Taylor of Chicago Commons, and Mary McDowell of the University of Chicago Settlement. The community rooms were used daily to study social literature and remedies for ethnic problems. In other rooms of the building young boys between eight and seventeen were being taught to read. Black and white working mothers were permitted to leave their young children in the daycare center for five cents a day.

Institutional House was an American prototype for the NAACP, the Urban League, and the Colored YMCA and YWCA. Dr. W.E.B. DuBois wrote that Rev. Reverdy C. Ransom's speech in 1906 at the second meeting of the Niagara Movement at Harpers Ferry did more to inspire the eventual founding of the National Association for the Advancement of Colored People than any other single event.

My father was one of twenty-two young men in the Institute's Bible class. Among the others in attendance were Oscar DePriest and Louis B. Anderson, who later distinguished themselves in Chicago politics—DePriest as Illinois' first black congressman, and Anderson as a Chicago alderman. The teacher of the Bible class was Mose Hardwick, a sixty-five-year-old ex-slave.

Hardwick was familiar with all of the books of the Bible and was a self-taught authority on the history of black people in Chicago. He was a tall, friendly man with the physique of a prizefighter and the strong features of a W.E.B. DuBois.

My father asked Hardwick to help him learn more about the city. Hardwick asked my father to visit him and his family in their home at 2949 South

Dearborn Street. Prior to moving there, they lived at 211 Third Street in downtown Chicago. Their present home was just a couple of doors north of Bethel A.M.E. Church, where Rev. Ransom was pastor from 1896 to 1900. Hardwick invited several other young men from the church, who were also newcomers to Chicago.

Hardwick's introductory lesson on Chicago was very graphic and one my father never forgot. I haven't either.

From maps on easels he had placed along the south wall of his very small parlor, he pointed out the Chicago River and Lake Michigan and a small house on the north bank of the Chicago River labeled "DuSable House, 1779" and "Kinzie House, 1804." "Jean Baptiste Point DuSable exercised the first ownership of real estate within the present limits of the City of Chicago," Hardwick said. "His claim to ownership was based not on federal tenure or purchase from the lord of the manor or holder of eminent domain, but by allodial tenure, that is, by right of the plow."

A 1779 British Army report described DuSable as a "tall, handsome, muscular built frontiersman who displayed great talents as a barterer. He was either a black freedman or a fugitive slave from Kentucky. He was intelligent, well educated, genteel mannered (his home was filled with fine, imported furnishings and paintings) and sufficiently American to have been arrested by the British. DuSable was married to a Potawatomi Indian named Catherine, and they had two children."

In 1800, DuSable sold his Chicago real estate and personal property to a white Frenchman named Jean La Lime of St. Joseph for 6,000 livres. Items in the sale were a wooden house, which measured forty by twenty-two feet, one horsemill, one pair of millstones, one bake house, a smokehouse, a dairy, a workshop, two barns, a large number of tools, household goods, furniture, thirty head of cattle, two spring calves, thirty-eight hogs, two mules, and forty-four hens. DuSable's house and chattel is prima-facie evidence that he was not simply a trader passing through the night; he was Chicago's founder in that he was its first landed proprietor. La Lime subsequently sold the DuSable House to John Kinzie in 1804. Kinzie, the first white American to establish a domicile in Chicago, fled the city in 1812 after stabbing Jean La Lime to death.

DuSable moved to East Peoria, Illinois, with a group of Potawatomi Indians and died sometime later at the home of an old friend, Glamorgan, who lived in St. Charles, Missouri, according to Hardwick.

Hardwick next directed his students' attention to a second easel, where he had placed a map that was dated 1830 and highlighted the south bank of the Chicago River. There, he pointed out a garrison called Fort Dearborn. Subjects identified in the general vicinity of the Fort were a wash-house, well shop, barn, garden for the garrison, and a little further south, near the mouth of the river, a U.S. Factors House. The third map in the room, dated 1840, outlined Chicago's new city limits which extended south to 22nd Street, west to Ashland Avenue, and north to North Avenue.

The total population of the city in 1840 was 4,417, of which 53 were blacks, a decrease of 24 from the 77 blacks included in the 1837 census. The 1837 count has been interpreted by some historians to mean that the count may have included fugitive slaves awaiting passage to a safe haven in Canada.

Hardwick emphasized that Chicago was the western center of the abolition movement and one of the most important stations of the Underground Railroad. Abolition activities were boldly described in ads appearing in Chicago-based abolitionist newspapers such as the *Western Citizen* and the *Western Herald.*

Only one of the seventy-seven blacks in Chicago at the time it was incorporated in 1837 appeared to be an owner of real property. However, the local census of 1844 reflected 155 free blacks in Chicago, which included 5 black real estate owners. Their properties were all located in the original 1st and 2nd Wards of the city in downtown Chicago on the following streets: Lake, Madison, Fifth Avenue (Wells), and two parcels on the corner of Clark and Harrison Streets and at Buffalo (Federal) and Harrison Streets.

Black realty ownership increased from five to ten parcels between 1844 and 1847. The additional 5 properties were also located in the original 1st and 2nd Wards. The Fugitive Slave Law of 1850 compelled many Chicago blacks to flee to Canada and dispose of their property at great sacrifice. The result was a net reduction in black property owners from ten in 1847 to seven in 1850, as revealed in the census of that year.

The 1850 census showed that John Jones, a black tailor, was the owner of property that had a value of $1,500. This was a significant economic achievement.

Jones had arrived in Chicago five years earlier from Greene County, North Carolina, via Memphis, Tennessee, and Alton, Illinois, with his wife and the total sum of $3.50. After pinching every penny of that $3.50 to furnish his house, he had to pawn his watch to purchase two heating stoves, one for his house and the other for his tiny tailor's shop. His rented one-room cottage was located on the northeast corner of Madison Street and Fifth Avenue (Wells).

Jones' original tailor shop was six and a half by thirty feet and was located at what will be the Clark Street entrance to the new State of Illinois Building, scheduled to be completed in 1983. For groceries he was extended $2 in credit by a black man named O.C. Hanson.

Jones became the undisputed business and civil rights leader for blacks in Illinois. As the leading black abolitionist in the state, he met and corresponded with John Brown and Frederick Douglass as well as Joseph Medill, editor of the *Chicago Tribune*, and Republican leaders such as Governor Richard Yates and Cook County Senator Francis Eastman. John Jones understood that freedom for wealthy and influential blacks was impossible without recognition of equality for all blacks. Ensconced in the surroundings of his merchant tailoring business for the Chicago elite, he was quoted in the Friday, January 2, 1874, edition of the *Chicago Tribune*: "We must have our civil rights; they must not be withheld from us any longer; they are essential to our complete freedom."

Jones' life-long battle for civil rights enabled him to become the first black to hold an elective office in Cook County and in the State of Illinois. Jones became a Cook County commissioner in 1871. Jones used a smooth rhetoric, black ink, and green bucks in a continuing battle against Illinois' "Black Laws." His victorious struggle made him the first effective black civil rights and business leader in the history of the state.

The "Black Laws" deprived black people of the right to testify in courts or to purchase property; moreover, blacks were taxed for public schools they could not use. A constitutional revision in 1847 prohibited free blacks from settling in Illinois and also prevented slave owners from bringing them into the state in order to free them.

The "Black Laws" were repealed on February 7, 1865, a political victory which can be attributed to John Jones' leadership. It had a heartening effect on black migrants coming into Illinois.

Before the Great Chicago Fire of 1871, Jones' real estate improvements were valued at $100,000. Included in his real estate holdings was the northeast corner of Madison and Dearborn Streets, commonly known as 119 Dearborn Street.

John Jones' contribution to the black community and to the city certainly merits the placing of his name on a school or public building. This honor had not been bestowed upon him as of 1981, 102 years after his demise, though there is a common impression that Jones Commercial High School is named for him. In fact, the school was named after a William Jones, who served as president of the Board of Education from April 11, 1840, to April 26, 1843, and again from April 26, 1851, to April 10, 1852. In 1857, William Jones established a fund of $1,000 for Jones students who could not afford the cost of textbooks. These were the first free textbooks in the Chicago public schools.

The day after John Jones' death in 1879, the *Chicago Tribune* reported that he had been the most prominent black citizen of the city. No single black to this date has been endowed with the overall power displayed by John Jones during his thirty-four years in Chicago. Jones' business was continued until 1906 by his son-in-law, Lloyd G. Wheeler, first black to pass the Illinois Bar and the grandfather of Lloyd G. Wheeler, III, the current president of the Supreme Liberty Life Insurance Company.

There is no reliable data on black property owners between 1854 and 1860. However, the 1860 census reveals that there were thirty-five black property owners in Chicago. The values of these properties ranged from $100 to $17,000. The John Jones real estate fortune escalated in the ten years between 1850 and 1860 from $1,500 to $17,000, compared to the more normal increase, for example, in the real estate investments of Maria Smith, a washerwoman, whose holdings rose only 150 percent from $1,000 in 1850 to $2,500 in 1860. Jones' real estate holdings were valued at $100,000 in 1870.

The Great Fire of 1871 stopped at Harrison Street, and only a small percentage of the black community was burned. However, another fire in 1874 started at 449 South Clark Street on the afternoon of July 14 and continued to burn in a northeasterly direction for twenty-four hours. The fire covered forty-seven acres. Eight hundred and twelve buildings were gutted at an estimated loss of $2,850,000.

The burned area included 85 percent of the black-owned property in the city.

The fire was the second major setback in realty ownership for Chicago blacks in less than twenty-five years, the first being the exodus caused by the Fugitive Slave Law of 1850.

The 1874 fire burned down and closed an era of black realty ownership in the area now known as the South Loop (Dearborn Park). The movement south of 16th Street into the 2nd, 3rd, and 4th Wards is reflected in the distribution of blacks by wards in 1880, 1890, and 1900. (The ward boundaries were the same in 1870, 1880, 1890, and 1900.)

Data on black housing for the sixteen years after the fire of 1874 are missing, but the 1890 census showed an increase of 208 colored owners of area real estate from 39 in 1870 to 247 in 1890.

Louis Travis' history lesson introduced him to a city that had offered a mixed reception to blacks. On the one hand, it had had a strong abolitionist tradition; on the other, blacks were hardly welcomed into full participation in the city's economic life. Nevertheless, there were signs of encouragement and movement. John Jones' political success as a Cook County commissioner in 1871 created an acceptance for blacks in politics somewhat akin to the climate generated by Jackie Robinson's baseball success in 1947. The first black police officer was appointed in 1872, and, later in the same year, a nine-man black fire company was commissioned by Mayor Joseph Medill. In 1876, John W. E. Thomas, a lawyer whose office was located at 181 Third Avenue, became the first black to be elected to the Illinois House of Representatives.

Another young lawyer, Ferdinand L. Barnett, founded the *Chicago Conservator*, Chicago's first black newspaper, in 1878.

These were the beginnings. The frontier still had openings.

CHAPTER 2

The Early 1900s:
Time of Change

C HICAGO'S SOCIAL PATTERNS BEGAN TO CHANGE UNDER THE
impact of growing immigration of Southern blacks. While black
Chicagoans of an earlier generation can still recall a relatively easy,
hostility-free mixing of the races in early Chicago, accelerated black recruit-
ment quickly changed all that.

The housing community had not been organized like the trade unions to
exclude the black workers by ritual or constitution, and consequently blacks
had been able to live in just about any area of the city. For example, the Joseph
Millers, who were the parents of Lovelyn Evans, lived at 4015–4017 Broadway for years, operating a large warehouse business at that address, the Millers Buena Park Fireproof Warehouse and Moving Company. Joseph Miller
employed a crew of thirty workmen composed of Swedes, Poles, blacks, and
Germans. Oneida Daniels Woodard and her parents lived at 315 Webster Avenue in the Lincoln Park area from 1908 to 1918. At the south end of town,
on 72nd and Vincennes, lived the Oscar Freeman family, who shared a three-
flat walk-up with white families without conflict.

Although black people in 1900 represented only 1.9 percent or 30,150
out of a city population of 1,698,575, the competition for urban space and
jobs with whites, especially recent European immigrants, quickly became a
threatening problem.

It was during this time that the managements of many businesses in Chicago began to recognize that hiring Southern blacks could be a strategic move
in their conflict with the unions. Blacks represented an almost inexhaustible

supply of cheap labor. Other groups, like Polish immigrants, had been exploited in the same way, of course, but the hostility of white labor unions
toward blacks offered employers the added attraction of deflecting some of
the animosity away from themselves.

Louis Travis' youngest brother, Joseph, was recruited in Atlanta by a
stockyards headhunter and shipped to Chicago by train with several hundred
other young blacks to break the stockyards strike of 1904. Uncle Joe and hundreds of other strikebreakers were smuggled into the stockyards the evening
of the same day that the regular white employees laid down their tools and
walked out.

The press constantly spotlighted the activities of black strikebreakers, in-
tensifying racial animosity. In fact, it was considered a plus for corporate-labor
relations to ship blacks back South on special trains after a strike was broken.
A sad irony of the American labor movement is that the racism of the labor organizations allowed management to keep black and white workers separated
and mutually hostile, weakening the power of the unions and prolonging the
struggle for improved working conditions and higher wages for all workers.

Living far south or north in the city was not convenient for the blacks
who were recruited to Chicago to work in the stockyards or factories located
south of the Loop. Proximity to the job was important because of travel time
on both the cable cars and streetcars. The new influx of blacks in search of
housing west of State Street forced the early black settlers to seek better accommodations east of State.

A white Unitarian minister, Mrs. Celia Parke Wooley, tried unsuccessful-
ly to rent a house on Wabash Avenue for an interracial community center. She
then purchased a house at 3032 South Wabash Avenue in 1903. Ida B. Wells
had outlined a proposal for such a center four months earlier at a meeting
held at Hull House. Within eight months after the center's opening, the first
black family moved into the 3100 block on Wabash. Between 1904 and 1912
the black population on Wabash Avenue between 31st and 39th increased
from .05 percent in 1904 to 100 percent in 1912. Between 39th and 47th on
Wabash the black population was approximately 50 percent by 1917.

The block-by-block racial transition was costly to both the white seller
and the black buyer. The loss to sellers could vary from $50,000 to $350,000
per block depending upon the price and quality of the average house or apartment building in the block. On the other hand, the real estate speculator who

urged the seller to move out and packaged the blacks who moved in realized as a profit the seller's loss plus an override of 10 to 50 percent, subject to market demands.

As a very young man in 1915, William Y. Browne, currently president of Riley-Browne Real Estate Company, observed brightly-colored handbills being passed out by employees of Frederick H. Bartlett and Company of 69 West Washington Street. The handbills carried a propaganda message advising whites to sell because a black invasion of the neighborhood was imminent. Hitler's Goebbels could not have prepared the troops better. The appearance of the first blacks in an all-white block triggered a response that caused the whites to treat them as invading enemy aliens.

Such a reception was received by the family of "de Lawd," better known as Richard B. Harrison, who played "The Lord" in *Green Pastures* on Broadway. The Harrison family became the first visible black buyer of real estate in the all-white section of Grand Boulevard (King Drive) when they purchased 3624 Grand Boulevard in March 1918. Blacks had lived on South Park Avenue in the 3400 block prior to moving to the 3600 block on Grand in 1919. After two bombings in May 1919, the Harrisons moved out in mid-June.

The three-story, fourteen-room, four-bath mansion was purchased for $8,000 by Attorney Ferdinand L. Barnett and Ida B. Wells Barnett, the parents of Alfreda Duster. The Barnetts were the first black family in the 3200 block on Rhodes, where Mrs. Duster was born in 1904. However, by 1917, Rhodes was 75 percent black between 31st and 39th Streets. According to Mrs. Duster, the family lived at 3234 South Rhodes for over fifteen years without any major incidents.

In 1919, blacks flanked Grand Boulevard on the west on Calumet between 31st and 39th and Vernon on the east. Both areas were about 85 percent black. Whites violently resisted surrendering Grand Boulevard; it represented a prominence and a golden era they did not want to forget. Gone were the days when Grand Boulevard would be the thoroughfare for the thousands of expensive carriages that augustly transported the rich and super-rich to the racetrack south of Washington Park, an eighty-acre plot located between South Park and Cottage Grove Avenue from 61st to 63rd Street. Washington Park Racetrack was moved to its present location in Homewood in 1908. This affected the South Side commercially; however, the area had already begun to decline at the close of the 1893 World's Fair.

After war was declared in 1917, the influx of Southern blacks to Chicago was overwhelming—to the point that blacks constituted 20 percent of the workers in the meat-packing industry in 1918, compared to 3 percent in 1909.

Many black professionals and business pioneers living in the South watched their clients board the Jim Crow cars of the New Orleans and Vestibule Limited heading north and then decided themselves to get on board the train going to Abe Lincoln's city on the lake.

The founders and officers of Supreme Life Insurance Company, the largest black-owned insurance company in the North today, all came out of the South: Frank L. Gillespie, founder, born in Osceola, Arkansas, in 1876; Harry Herbert Pace, president, born in Covington, Georgia, January 6, 1884; Truman Kella Gibson, Sr., treasurer, born in Macon, Georgia, August, 1882; W. Ellis Stewart, secretary, born in Columbus, Indiana, 1892; Dr. M.O. Bousfield, vice president and medical director, born in Tipton, Missouri, August 22, 1885. (Blacks were treated with the same Jim Crow attitude and restrictions in Columbus, Indiana, as they were in Columbus, Georgia.) Robert S. Abbott, who founded the *Chicago Defender* in 1905, was born in St. Simon Island, Georgia, in 1870 and migrated to Chicago in 1896. Anthony Overton, founder of the Victory Life Insurance Company, the Douglas National Bank, Overton-Hygienic Products Company, the *Chicago Bee* newspaper, and the *Half-Century* magazine, was born a slave in Monroe, Louisiana, in 1864, and moved to Chicago in 1911. In 1919, he was a millionaire.

The trains could not bring blacks to the North fast enough to fill the job vacancies left by more than 350,000 Illinois men who had either enlisted or been drafted into the 1917–18 European conflict.

Many of the newcomers felt that they knew Chicago through the wide circulation of Abbott's *Chicago Defender* in the South. What also helped was their acquaintance with the Sears Roebuck and Montgomery Ward catalogues, which tended to minimize the difference between rural and urban dress.

By 1918, the mass debarkation of blacks in Chicago had burst all the prescribed black housing belts. Friction was developing with the competition for the right to lay down one's body in the squalor of fourth-rate dwellings. On a single day, in July, 1918, the Chicago Urban League received 664 applications for only 55 available dwellings.

Blacks participated in the American armed forces in World War I in the largest numbers since the Civil War, the war against slavery, in hope that the

new war to save democracy would advance the struggle for equality and justice at home. But, of course, there were two separate American armies, until
President Truman started desegregating the Armed Forces in 1945. A new
integration policy was not adopted by the Army until 1949; similar policies
were subsequently adopted by the Navy and Air Force.

Black soldiers returning in early 1919 were overwhelmed with an outburst
of gratitude and affection from both black and white Chicagoans. However,
after a very brief feast on the affection of all Chicago, they soon discovered
that there were no jobs for yesterday's black heroes except a few low-paying
menial ones.

But Chicago never had a serious love affair with the returning "Black
Devils" of the 370th Infantry—formerly the Eighth Illinois National Guard.

A family friend, Mae Robinson, who lives in the Rosenwald apartments
near 46th and Michigan Boulevard, remembers that in 1919 when she was
a student at the Haven Elementary School (15th and Wabash) "the school
permitted only the black children" to attend the "Black Devils" celebration at
the spacious Coliseum on Wabash. In contrast, in 1919, the entire school was
dismissed when the white soldiers returned.

CHAPTER 3

Racial Strife:
I Never Learned to Swim

M Y FATHER, DREAMING OF BETTER DAYS IN CHICAGO, HAD
a rude awakening on June 5, 1900, when he reported for work as
a strikebreaking construction laborer at Mandel Brothers Department Store at 1 North State Street (now Wieboldt's).

Louis Travis' oldest brother, Otis, had been working as a strikebreaker since February, but he had failed to warn Louis of the danger that surrounded the job. Uncle Otis had already learned to accept strikebreaking as a way of life for black workers. His first job in Chicago had been as a scab at the stockyards in 1894. White meatpackers had struck in sympathy with the American Railway Union in dispute with Robert Todd Lincoln's Pullman Co. The black stockyards strikebreakers had participated from two motives: they needed the jobs, and it offered an opportunity to protest the anti-black clause in the American Railway Union Constitution.

My father, however, like many of the Southern immigrants, had a lot to learn about the harsh realities of life in a Northern city. That first day, Louis Travis wandered off the job site without protection—without realizing he needed protection. He walked up State Street to do a little sightseeing, casually inspecting the tall buildings of the Loop.

He had reached State and Lake when he ran into some union men. They quickly recognized that he was a strikebreaker because of his construction clothes. Gathering in front of him in a tight, angry little knot, they yelled at him: "Scabbing coon!" they shouted, shaking their fists.

As my father used to tell the story, he wheeled around immediately and headed south on State Street at a steady trot that quickly turned into a full gallop as the whites pursued him, shouting. His fleet-footedness, and a friendly cop, saved him after a sweaty sprint back to the construction site at State and Madison.

Though my father usually told the story as if it had been a huge joke on him, the very real pain and fear of such an experience always came through. Resentment between union members and black strikebreakers had escalated to the point that union members publicly burned blacks in effigy.

In spite of all this, my father and his two brothers decided not to go back South because Chicago offered them more freedom and opportunity. It was true that both trained and untrained blacks found their freedoms restricted in the North, but they preferred the Northern situation to the Southern suffocation born of the fear with which they had grown up.

My father and his brothers were laborers, and, like many blacks, they took great pride in doing their jobs well. They stayed and later became part of a cadre of the best workers in the packing houses.

Just before the United States entered the war in 1917, my mother, Mittie, was invited to Chicago to visit her middle sister, Claudie. She immediately became fascinated with the people and the bright lights of Chicago's 31st and 35th streets and South State Street, the focus of social activity for the black community. In her hometown of Birmingham, Alabama, she had never seen such glitter.

Besides, during this visit Mittie had met Louis Travis, a dude with a fondness for black women and black derby hats. She married him within five months of her arrival and never went back South except for brief family visits and funerals.

My folks lived first in a frame shanty at 3715 Butterfield (now Federal Street), with wooden sidewalks and on a street laid with wooden blocks. During the war, however, the Urban League helped them move to a stone-front house at 3514 Calumet Avenue, with concrete sidewalks and a street paved with asphalt. They had been there for only a few months when the Armistice was signed on November 11, 1918.

But Louis and Mittie Travis were carrying out their lives against a background of impending violence. The return of thousands of robust, healthy ex-servicemen arriving in Chicago to look for work—and their failure to find it—built up to the violent summer of 1919. My mother became pregnant with me in May 1919, and the nine months that she carried me were among the most violent periods of racial confrontation in the history of Chicago.

In May, a neighbor's home on the next street was fire-bombed. This bombing of the Richard B. Harrison home at 3624 South Grand Boulevard (now Martin Luther King Drive) was just one of a series of violent acts directed at black-occupied homes. Black and white realtors' offices and homes were also hit if it became known that the whites had sold or leased to blacks outside of the "Black Belt." The expansion of the "Black Belt" in Chicago could be measured by the bombings: between July 1, 1917, and March 1, 1921, bombings occurred on an average of once every twenty days.

And on July 27, 1919, Chicago ignited into one of this country's bloodiest race riots.

My first cousin, Joe Crawford, now age 72, was living with his parents and two brothers in a racially integrated, three-apartment building at 5915 South Wentworth Avenue, adjacent to the Englewood elevated tracks, when the race riot broke out. On July 28, the second night of the riot, a white woman who lived on the second floor in the same building told my Aunt Claudie that she had heard that a group of teenagers had planned to give the entire Crawford family a public flogging if they did not move out of the neighborhood.

An hour had not passed before there were knocking and loud angry voices at both the front and rear doors of the Crawfords' first floor apartment.

"Niggers, come out and get your asses whipped or stay in there and be barbecued," were the words Joe Crawford heard, loud and clear. Cousin Joe and his two brothers, Ralph and Cornelius, along with my Uncle Bee and Aunt Claudie, slipped single-file through a small bathroom window directly under the "El" tracks. The giant iron legs of the "El" provided perfect cover for them to move in a squatting position down the alley until they reached LaSalle Street. There they saw a dim light from a cracked back door about fifteen feet away and a black woman beckoning for the five of them to come in. The stranger who offered the Crawford family a haven was Mrs. Ruth Embry. They were fed and bedded down in her home for the next forty-eight hours.

The heavy rain on the fourth night of the riot provided cover for them to make a three-and-a-half-mile trot to my parents' home, which was in the heart of the "Black Belt" at 3514 South Calumet Avenue.

Frank Alexander, now turned eighty, a former Pullman porter, was living between Wabash and State on 36th Street during the riot. Because of his light complexion and straight black hair, friends advised him to stay off the streets for his own safety. Wisely, he followed that advice.

William Y. Browne, now owner of Riley-Browne Realty Company at 63rd and Langley, lived at 6530 South St. Lawrence during the riot and remembered that Woodlawn area blacks were heavily armed. They were ready to meet a rumored threat of an invasion by whites. At least eight blacks were injured at the street-car transfer corner on 63rd Street and Cottage Grove Avenue.

In the aftermath of the riot, the national office of the NAACP cooperated with the Chicago Branch in offering counsel and legal assistance to all the riot defendants. Members of the Cook County Bar Association, an organization of black lawyers, tried some of the cases that resulted in complete acquittal. In the end, sixteen black and eight white persons were tried for murder and manslaughter. Three blacks and two whites were convicted.

Thus the first score of years of the twentieth century ended on a sour note for Chicago's blacks. The next decade held an economic depression for blacks and reinforcement of racial hatred evident in the resurgence of the Ku Klux Klan, whose membership swelled to four million by 1924. The Klan in 1925 was permitted to march 40,000 strong down Pennsylvania Avenue in their white-sheet regalia past our nation's Capitol. Many non-sheet-wearing whites supported the Klan ideology because whites were beginning to feel the economic pressures of black competition for living space and jobs in urban areas.

It started when a gang of whites hurled rocks at a black teenager named Eugene Williams at a beach on Lake Michigan near 29th Street. Williams was hit in the head and drowned.

The tragedy forever affected my parents' attitude toward Lake Michigan. Mom is now eighty-four years old and has never put even a toe into Lake Michigan's water. My father never wore a swimming suit after that bloody Sunday. Blacks continued to barely tread water.

I was never permitted to learn to swim. For six years, we lived within two blocks of the lake, but that did not change their attitude. To Dad and Mama, the blue lake always had a tinge of red from the blood of that young black boy.

The clouds of racial hatred that had hovered over Chicago for months thickened on that July day, looming lower and darker to the west of Wentworth, the boundary of the "Black Belt," as the racial temperature continued to rise. The murder of Williams was the culmination of the racial inequities and humiliations heaped upon black soldiers who returned to find that the democracy they had fought for in Europe still did not exist for blacks at home. They had been drawn up sharply by the competition for poor but expensive housing, frequently punctuated by bombings; by educational material for children that included sickeningly offensive images of twentieth century Uncle Toms, Topsys, and Little Black Sambos, purveyed by a school system that failed to educate; and by gang attacks by Back of the Yards hoodlums that resulted in the murder of two blacks five weeks before the riot.

Though racial violence had flared briefly in the city before, the race riot of 1919 was too hot and intense to be extinguished quickly. It took military assistance as well as a thunderstorm and heavy rain that started Wednesday night and lasted through Thursday, July 31, to bring the conflict under control. But by that time 38 men and boys, including 23 blacks, had been killed. At least 537 people were injured, 342 of them blacks. Anna Mary Grinnell, now 96 years old, described an incident in which 4 of the whites killed in the riot had participated.

Mrs. Grinnell and her husband ran a bakery at 3308 South State Street, living in an apartment on the second floor with their eighteen-month-old daughter. They spent most of Monday night, July 28, lying on the floor of their apartment to avoid bullets fired by whites from the windows of automobiles racing up and down State Street at high speeds. Through the night, groups of whites in auto caravans kept shooting wildly from both sides of the cars, using rifles and handguns in rapid fire.

One car with four occupants passed 33rd and State. But by this time blacks had set up army-like barricades to defend their community with sniper fire. All four whites in the car died from gunshot wounds before the car reached 35th Street.

The Grinnells spent the anxious hours trying to figure out away to get their child to safety. Blacks were unable to travel north of 16th Street to get to the Loop train stations. The white man who delivered flour for their bakery offered to take Mrs. Grinnell and the child to the depot, but he couldn't come south of 16th Street for fear of blacks. So Mr. Grinnell tried to make arrangements to get his wife and child to 16th Street, where the friendly flour man could meet them and escort them through to take a train for Ohio. But before the arrangements could be made, the riot ended.

CHAPTER 4

Hard Times

C HICAGO'S BLACK POPULATION REACHED 109,594 IN 1920, and an estimated 20 percent of the blacks were unemployed. Although they were indigent, most would not accept free transportation to the South, where there was a critical shortage of sharecroppers. They preferred to sleep in the cold halls and doorways of Chicago when they could not get accommodations at the police stations.

Fortunately, my father retained his job in the stockyards during those hard times, and that is where he was when Mother gave birth to me at noon, February 25, 1920, in St. Luke's Hospital at 14th and Michigan.

My earliest accident happened at Riverview Amusement Park on the Northwest Side of Chicago when I was about three and one-half years old. I fell from a beautiful, hand-carved merry-go-round horse, then rolled off and under the revolving platform. I was rescued by the brake-man-operator and an hysterical mother. I remember vividly on another visit to Riverview that we witnessed a game called "Dunk the Darky in the Water." Black men sat on a seat above a pool of water with their heads stuck through a hole in a white canvas. For a dime, a customer could buy three balls. If the player successfully hit the "darky" on the head, he would fall into the water. This generated a great deal of laughter that was repugnant to me even at age five. The game was still being played when I was drafted into the Army in World War II in 1942.

In May 1925, we moved to 3609 South Cottage Grove Avenue, the first black family to move into the building. The white boys in the building tried to scare me by making sounds like an alley cat: "meow...meow...hiss...hiss." They were older boys who, with their green and gray eyes, looked to me quite a bit like mean old alley cats, sitting there at the top of the stairs. It was my first real contact with white folks.

The integration experience did not last more than a year, before the last white family moved out. Within that same period of time, the whole block turned black with the exception of a white boy named Wayne, whose folks operated a Singer Sewer Machine repair shop on the ground floor at 3615 Cottage Grove. We were playmates at a time when black and white children in the city rarely played together. Wayne's family stayed for three years after the neighborhood changed. He and I stayed in touch with each other until he was killed in the Normandy beach landing in World War II.

As an only child, I always slept by myself, except when my cousin Frank came over for a visit. Frank was the son of Mama's younger sister, Willie, who came to Chicago from the South in 1918. Sleeping alone was not a problem until we moved to 3609 South Cottage Grove Avenue, only two blocks from Lake Michigan. Some nights I heard spooky and eerie sounds that made me shiver and put my head under the blanket, hoping not to be discovered by whatever was making the noise. This spooky situation lasted for several weeks before my father took my fright seriously enough to explain that the noise was from fog horns on the large ore ships sailing in the fog near shore off 36th Street. He assured me that it was not a ghost from the funeral parlor down the street.

The silent movies of this period were filled with plots about ghosts and trap doors. I remember seeing *Uncle Tom's Cabin*, in which Uncle Tom actually came back as a ghost after he was killed. We saw these movies at theatres such as the Lyceum at 38th and Cottage Grove, the Pickford near 35th and Michigan, and the State Theatre at 35th and State, all of which had predominantly black audiences.

The pictures had subtitles and were shown with the accompaniment of a live piano player playing mood music, ranging from a progression of minor chords sounding like spooky footsteps to the rhythmic beats and scales of galloping horses.

Nineteen hundred and twenty-five was an eventful year for me. It was the year that I decided to become a businessman. I was five. This decision was triggered by a big green Buick with side-mount tires driven by a black man who owned four or five adjoining storefronts across the street from us at 3606–3616 South Cottage Grove. Sometimes this man brought a little boy along with a tricycle. He would lift the tricycle out of the back seat of the green Buick, and the little boy would ride up and down the street in front of the stores. I wished the man with the big green Buick were my father; I wanted to ride a shiny new tricycle.

The man was Charles Murray, who had developed a hair pomade. Murray was successful. Nearly every man I knew, except Uncle Otis who wore his hair natural, used Murray's Pomade. Murray's Pomade and Overton Products were to the 1920s what Fashion Fair and Ultra Sheen are to the 1980s. I did not know if my father would ever own a big green Buick, but I knew that I would someday use Murray's Pomade, which I did when I finally had some hair. I tried to look like the picture on the orange can of Murray's.

I finally met the boy with the tricycle ten years later in a freshmen Spanish class at DuSable High School. Charles Murray, Jr. and I became good friends and saw each other regularly until he married and dropped out of school to pursue a career as a wrestler. After the death of Murray, Sr., Mrs. Murray sold the Murray label to a white firm in Detroit.

A few weeks after I first saw Murray and the tricycle, a man opened a barbershop in the store at 3613 Cottage Grove. I asked him if he needed a young barber. "No," he said, "but I need someone to pass out my business cards." He agreed to pay me fifty cents, and I started work immediately.

I was not satisfied with simply passing out the cards on one side of the street; I had to cover both sides. Running across the street, I noticed a big red streetcar headed straight at me. I dodged the streetcar just in time just in time to be hit by a Model T Ford coming up on the right side parallel with the streetcar. When I woke up, I was in Provident Hospital at 36th and Dearborn. My mother and a doctor dressed in white were standing at the foot of the bed.

My mother was wringing her hands and asking, "Is he going to be all right?"

"He doesn't seem to be too badly injured," the doctor said. "All he seems to have is a fractured left leg."

Mom began to smile a little. But she didn't seem convinced until she leaned over the bed and tickled my right foot. I giggled. She smiled at the doctor and said, "Yes, he's going to be all right."

My first job ended at age five with my employer's bringing me a hand basket full of apples and oranges and an extra dollar for service beyond the call of duty.

My next venture came just three weeks before Thanksgiving in 1925 as a result of an ad in the funny paper. The ad offered a toy train in exchange for the sale of 200 miniature, pencil-sized, multicolored bottles of perfume. Each color represented a different fragrance. My mother mailed the newspaper coupon, and I received the shipment on December 1. My thought was to sell the perfume fast enough to get the train for Christmas. Again, I did not succeed. Everybody I attempted to sell sniffed the bottle of perfume and frowned. However, for reasons I did not understand at the time, some people gave me ten cents and told me to keep the perfume.

Santa Claus did not leave a train for me, but he did leave a player piano for the family. The piano had two functions: you could play it manually like an ordinary instrument, or you could put a roll on it and by a see-saw pumping of the feet, watch the keyboard move rapidly with the sounds of Jelly Roll Morton, Scott Joplin, and many popular tunes of the day. My father had learned to play the piano skillfully without the ability to read music. But he was determined that I was going to be a music-reading piano player.

I took my first lesson from Elmer Simpson in January 1926. I wanted to learn to play like my father, but I found learning to play very hard work requiring a lot of discipline. By late spring, my music teacher had me ready to appear in a children's program at West Point Baptist Church, a black church still located on the northwest corner of 36th Street and Cottage Grove Avenue. This piano debut started me on a music career that did not end until I was twenty-six years old. The self-discipline I acquired in the many hours required to learn a single number on my instrument made it easier for me to go from music to hard academic studies at age twenty-seven.

I studied music under a series of teachers for twelve years. Three of my teachers were blacks, and two were German (whether German Jewish or otherwise German, I didn't know—we blacks were not aware of any difference). From both black and white teachers, I learned sonatas of Mozart, the preludes and nocturnes of Chopin, and other standard pieces by European composers. My instructors taught me very little American music and no black music. Although my interest was always in jazz, my teachers said I had the touch, talent, and flair of a concert pianist. But I couldn't see such a career, largely because I knew no blacks who made a living playing concert piano, except some who played in the black churches.

My initial formal education started in a private kindergarten where I was considered a very bright child. My parents were proud of my progress. They always had me counting to one hundred or saying the alphabet and reciting simple poems and rhymes for their friends. I was pleased with myself and with school. Then suddenly my whole world changed.

My father became ill, and my mother could no longer afford the tuition, so I went to a public school, Doolittle School, just east of Cottage Grove at 35th Street. My teacher was a white lady named Mrs. Green. For reasons unknown to me now or then, I did not like Mrs. Green, and she returned the emotion. I found the teacher and the school so distasteful that I was playing hookey after my third day.

To me it seemed that I walked around for months, although I'm sure that it was only a few days of kicking cans and other stuff in the alleys while my parents thought I was in school.

Sitting on a stoop one rainy morning, I was picked up by a truant officer, who took me back to Doolittle. I was glad that I had been caught and happier still when Mrs. Green refused to accept me back in her class and had me transferred to another teacher. I had no problem with the new teacher, but neither can I remember her name. No problems and no names is a posture I maintained for the next eleven years that I was in public school, with the exception of two elementary teachers and two high school teachers, who I thought made a contribution to my education.

When my parents learned of my hookey-playing, they both beat my behind and grounded me from all activities, including the Saturday afternoon movie matinee, for one month. From that point through college, I never missed a full day in school. Of course, occasionally I cut classes to catch famous bands like Duke Ellington's and Jimmy Lunceford's when they came through Chicago during my high school days. But I was never excessively absent.

"Black boys are not admitted here" is the greeting my cousin Frank and I received when we attempted to buy two tickets at the Oakland Square Theatre at 39th and Drexel Boulevard in 1928. We wanted to see Douglas Fairbanks in *The Three Musketeers*, but the ticket seller told us that if we did not move from in front of the theater, she would have that big burly usher at the door "kick our nigger behinds." We turned and saw the blonde, blue-eyed, burly usher glaring at us. We ran.

Holy Angels Catholic Church around the corner on Oakwood Boulevard treated blacks better. Well, at the time it seemed mighty nice that we were allowed to sit in a section reserved for blacks, the six back pews on the right side. The Oakland Square Theater folded long ago, but Holy Angels remains an influential community institution under the leadership of a black pastor, Father George Clements.

In 1929, at age nine, I became a *Chicago Defender* paperboy. I still remember vividly the first issue that I sold, with its red headline over the picture of a black man hanging from a tree. I sold my twenty-five copies of that issue in less than an hour and realized a dollar profit. Ordinarily it would take three or four hours to hustle that many papers on Saturday. In those days, the headlines were always red in the *Defender*, but not always as dramatic. My *Defender* business continued to prosper right up until "Black Thursday," October 24, 1929, the day the stock market failed. Before the year's end my customers were more concerned about feeding their stomachs than feeding their minds.

The Depression hit everybody, including my Uncle Otis. Up until the Depression I remember Uncle Otis as a high-spirited person who occasionally gave me a nickel for an ice cream cone or a dime to see the Saturday afternoon matinee. During the good days he would bring his pretty girlfriends around to see my parents. My mother always hoped he would marry the one named Mildred. Even though I was a child, she appeared to me to be both attractive and sophisticated. As a matter of fact, I still think of her as the model for Duke Ellington's "Sophisticated Lady." I missed seeing her almost as much as my uncle must have after he lost his job, his savings, and his spirit.

Uncle Otis was laid off his job on December 22, 1929. He had always been thrifty and had saved his money in the Binga State Bank, the financial rock of the black community, located one door north of the northwest corner of 35th and State. The family never knew exactly how much money Otis had saved, but he managed to live comfortably without apparent worry until July 31, 1930. On that day, the examiners closed the doors of the Binga bank. Thrifty Uncle Otis became destitute with the turn of the examiner's key in the front door of the bank.

Otis Travis died in 1933, broke and broken-hearted, without having recovered one penny of his savings. Many savers suffered such losses in those days before deposits were insured by the Federal Deposit Insurance Corporation.

Hard times, indeed.

CHAPTER 5

If Bad Dreams Were Money, Blacks Would Be Rich

THE 1920S ROARED LIKE AN ECONOMIC LION FOR WHITE folks, but they barely meowed for blacks.

Chicago's black population increased from 44,000 in 1910 to 109,000 in 1920, an increase from 2 to 4 percent. By 1950 the total had increased to 492,000, or 14 percent of the total population.

The city's geographical limits within which most blacks would be housed were established by 1920. The growth pattern would be continuous and not leap-frog. The exceptions, to name a few, were Lillydale, Morgan Park, and Robbins. Some of the old settlers, in an effort to escape from the influx of Southern migrants, relocated in areas that were a long ride away via the interurban street car. Morgan Park attracted middle-middle-income blacks, that is, middle-middle on the scale of black employment opportunities—clerks, Pullman porters, dining car waiters, and semi-skilled laborers. Lillydale and Robbins attracted lower-middle class blacks in search of space to rear large families. Both Robbins and Lillydale have dramatically improved the quality of their housing stock within the past twenty years.

The industrial depression that embraced the city during the last six months of 1920 caused the lay-off of some 20,000 blacks, many of whom drifted to pool halls, police stations, and doorways for shelter. On the shore of Lake Michigan north of 31st Street, the homeless sought shelter in a "Village of the Deserted" in make-shift shanties made of rocks, newspapers, and other junk.

The economic depression, however, did not relieve the housing crisis for the employed black, who was still forced to pay extremely high rent for furnished or unfurnished quarters. At the same time it was estimated that 25 percent of the units in north Kenwood were vacant.

In 1921, whites began to demand both apartments and houses in the Kenwood-Hyde Park area, suddenly a highly desirable area. The Hyde Park Owners Association launched a campaign to move out the 1,000 black families who were living between 39th and 55th Streets between Lake Michigan and Cottage Grove Avenue. They tried to move them back into the old, defined "Black Belt" north of 39th Street. But they learned that many had paid cash money for their property, some of it realized from the sale of their homes in the South, and there was no legal way to move them out. In this instance, violence was not used. The blacks had landed. The beachhead had been established.

But blacks' penetration of the southeast area was still painfully slow, because the whites' defenses were many, including neighborhood associations and individual opposition, restrictive covenants, and local political actions to restrict blacks to certain areas.

Waking up a black in Chicago was always a continuation of the previous night's bad dream. If bad dreams were money, all blacks folks would be rich.

An attempt to capitalize on bad dreams created a dream book industry that is still not well known outside the black community. There were more than twenty dream books or policy games [editor's note: policy games were immensely popular, though illegal, lottery-like gambling games]. The most popular during the '20s and '30s were *The Three Witches*, *The Gypsy Witch*, *The Japanese Fate*, *Aunt Della's*, and *Aunt Sally's*. These books were best sellers whose popularity was exceeded only by the Bible in the black community. Dream books were used to translate the meaning of a dream into policy numbers, which were usually a combination of three numbers. For example, a dream of Death Row translated into 9-9-29, and the name "Henry" translated into 27-31-33.

The black millionaires of the 1930s were the policy kings, such as "Big Jim" Martin of the West Side and, on the South Side, "Giver Dam" Jones and his brother Teennan, and Illy Kelly and his brothers Walter and Ross. Pop Lewis was a cultured college-trained gentleman, who ran the Monte Carlo Wheel and owned the Vincennes Hotel at 36th and Vincennes, with its 200 rooms, ballroom, and banquet halls featuring full orchestras.

There were other successful operators, but none compared with another set of Jones brothers—Eddie, George, and McKissick. Their headquarters at 4724 Michigan employed as many as 250 people, a number which does not include several hundred working their stations and runners. At the height of the Jones brothers' career they grossed $25,000 per day. An efficiency expert once said that the Jones' wheels operated like clockwork, as efficient and as well run as many of the marble-lined banks and brokerage houses on LaSalle Street, and many times more profitable. In addition to a villa in Paris, a summer home in Peoria, and a villa in Mexico City on Compe 73, they owned four hotels: the Vienna Bathhouse, the Grove, the Garfield, and the Alpha. They were the first blacks to own a piece of real estate at 47th and King Drive. They opened their Ben Franklin Store at 436–44 East 47th Street in 1937 which was considered such a major achievement that thousands of people filled the street, and celebrities such as Joe Louis and Bill (Bojangles) Robinson appeared.

One of the most prominent lawyers in the city dubbed the opening of the store "a milestone in the progress of our business." The Franklin Store property was the first to be owned by a black in the heart of the business district on 47th Street. According to the late Dr. Bishop Smith, a black could not rent a ground floor store between Forrestville and Prairie on 47th Street for any retail purpose. The only exceptions were barber shops, beauty shops, taverns, and the Morris Eat Shop, which was located at 410 East 47th Street.

A nickel bet on the right combination of numbers could make a player a five-dollar winner. Five dollars represented two days' pay for me at the Quality Laundry in the summer of 1939. Policy was and still is the poor man's sweepstakes. Some people played seven or eight different combinations of numbers a day, because they had bad dreams in multiples.

Not everyone turned to dream books to find the meaning of their bad dreams. My Uncle Otis sought a solution for the bleakness of black life in the Marcus Garvey movement in the early 1920s. The name of Marcus Garvey was always spoken with reverence in our home.

Uncle Otis had described Garvey, that twentieth-century dreamer, as an "unsynthetic" black man. He was short, with a slightly rotund trunk under an average-sized neck and shoulders, which supported a large head. Garvey's speeches on black nationhood stirred his audiences into a fever of excitement, his colorful style leaning heavily on rhetorical questions.

"Where is the black man's government?" he would ask. "Where is his president, his country, and his ambassadors, his army, his navy, and his men of big affairs? I could not find them, and I declared, 'I will help make them!'" Such a speech always had his audience foot-stamping, shouting, and clapping.

Garveyism generated more serious street talk than any other subject along "The Stroll," which was State Street between 31st and 39th Streets, in the '20s. Robert S. Abbott, founder of the *Chicago Defender*, could be found holding court on the corner of 35th and State with a big cigar in his mouth, discussing the similarity of the Garvey scheme with that of "Chief Sam," who, earlier in the century, flimflammed some black people with a scheme to establish a black kingdom in Africa. Like Garvey, "Chief Sam" had purchased some second-hand boats for a black exodus to the homeland.

Another heavy topic on "The Stroll" might be Jack Johnson, the "Great Black Hope" and first black heavyweight champion of the world. The last three of Johnson's four marriages were to white women and were eagerly discussed in the black community.

Johnson's victories in the ring were interpreted by blacks and whites alike as a "Black Manifesto" against white supremacy. With each blow, Jack Arthur Johnson was laying to rest the nineteenth century myth of the white superman. The reaction to Johnson's championship victory over Tommy Burns on December 26, 1908, in Sydney, New South Wales, was pandemonium. Black jubilation was met with white mob violence and police suppression after the defeat of the "White Hope" Jim Jeffries on July 4, 1910. There were disturbances in many cities, and victory celebrations turned into brick and bottle-throwing riots by whites.

Johnson was finally stopped by a conviction under the Mann Act, passed in June, 1919, after a press blitz on Johnson's activities with white women. This "white slave traffic" act was sponsored by James Robert Mann, Congressman from Illinois. It prohibited transportation of women across state lines for unmoral purposes.

Johnson was convicted under this act for associating with his favorite lady of the evening, Belle Schreiber, who was the star Daughter of Joy at Chicago's Everleigh Club, located in the red light district at 2131–33 South Dearborn Street. Johnson allegedly sent money to Belle in Pittsburgh so that she could come to Chicago for a specific and immoral purpose. The Ku Klux Klan mentality of many Americans dictated that the black hero must be punished for this act, though there is no record of any white convictions for similar transportation of black women from the South to the North.

Johnson's conviction was reversed on appeal, but he had gone into hiding and remained a fugitive until he gave himself up to the U.S. government in Mexico. He served a year and a day in a federal penitentiary at Leavenworth, Kansas. As a result, blacks were "white-lined" out of the contest for the heavyweight championship for two decades after Johnson's reign.

Thirty-fifth and State Street was home to thousands of black Chicagoans who sought breathing space outside of their cubicle rooms and kitchenettes. People walked, talked, laughed, and gestured around the intersection all night long. The attraction was the theatres, nightclubs, and lively businesses of the area.

This intersection spawned a lively round of interests. There are many examples. The business empire of Anthony Overton was led by his cosmetics company. In his "fleet" of businesses he had the Victory Life Insurance Company, *Half Century* magazine, the *Bee* newspaper, and his Douglas National Bank, all located on the east side of State Street at 36th.

On the northwest corner at 35th Street was Jesse Binga's office building, known as the Binga Arcade. Next door, to the north, was the Binga State Bank.

Jesse Binga had been a railroad porter. In 1908 he founded a private bank. He married the sister of "Mushmouth" Johnson, who ran a lucrative gambling business, and much of the Johnson foundation went into Binga's bank. In 1920, Binga's bank became a state bank.

Binga built the Binga Arcade in 1929. It was a five-story building of imposing design, with office space and a dance hall on the roof. Binga had been warned that such a building at such a location would not prove a really practical investment, but the building represented a dream. In 1929, when the Depression started, Binga was riding high—he had become chairman of a new and thriving insurance company, and his bank had nearly $1.5 million in deposits.

But on July 31, 1930, Binga's bank was shut down by the state examiner. Banks were closing across the country, and controversy surrounded Binga's various real estate deals. Depositors started a run on the bank, and that was the end of it. Eventually Binga served time in jail for embezzlement.

Binga remained a figure of controversy to Black Chicago. Some said he was simply a crook. Others said he was merely a creative businessman who ended up taking too many risks, and that without the Depression he might have continued as Black Chicago's foremost businessman. Other said he was a victim of circumstances brought down by the white system, and that his mistake had been in overextending the bank by making too many first mortgages to blacks desperate to buy homes.

At 37th and State stood the first and largest black-built high-rise office building, developed by the black fraternal organization, the Knights of Pythias. This structure was converted to residential use during World War II, and its shell remained standing until 1980.

State Street was both Wall Street and Broadway to the black community in the twenties. The white lights of South State went on after the red lights of New Orleans' Storeyville section went out in November, 1917, when New Orleans' mayor, on order of the Secretary of the Navy, closed down the houses of prostitution. That produced instant depression among the jazzmen who had played those houses and the honky-tonks of Storeyville. Many of those talented musicians, along with their jazz-loving fans, rode the rails north to Chicago.

That shift from New Orleans to Chicago made State Street, and its cross streets at 31st and 35th, the jazz mecca of America. The Royal Garden, the Sunset Cafe, the Pekin, the Dreamland, Elite #1, Elite #2, the Entertainers Club, and the Plantation on 35th Street, where King Oliver, the great New Orleans' trumpeter, played nightly, were centers of entertainment for black and white Chicagoans. Jack Johnson's Cafe de Champion at 42 West 31st Street was a forerunner in entertainment for "black and tan" audiences in Chicago.

Other New Orleans jazzmen who kept the South Side jumping were Louis Armstrong, Freddy Keppard, Johnny and Baby Dodds, Sidney Bechet, Perez St. Cyr, and Jelly Roll Morton, who was the most popular underworld pianist around.

Underworld characters, jazz, prostitution, alcohol, and dope moved through the residential sections of the black community the way the Illinois Central Railroad ran through the little towns and cities between Chicago and New Orleans. Vice first surrounded and then infiltrated the "Black Belt." It was all but impossible for black families to escape the stench of corruption and immorality, because it operated under a protective political umbrella. Blacks were powerless to stamp out the vice and powerless to flee from it, since they could not freely move about the city in search of more wholesome neighborhoods.

But, of course, all blacks did not regret the introduction of vice into the black community. It offered color in a drab existence and money in a time of restricted opportunity. Black jazz musicians could not have exploited their talents without the permissive sponsorship of the vice operations.

The comfortable identification that Cab Calloway, the entertainer, had with vice in Chicago is described in his autobiography, *Of Minnie the Moocher and Me.* He tells about his first wife, Betty, a tall, light-skinned beauty who earned $50 a day and gave him more than $200 a week:

> *On July 26, 1928, we were married. By that time we had moved out of the Joneses' house to live with a woman named Mae Singleton in another house on the Southside. Mae had one fine house, and she did a beautiful business. She had two or three prostitutes living in there. You might think it would bother me to be living in a house run by a madam, but it didn't. It was a damned comfortable life.*

But it was hell for those blacks who were trying to build a strong, moral family. A further extension of the vice virus could be found in the typical jazz club environment on the South Side in the twenties and thirties as Earl "Father" Hines, the famous pianist, described it in his autobiography, *World of Earl Hines:*

> *The club where I was working brought in, as I said, a lot of underworld people, and among them many pimps. They used to hang out there until their girls finished working at two or three o'clock in the morning. Then they would bring them there to thrash out whatever went on during the day. The big-time pimps had Packard's and Pierce-Arrows, and I often wished I could get a car like they had. They were dressed up at all times...*

The infectious environments described by both Calloway and Hines are models that laid the groundwork for the moral and social disorganization of the urban black community.

CHAPTER 6

Listening Back

IN 1931, UNCLE OTIS WAS STILL UNEMPLOYED, AND UNCLE JOE and my father had been cut from six ten-hour days a week to three eight-hour days. And in January, the Willard Elementary School, where I was enrolled, went on a double shift that cut my school day almost in half.

Fortunately for me, the lost classroom hours were recovered at home in a totally different educational environment. Those harsh realities of the thirties had an unexpected benefit—they allowed me to listen to my uncle and my father discuss the issues of the day and the personalities of Black Chicago. Those discussions shaped my views as a young black man.

My home study took place at least three afternoons a week when I came home to find my father and his brothers sitting around the dining room table, sometimes sipping home brew, talking about the good old days—what they called "the silk shirt days"—when the overtime pay of the better days of the twenties had given them some economic freedom. They let me sit on the floor and listen to their discussions, which ranged from Abyssinia to Zanzibar. I was only barred when they started talking about women, since at the age of ten, I was judged too young to fully participate.

My mother seldom took part in these skull sessions, but when she talked, she made it clear she had her own views. I remember once, when I was five years old, some older white boys in the building we had integrated at 36th Street and Cottage Grove Avenue called me a "black son of a bitch." They said it in such an ugly, frightening tone that I ran to my mother and repeated the phrase. She only smiled.

"Have you ever seen black velvet?" she said. She took a velvet jacket out of a drawer and showed it to me.

I touched it. "Yes. It's soft and pretty."

She put her arms around me. "This is the best and most expensive material in the world," she said.

"Is it?"

"You're my black velvet," she said. For me, that simple exchange provided a structure for the resolution of most of the future problems I was going to have about my color. If I had gone to my father or his brother Joe that day, however, I know they would have advised me to "punch the honkies in the mouth."

Dad and his younger brother were tough, no-nonsense, strike-breaking laborers. They fought any black or white man who crossed them. Uncle Otis, on the other hand, was gentle and philosophical. Their differences kept their talks spirited. I found it especially exciting when they talked about such heroes as Jack Johnson, Marcus Garvey, Booker T. Washington, or W.E.B. DuBois.

Uncle Joe, who was the family playboy, opened the Johnson argument one night with a smile. "Any black man who achieves the world's heavyweight championship deserves the best that womanhood can offer."

That got a sardonic grin from my mother: "Does that mean the best white prostitute?"

"I didn't say anything about pay-for-play girls," Uncle Joe said.

Uncle Otis tried to lift the discussion to a higher level. "Jack Johnson's contribution to vertical black pride should not be diminished by his taste in horizontal relaxation," he said.

My father agreed: "That's right. Jack's victories have lifted more bent backs and bowed heads than any other event since the Emancipation Proclamation."

But Mama wasn't having any of that. She glared around the table at the men: "Name one instance when Jack Johnson took a public position on behalf of colored people."

There was a long silence.

"I'm going to bed," Dad said finally. And that was the end of that discussion.

Mom had little sympathy with black males' need for symbolic props to their masculinity in a society that offered them little else. Nor did she understand the argument that Johnson took no public positions for black people because whites kept him off balance outside the ring.

But Mama had another go at it at a subsequent session. It came about at the end of a talk about the Garvey movement.

"We don't have a black army, navy, or such," my father said, rubbing his chin and referring to Marcus Garvey's favorite challenge to blacks. "The Garvey movement has failed."

"No! Garvey did not fail," Uncle Otis said, speaking with a special deliberateness. "He gave colored Americans a pride that never surfaced before on any continent. He's laid a foundation on which all the colored people of the world could coalesce."

Dad dismissed the argument with a gesture of his big, calloused fist: "How do you bring people together on a sinking ship? Didn't the black-owned Black Star Line fail?"

"Yes," Otis admitted, looking straight into Dad's eyes. "It was an economic failure, even though whites occupied most of the important administrative and operational posts. There weren't any trained blacks with experience in the steamship business. But it was a psychological success."

Dad snorted.

"Yes, it was," Otis said. "That venture, like the other Garvey enterprises, created a spirit that has yet to be parallelled in any other black movement."

Dad was silent.

"Louis, you must have felt that spirit the last time we heard Garvey speak at the Eighth Regiment Armory at 35th and Giles," Otis said. "Chicago may have had only 9,000 contributing members in the Universal Negro Improvement Association, but more than six million people worldwide were committed at the peak of Garvey's influence. Any movement that can attract that much attention is never a failure."

That was when my mother, who had been sitting silently in the doorway between the kitchen and the dining room, made her move. She coughed as if to clear her voice.

"Garvey was a sensible and sensitive man," she said placatingly. And then she produced a book, as if she had been already prepared for this discussion. "I want to read you this poem 'The Black Woman,' because it reflects his inner soul on Negro purity and beauty."

She made sure she had their attention, and then she read out in a clear voice:
Black queen of beauty, thou hast given color to the world!
Among other women thou art royal and the fairest!
Like the brightest jewels in the regal diadem,
Shin'st thou, Goddess of Africa, nature's purest emblem.

Black men worship at thy virginal shrine of purest love,
Because in thine eyes are virtues steady and holy mark,
As we see no other, clothed in silk or fine linen,
From ancient Venus, the Goddess, to mythical Helen.

My mother rose from the chair after reading the poem, walked over to my father, and placed her right hand on the back of his neck. She looked with airy confidence at the other two men.

"How did you Jack Johnson fans like that message?" she said.

Dad's face lit up with a broad smile. Uncle Joe scratched his head. End of that discussion.

I saw a graphic illustration of the wide-open nature of vice in 1926, when I was six years old and living at 3609 South Cottage Grove Avenue. I often saw black and white women stopping men on the street. At that time, I thought they were lost and were asking for directions. But it seemed strange that the man would follow the woman into a nearby alley or hallway. One day some older boys curiously followed the "lost" lady and her new "friend" into a hallway and were immediately chased out as the woman cursed them for harassing her "client."

At dinner that evening, I described my itinerary to Uncle Otis and Dad. Both laughed noisily, nearly choking on their food. Later that night, after I had gone to bed, I could hear them discussing the "lost" lady through a crack in my bedroom door.

"You know, that boy wouldn't have seen anything like that episode of our red light district if the law hadn't closed all the whorehouses down. I think it's a damn shame they turned all those whores loose in our neighborhood," my father said.

Uncle Joe responded with a Chicago history lesson: "Colored folks have always lived on the edge of this city's vice district," he said. "That's just the way it's always been. And now that they're closed, we are the vice."

"Listen, you know the district would still be open if some rich white merchant's kid hadn't been killed in a whorehouse," Uncle Otis put in. "The bitches would still be legal, licensed, and confined to their houses between 18th and 22nd Streets." Some 260 houses of prostitution had been in operation between 18th and 22nd Streets, from Wabash on the east to Wentworth on the west, in the area called the Levee.

There was silence as the men considered this. Then Uncle Joe spoke.

"My old lady's sister lost her job as a maid there and she hasn't had a regular job since." Over 2,000 black women had worked as maids or personal servants in those houses. Like Amy Lou, Uncle Joe's friend's sister, they made good money, because in addition to their wages, they got healthy tips from the wealthy patrons.

Dad agreed that these facts were well known in the black community. "And Frank Brown says when he was tending bar at the Everleigh Club, they had a $15,000 gold-plated piano that was made to order. And they had three eight-piece orchestras that played alternately dusk to dawn, seven nights a week."

By this time I was so interested in the wider implications of the discussion that my "lost" lady had evoked that I got up and cracked my bedroom door open a little wider. Uncle Otis was sitting with his back to the dining room window, and I could look directly into his face across Dad's shoulder. Otis was rubbing his hands and looking quizzically at Dad and Uncle Joe.

"Do you think a block club protest would get rid of the street-walkers?" he said. But his expression changed and he answered his own question before the others could speak.

"No! There's too much money in it. The papers say the graft from prostitution is more than $15 million a year. And Mayor Big Bill Thompson, the black folks' favorite Republican, died leaving over $2 million in currency."

Dad shook his head. "Clam it, Otis! Booker T. Washington said black people have to wipe out vice in their own communities."

"How can we do that when the white man pays the fiddler and calls the tune?" Otis said. "It's like attacking elephants with bean guns."

"My boy deserves a better environment. I'm going to move," my father said glumly.

"Move where?" Otis jeered. "You can't escape the whores. The landlords will make room for them as long as they pay double rent. You haven't got the money. You haven't got the political power to fight it."

He watched my father's face as his words sank in.

"And you can't move away from it," he said. "Face it. You're black."

I watched them sitting there in the long silence that followed. Then I got up and quietly tiptoed back to my bed.

CHAPTER 7

Hoover's Depression and
Grandma's Session

I N 1930, President Herbert Hoover promised two chick-
ens in every pot and a car in every garage. Black Americans hardly noticed. They knew the promise wasn't for them.

Almost half of Chicago's black families (the black population was
233,903) were receiving some form of public welfare that year. Without aid,
they could not have afforded the 10 cents for a quart of milk, 29 cents for a
dozen eggs, 5 cents for a 20-ounce loaf of bread or 7 cents for transportation
across town to try to find a job.

The search for work sent 200,000 boys, girls, men and women crisscrossing the country as stowaways on freight trains. The railroad detectives ignored
their human freight since there were not enough jails to accommodate the
ride-stealing, light-traveling "Hoover Hobos" moving from city to city, town
to town, looking for the prosperity their president had promised was just
around the corner.

Several members of my family joined the wandering freight riders. Both
Uncle Glenn, my mother's step-brother, and cousin Ralph, my Aunt Claudie's
oldest son, had become experts at hopping freights.

Uncle Glenn showed up at our back door suddenly one summer afternoon after having paid a very high price for a freight ride: six months earlier
he had lost both legs up to the knee riding the rails. But this had not stopped
him from freight-hopping. He could still get around almost as quickly as a
normal man, wearing special inverted shoes strapped to his knees. He would
use his strong arms to hoist his body into the railroad car. He left Chicago as

suddenly as he came one morning, heading for the freight yard. We never saw or heard from him again.

Cousin Ralph was the globe-trotter in the family. He told us he had ridden freight trains through forty-two of the forty-eight states. A gregarious, loud-laughing, fun-loving individual, Ralph had a capacity for deep scholarship in many subjects, ranging from the Bible to Buddhism, and he was the first member of our family to attend college. He studied at Oakwood Junior College, a Seventh Day Adventist school in Huntsville, Alabama, and during his frequent visits with us, he introduced me to the thoughts of such men as Dr. W.E.B. DuBois, Booker T. Washington, and George Washington Carver. Then again, on several occasions he took me to see a burlesque show at the Rialto Theater on State Street, just north of Van Buren. That was cousin Ralph, a man who enjoyed all seasons. When I was eleven, he took my mother and me to see a Paul Robeson concert and introduced us to the great singer after the recital.

Even more exciting was the first time Ralph took me to Washington Park to hear the "Reds" give a lecture on the bourgeois injustices of tenant evictions. The joint efforts of blacks and whites to resettle evicted families was the first integrated action I had ever witnessed in which the races acted as equals. Not surprisingly, during this period I thought that any white person seen associating with a black was a Communist.

Ralph was a wrestler, and he was always challenging me or my father when he was in town. He was a feisty man and a fervent believer in Adventistism. In fact, this led to his death years later. He was preaching in a bus station in Kansas City when some policemen tried to get him to stop. He refused to leave the station, and he was shot to death.

With all of its sorrow, the Depression brought some free excitement for kids called "Put the furniture back in." Every day someone was evicted on our block for non-payment of rent. Before the bailiffs had put the last piece of furniture on the street, someone would contact the Communist Red Squad that met in Washington Park. The Squad would send a group of men to put the furniture back into the apartment. On other occasions they would arrive just as the furniture was to be removed by the bailiffs and would advise the tenants to sit on the furniture to prevent its removal. The seated tenant was soon joined by neighbors and the squad who would lead in the first chorus of an old spiritual, "I shall not, I shall not be moved," the theme song of the resistance in the thirties.

The Communists held mass meetings daily in Washington Park. There was usually one very large crowd listening to a prominent guest speaker, and at the same time there were dozens of smaller groups listening to lesser-known personalities. Cousin Ralph told Dad and his brothers after returning from the park one evening that they could get a liberal education in Washington Park by simply moving from one bench speaker to another.

"What subjects were you educated in today?" Dad asked.

"The Scottsboro Boys," Ralph said.

"Who was the speaker?" Uncle Otis.

"Some white New York lawyer who was at the nine boys' first trial in Scottsboro, Alabama."

"Weren't they arrested on a freight train in Paint Rock, Alabama?" Uncle Otis asked.

"Yep! But they shipped the niggers by open truck to Scottsboro, the Jackson County seat, because they didn't have a cage big enough for them in Paint Rock," Ralph said.

Cousin Ralph spent the rest of the evening relating what the New York lawyer had said to the big crowd in the park. According to him, the nine black boys were arrested for fighting seven white hobos who had been trying to force them to jump from a moving freight train. Instead, the black boys beat and kicked all of the white hobos off the train except one. They spared the last white hobo because the train had picked up too much speed for them to put him off without causing him serious injury or possibly death. The bruised and infuriated white boys hitchhiked ahead to Scottsboro, where they pressed charges with the sheriff against the blacks for beating the hell out of them. Deputy Sheriff Charlie Latham put together a posse to capture the blacks on the freight train. They were arrested at the next scheduled stop, which was Paint Rock. To everyone's surprise, in addition to the nine blacks and one white boy on the train, two young white female hobos, wearing men's caps and overalls, were also aboard.

Only twenty minutes had passed after the arrest had been made when the younger girl, who identified herself as Ruby Bates of Huntsville, had accused the nine blacks of raping both her and her girlfriend, Victoria Price. The nine boys were arrested on March 25, 1931. They went to trial on April 6, 1931, and three days later, April 9, 1931, eight of the nine were sentenced to die. Roy Wright, who had barely reached his thirteenth birthday, was sentenced to life in prison.

A death silence fell over the dining room. Everyone at the table was stunned at the severity of Judge Hawkins' sentence and the swiftness of the trial. It seemed like an hour of silence passed before Uncle Joe asked Ralph, "How did the Washington Park crowd react to this?"

"Shock," Ralph answered. "Just plain shock!"

Uncle Otis cut in, "Those boys were lucky they weren't arrested in my home state of Georgia; there they might have been given an instant trial. I understand the lynching quota for niggers in Georgia was something like eleven a year compared to an average of six in Alabama between 1882 and 1927. Alabama was about 40 percent less."

Ralph gave a grim chuckle. "You fellows have been away from the South so long that you have forgotten 'Uncle Charlie's first commandment,' haven't you?" he said. "The first commandment is, 'Don't ogle or touch Charlie's ladies unless you have already made your peace with God.'"

Uncle Joe, jumping from his seat, shouted, "Damn, man! How can any civilized court sentence eight teenaged boys to die on the word of two white prostitutes?"

"Easy," Ralph said. "Black men in the white man's scheme of things are a sub-class. Keeping this premise in mind, then you will understand the white man's rage when he discovers that his woman has been violated by a lower order of being."

Uncle Joe smiled. A cynical, streetwise Chicagoan now, with a streak of the playboy in him, he was often amused at Ralph's fervor in explaining just how White America worked. "Aren't you drawing some pretty broad conclusions from one incident?" he said.

Ralph stared at him seriously. "The real issue is not the violation of the white woman, but a systematized program devised by the white man to detour the sub-class from economic and political parity for another two hundred years."

Uncle Joe smiled again. "Those are some pretty strong words, Ralph."

Ralph was scowling now. "The Anglo judicial system condones black genocide by refusing to deal with black-on-black killing or crime seriously. The legal and social institutions do not see the individual black man as a personality, but as a blur of an impersonal mass. Therefore, many blacks have been brainwashed into accepting this indistinctiveness and have adopted a self-defeating 'nigger ain't nothing' attitude response to his social and legal individual invisibility.

"In the absence of individual distinctiveness, blacks have taken on a group guilt complex exhibited by such remarks as 'We tore up the neighborhoods,' 'Why don't we learn how to act,' and 'Why can't we behave like white folks,' or the acceptance of the white man's highest commendation: 'You are not like the others.'"

Everybody let his words hang in the air while they studied each others' faces. Then Dad said, "Ralph, you didn't finish telling us what happened to the Scottsboro Boys. Did they try to escape?"

"You have got to be kidding," Ralph said.

"The NAACP ain't going to let those black boys burn," Dad said.

"They will if they don't dismiss those white New York lawyers hired by the International Labor Defense. Everybody knows the ILD is a Communist group. As a matter of fact, Walter White, the Executive Secretary of the NAACP, said, 'The prejudice against Communism and blacks combined guaranteed the Scottsboro Boys going to the electric chair,'" Ralph said.

The ILD attorney defending the Scottsboro boys, Walter Pullack, took the case to the Supreme Court. On November 7, 1932, the Scottsboro Boys were guaranteed new trials based on the landmark decision in *Powell v. Alabama*. The decision of the lower court was reversed on the grounds that their rights under the Fourteenth Amendment had been violated and that they had not received adequate counsel at Scottsboro. On April 7, 1933, Ruby Bates took the witness stand and denied she or Victoria Price was raped. On October 25, 1976, Governor George Wallace approved the pardon of Clarence Norris, the only survivor of the Scottsboro Boys.

But the Communists never managed to make a dent in blacks' loyalty to the party of Abraham Lincoln. In the presidential election of 1932, most stayed with the Republicans in spite of disillusionment with Herbert Hoover and his promises of prosperity just around the corner.

The Roosevelt era began just four months prior to the opening of the Century of Progress World's Fair on Chicago's lakefront. The white newspapers were saying eagerly that the fair would attract enough visitors to restore the prosperity the city had known in the twenties. But Black Chicago was less optimistic.

The World's Fair of 1933 found the Chicago Urban League with a full-time staff of one. That was the Executive Secretary, A.L. Foster, who tried to get both white collar and menial jobs for the blacks at the World's Fair. But the placement of menial jobs was given to a white employment agency. According to Willie Randall, the orchestra leader, the only black professionals working on the fair grounds were musicians, members of the Freddie Williams Orchestra, playing at the Jensen Pavilion.

The Chicago World's Fair of 1933 and '34 was commercially successful. Nearly 28 million people went through its turnstiles.

One person attracted to Chicago by the Fair was my maternal grandmother, Winnie Strickland Simms.

Grandma arrived by train from Birmingham, Alabama, on May 30, 1933, two days after the fair opened its doors. For Grandma's announced four-week visit, she brought with her two large trunks, three tightly packed carpet bag suitcases, three Bibles, and a three-volume set of *Patriarchs and Prophets*, a five-volume set of *The Greatest Controversy*, a three-volume set of *The Desire of Ages*, four *Christ in Song* books, and my Aunt Delia's thirteen-year-old son, Joseph Strickland. Grandma was a vociferous believer in the Seventh Day Adventist faith.

I was twelve that year and I couldn't take my eyes off Grandma and all that baggage. When I raised my eyes to her face, they were caught by a cold school-teacher-like stare. She reached out and gave me a quick pat on the back, but her eyes kept staring into mine.

Grandma's voice was soft but stern; she seldom smiled. Prior to her marriage to Grandpa, she was a rural schoolteacher. My mother was convinced that Grandma was smarter and better educated than any of her six daughters, although she was born a slave in 1860 on a Georgia plantation owned by a white Seventh Day Adventist family.

Adventistism wrapped itself around Grandma early in her life and she, in turn, brought that truth to her children and grandchildren with such conviction and force that almost all of my relatives are practicing Seventh Day Adventists.

I will never forget the commanding tone of Grandma's voice on that first Friday when she reminded my father, who was not an Adventist, that all cooking for Saturday's meals would be prepared on Friday, before sundown, because at sundown on Friday we opened the Sabbath, which meant much singing, prayer, and scripture reading. Adventists kept the Sabbath on Saturday instead of Sunday.

That first Friday evening, Grandma handed me one of her *Christ in Song* books and said, "Junior! I want you to open the Sabbath by playing and singing 'Don't Forget the Sabbath' on page 653."

I sheepishly began to sing out of key in a high-pitched voice: "Don't forget the Sabbath the Lord our God hath blessed, of all the week the brightest, of all the week the best; it brings repose from labor, it tells of Joy divine, its beams of light descending, with heavenly beauty shine. Welcome, welcome, ever welcome, blessed Sabbath day."

My grandmother and the group joined me in singing the second and third verses. Grandma seemed pleased with both my piano playing and singing and requested in a cheerful voice that I play and sing the following hymns: "Another Six Days Work Is Done," "Blessed Be the Tie That Binds," and "Rock of Ages, Cleft for Me." I had never tried to perform church songs before, or any song without practice, but I was pleased to find myself playing them easily.

That particular Friday marked the beginning of my 106-week engagement as the family musical director for opening and closing the Sabbath. The closing of the Sabbath ritual took place on Saturday afternoon at home, after church, and commenced just before sundown. Grandma used the sunset table published in the *Morning Watch* to determine the exact time the sun would go down.

Grandma was so bent on our being prepared for the second coming of the Lord that she kept my cousin Joseph and me in some form of religious services five days a week. Mondays, we had prayer meetings at home; Wednesday evenings, we would go to prayer meetings at church; Friday evenings, we held an opening of the Sabbath Ritual. We attended both Sabbath School and church on Saturday; and on Saturday evenings we held a closing of the Sabbath service; and then there was a Sunday evening service, which we always attended. Sunday evening at the Shiloh Seventh Day Adventist Church (which was located on the northeast corner of 46th Street and St. Lawrence Avenue and is currently located at 7000 South Michigan Avenue) was the closest thing to a movie I would experience for the next two years, since we often had as guest speaker a traveling Elder of the Church. Some were great orators. Often they would present slide shows. Those evenings offered entertainment plus news about the outside world.

Also forbidden was the adornment of one's body with cosmetics and worldly dress styles. Grandma was so modest in her clothing selections that she literally followed the dictates of Disciple Timothy: "In like manner also, that women adorn themselves in modest apparel, with shamefacedness and sobriety; not with braided hair, or gold, or pearls, or costly array." (Tim. 2:9) Grandma was careful not to wear any powder or jewelry and restricted the color of her dress and outer coats to two colors, black and blue.

Adventistism not only dictates the type of dress you wear, but it also restricts the food that dresses the lining of your stomach. (A recent medical survey indicated that Adventists as a group enjoy the best health and the longest life span as a result of their dietary habits.) As a true believer of the Adventist faith, Grandma never prepared or ate pork or fish with shells. The only fish that we ate had fins and scales in keeping with the eleventh chapter of Leviticus in the Bible.

> "And the Lord spake unto Moses and to Aaron, saying unto them. (Lev. 11:1)
>
> "Speak unto the children of Israel, saying these are the beast which ye shall eat among all the beasts that are on the earth. (Lev. 11:2)
>
> "Whatsoever parteth the hoof, and is cloven footed, and cheweth the cud, among the beast, that shall ye eat. (Lev. 11:3)
>
> "And the swine, though he divide the hoof, and be clovenfooted, yet he cheweth not the cud; he is unclean to you. (Lev. 11:7)
>
> "Of their flesh shall ye not eat, and their carcass shall ye not touch; they are unclean to you. (Lev. 11:8)
>
> "These shall ye eat of all that are in the waters: Whatsoever hath fins and scales in the waters, in the seas, and in the rivers, them shall ye eat. (Lev. 11:9)
>
> "Whatsoever hath no fins nor scales in the waters, that shall be in the waters, that shall be an abomination unto you." (Lev. 11:12)

To add variety to our daily diet, Grandma would prepare complete vegetarian meals at least three days a week. Her recipes were famous among friends and family. I enjoyed vegetarian meals, but before we could get to the food, we had to show her clean hands, a clean face, and orderly clothes. Then we had to quote a different Bible verse and its biblical source at every meal for 30 consecutive days. My love for Grandma's food and after-dinner stories inspired me to memorize 180 verses within a 60-day period.

Grandma would always tell one or two stories about the olden days after dinner. One evening she talked about the eating, cooking, and working habits of the slaves on the plantation where she was born. Her slavemaster, being a Seventh Day Adventist, made them follow the eating doctrine of the Seventh Day Adventist Church and keep the Sabbath on Saturday. The slaves on the next cotton farm kept Sunday and ate swine.

"Grandma, why did those slaves eat pigs?" Cousin Joe asked.

Grandma replied, "Slaves did not really eat the pig, but they ate the hog leftovers, such as the jowls, or chitterlings and the fat of the back. The slave-masters' primary use for chitterlings, the small intestines of the pig, was to obtain the intestinal grease by boiling the intestines, to be used for soapmaking. The rubbery remains of the gut were the leftovers. They were given to the slaves and they creatively turned them into a delicacy."

"Grandma, what's the good part of the pig?"

"There is no good part. However, the slavemaster ate the muscle cuts of the pig, such as pork chops and pork roast. The price that many of the slave-masters paid for eating low on the hog was a painful and crippling leg and arm disease known as trichinosis. You get trichinosis from eating half-cooked pork. Chitterlings were boiled to a rubbery substance before the slave received them, so few field slaves suffered the disease. Lots of house slaves were afflicted with trichinosis because they ate in the kitchen of their masters the same meals their masters were eating in the dining room."

"What kind of bread did the slaves eat?" Cousin Lucille asked. "Did they eat biscuits?"

Grandma smiled and said, "White folks didn't eat many biscuits because white flour was scarce. The slaves ate hoecake, a corn meal mixed with water and baked on the blade of a field hand's hoe over an open fire. Remember, children, most slaves didn't have pots and pans."

"Grandma, did you ever see a slavemaster beat a field hand for not working?" Junior asked.

"It's past your bedtime," Grandma said. "Good night and don't forget to say your prayers."

We didn't.

CHAPTER 8

Changing Tides: Boyhood to Manhood

I WAS AWAKENED BEFORE DAYBREAK ON MAY 4, 1935, BY MY mother's shrieking: "Junior! Junior! Your father is sick. We have to rush him to the Cook County Hospital."

The fear in my mother's voice frightened me almost as much as my concern about the seriousness of my father's illness. I knew that Dad would only go to the County Hospital as a last resort because he had always talked about the discrimination and graft demanded by the white nurses and interns and the fatal "black bottle" for those who did not cooperate.

Dad looked awful. He was sitting in a bent position on the side of the bed with both hands hugging his stomach tightly. He looked at us but he couldn't answer our desperate questions. His lips looked bloodless and his skin was ashen. Though the house was cool, he sweated profusely.

The fifteen minutes Mama and Grandma spent dressing Dad and walking him down the stairs seemed like hours. As we approached the hospital, Dad uttered his only audible sound other than those painful groans. "Boy, you are the man of the house now, and you have got to take care of your mother," he said in a weak voice.

My mother started crying quietly after Dad disappeared behind the swinging doors with the men in white.

"Mama, you know Daddy is going to be all right," I said, trying to sound like I believed it. She would nod her head up and down in a positive motion and start crying again. I put my arm around my mother's shoulders.

"You know Daddy would be ashamed to see us crying."

The words brought a quiet smile to both our faces. We were still smiling when the nurse informed us that the doctor would be down. Within fifteen minutes the doctor greeted us with a hand shake and told us my father had a ruptured appendix "and could not have lasted another hour."

During the three months he was at home recuperating, the Travis household endured some hard times. During the early 1930s there were no job benefits, hospital insurance programs, social security, or unemployment compensation. (Congress passed the Social Security Act in August 1935.) I tried to fill the void in the family income by taking two newspaper routes. I delivered the morning papers between five and seven a.m. before going to school and the evening papers between four and six p.m. after school. My seven dollar per week contribution helped, but it was not enough to feed Dad, Mama, Grandma, Cousin Joe, and myself. The landlord permitted us to stay with the understanding that we would pay the back rent once my father was able to return to work.

Grandma worked at being an innovative cook. She stretched the budget down to serving the pot liquor from the greens with corn bread as a total meal, putting us on a greens, beans, and hot-water corn bread diet. For four months we had lima beans, cow peas, pinto beans, or black-eyed peas with corn bread for breakfast, lunch, and dinner; and then she would switch to string beans, turnip tops, and cabbage. On rare occasions she prepared boiled turnip greens and we would have Alaga syrup (acronym for Alabama and Georgia) and corn bread for dessert. Grandma was always combining grain (corn bread) and legumes (cow peas, black-eyed peas, etc.) to provide protein for the family.

Dad returned to work in August 1935. Shortly after that, Grandma and Cousin Joe decided to leave Chicago for McRoberts, Kentucky, to stay with Aunt Delia, who was Joe's mother and Grandma's youngest daughter. I was both sorry and glad to see Grandma leave. I was glad because I knew I wouldn't be involved in church activities five days a week anymore. As a matter of fact, I became a church drop-out for the next fifteen years. I was sorry to see her leave because I would miss her presence and good advice. She was very philosophical, and she had a quotation for every problem and occasion. She used to say to me when I suggested that we eat a fourth meal:

To bed, to bed said Sleepy Head,
wait awhile said Slow,
put on the pot said Greedy-Gut,
let's eat before we go.

After hearing that quotation, I usually went to sleep without a snack. Grandmother was also a stickler about punctuality. She would always say: "Time and tide waits for no man."

Only six months of time and tide had passed before a Western Union man delivered a midnight telegram to our apartment which read: "Mother passed this afternoon...come at once." My mother and her sister, Willie, left by train the next afternoon and took my cousin, Frank, and me along. We caught the train at the 12th Street Station for Cincinnati, Ohio, which was the transfer point for trains going into Kentucky. It was my first journey to the South.

It was in the beautiful Cincinnati train station that Mr. Jim Crow kicked me into my assigned corner by refusing to sell me a hot dog at the soda fountain. The next blow occurred when we were herded into a Jim Crow coach, situated—that's right—next to the train's engine. The coach filled quickly, black passengers sitting at one end and baggage at the other. It also sheltered layers of coal dust, soot, and a foul-mouthed conductor.

Our Cincinnati-to-Lexington, Kentucky, train stopped at every town and continued to pack blacks into the Jim Crow car like captives packed into a slave ship in the days of the "middle passage" from Africa. Women, cradling their babies, stood while the conductor occupied four seats for his "office." My mother had Frank and me give up our seats for two of these women, so I rode standing halfway across Kentucky. At Lexington, late at night, we were to catch the double-engine mountain train, which would take us to McRoberts, a mining town.

When we got off at Lexington, we were directed to the rear of the train station where the "for colored only" facilities were located. The ticket and information window there was only manned after the white folks had been served on the other side of the ticket office. The "colored" people's waiting room was dimly lit and much dirtier than the white facility, which was bright, cheerful, and clean. The contrast reminded blacks of their inferior status. It worked.

At daybreak, we saw the train that would take us into McRoberts coming upgrade. The quality of the accommodations on this train "for colored" people was consistent—our coach was dirty with coal dust and soot, and the conductor's language was just as bad as on the other train.

"McRoberts! McRoberts! McRoberts! The end of the line." I looked up. McRoberts, sandwiched in a valley between two ugly coal mountains, seemed like the end of my world.

Uncle Ben met us at the train depot wearing his Sunday suit and a sheep-ish grin.

"Glad you all could come," he greeted us in his Southern drawl. Uncle Ben's smile was the brightest thing we would see in the mountainous, bumpy, three-mile ride we took in his Model T Ford from the train station to his home. Uncle Ben was a coffee-colored man with a kind, round face.

The white folks we saw sitting and standing along the road as we drove to the black section of McRoberts stared at us through bloodshot eyes. The leers on their pale, scrawny faces showed that they recognized us as strangers because of our "big city clothes."

Almost every man we saw along the roadway was dressed in faded blue denim loose-fitting overalls and a bright blue or red bandanna around his neck.

The houses and shacks along the road were painted in a sad rainbow of shades, with the dominating colors being red and white until we reached the black people's section, where the houses were unpainted and the wood was rotted. Clusters of black children were playing in front of the shacks and in the roadside gutters. Old black women wearing red bandannas watched over the noisy children as they sat in their rocking chairs on the sagging front porches.

"That's the house where Delia lives," Uncle Ben said finally, pulling to a stop.

Aunt Delia, who had been standing on the porch with some other people I did not recognize, started running down the hill, grinning and crying with her arms outstretched to hug the first one of us she reached. Aunt Delia had added at least sixty pounds and a substantial stomach to her frame since her last visit to Chicago five years earlier. Mother and Aunt Willie ran up the hill to meet her. The collision point found three sisters hugging, kissing, and crying, joyful at seeing each other, yet saddened by the loss of their mother. Their three-way conversation sounded like a choral counterpoint, with the main theme being a list of names of all the relatives who had arrived for Grandma's funeral.

When we reached the front porch, I realized the people I hadn't recog-nized from the road were aunts, uncles, and cousins from various parts of the country. After enjoying a moment of pride for having so many relatives, I be-gan to worry about where we were all going to eat and sleep.

Initially, we were only to stay two nights, but there was a spinal meningitis epidemic in McRoberts that resulted in canceling the funeral for five days.

On the fifth day we were permitted to have a graveside service for Grandma, because indoor public gatherings were prohibited for the duration of the epidemic.

I had not really accepted the finality of Grandma's death until we stepped out of the funeral cars at the gate of the graveyard. There we began a slow walk up a winding path on a steep and lonely Kentucky hill, behind the pallbearers carrying a pine box. My mind was churning with thoughts about Grandma. Those thoughts made my throat dry, but I could not cry.

Grandma's body was lowered into a dark six-foot hole on the hillside of a Kentucky coal mine, but she will never know how dark it was because her eyes were forever closed.

Uncle Frank, Uncle Russell, Uncle Elliott, and Uncle Ben had toiled in the mine holes of Kentucky, Alabama, Illinois, and Pennsylvania all of their working lives. They were lowered by cage into the deep dark holes daily. Their eyes were open, but they did not know how dark it was because the nature of their work had blinded them mentally and dwarfed them physically. I reflected on this as I talked with them during that visit.

Four of my mother's five sisters married Alabama coal miners who tried to escape. Each uncle tried to retrace his liberation route nightly for the rest of us during Grandma's five-day wake.

The stories would always begin in the early evening, after the women had cleared the kitchen. My uncles would pull their chairs around the woodburning cooking stove and place large tin cans to the right of their chairs to relieve their mouths of tobacco juice and clear their lungs of the coal-colored spit that always followed their frequent coughs. Every night, as the old iron stove turned fire red, their stories became more intense.

Uncle Elliott was considered the firebrand of the group. Uncle Russell always referred to him as the family Indian because of his reddish complexion and coal-black curly hair. Uncle Elliott's temper seemed to rise with the heat in the old iron stove.

"What took place between you and your foreman in the Alabama Edgewater coal mine that caused you to leave town so hurriedly?" Uncle Russell asked him one evening.

"Nigger! You know what happened!" Uncle Elliott said.

Uncle Russell flinched and stared at Elliott. "All I know is that three carloads of white folks came to my house looking for you. They'd been drinking, and some of them were carrying guns. When they were leaving, I heard one of them say, 'Let's check the freight yard for that coon.'"

Uncle Elliott grinned. "The bastards were on the right trail, but they were an hour late. I left the mine running after I hit that cracker on the left side of his head with a methane detector." They explained that a detector was a small stainless steel box half the size of a book, used to test the mine air for gases. "I didn't even stop at the bathhouse to change clothes. I did a one-mile dash in those steel-toed regulation shoes all the way to the freight yard and caught the first thing smoking." He stopped to smile at the memory. "The direction the train was going was not as important as putting the maximum amount of space between me and Edgewater, Alabama," he said.

"I still don't understand why you would start trouble with white folks in the mine," Russell said softly.

"You don't understand!" Uncle Elliott said. "The problem didn't start in the mine but in my mind, when I was born a black male in Alabama."

I sat up at that. The table reminded me of all these discussions my father and his brothers used to have around our dining room table. There was a lot to be learned when the men got to talking like this.

"I resented, as a kid, having to knock on the back steps of a cracker's house to get permission to step up to the back door to beg for a ten-cent grass-cutting job," Elliott went on. "My stomach and chest sheltered a silent rage when my young wife had to work in the company-owned shacks of those cracker miners for three dollars per week, plus lunch. She cleaned the house, washed and ironed the clothes, nursed their kids on her left breast and ours on the right breast, wiped their red snotty noses, and cleaned their dirty chalk-white behinds."

"But nigger mammies have always done those things," Russell said mildly.

"Damn it, Russell! That does not mean that they did not resent having to do them," Uncle Elliott said. "That 'kick me in the ass because I like it' mentality has kept most blacks in a crap-game kneeling position all of their lives!"

"I still don't think that we should do anything that is going to make white folks mad," Uncle Russell said in a reasonable tone. He was sitting straight in his chair, staring down at his hands with great concentration, as if making a great effort to understand Elliott's rebelliousness.

"I wouldn't have hit that honky if he hadn't threatened to beat my black ass. He wanted me to apologize for implying that he was lying about my work performance."

Uncle Russell looked up from his hands and straight into Uncle Elliott's eyes. After a moment he said, "Always remember that although the man cannot write, he is boss because he is white."

(In many instances, the white mine foreman could not read or write; hence, it was commonplace to see a black laborer with a seventh or eighth grade education assisting his white boss by making out daily reports which required both math and writing skills. In many sections of Northern West Virginia, Ohio, and Western Pennsylvania, black miners held such local offices in the United Mine Workers Union as president and secretary, even though they were outnumbered by Eastern Europeans. It was their proficiency in speaking and writing English that won them the positions.

(Black appointments to the mine committee can also be traced to the language factor. The United Mine Workers contract said all committee-men shall be American citizens, or miners who have made application for citizenship, and are capable of handling the English language comfortably. According to Professor Herbert R. Northrup of the Wharton School of Finance and Commerce, no black was elected to union vice presidency in Alabama until 1944.)

Uncle Elliott turned to Uncle Frank. "You explain it to him," he said. "You left your kneeling position in the Edgewater mine because you had trouble with your boss, didn't you?" The Edgewater mine, they told me, had a four-foot ceiling, which meant that the miners worked on their knees, using pieces of worn out auto tires as knee pads, as they drilled, picked, and cleaned the rock from the coal before loading it by hand for eight hours daily. The only lights in the work area were the bike-sized lamps on their hats.

"Yes. We moved to West Virginia to work in a new coal mine, but it wasn't because of any racial friction," Uncle Frank said. "We weren't there long before I was recruited to break a strike in a little coal town called Edenborn, near Uniontown, Pennsylvania. The Pennsy mines were the first I ever worked where I didn't have to do any crawl mining. The mines' ceilings there are all six feet or better." Uncle Frank stopped and coughed a long, racking cough. Then he spit painfully into the cuspidor at his elbow. The others turned their eyes away, aware that his cough was getting serious. Uncle Frank was displaying early symptoms of the totally disabling black lung disease, and all were aware of it.

(Several studies in the mid-1930s showed blacks overrepresented in mine jobs that were both dangerous and unhealthy and underrepresented in the more desirable outside jobs and indirect labor jobs connected with the mines. Of the 2,411 blacks studied by James T. Lang in his "Negro Miners in West Virginia", only eleven were in positions which, even by the most liberal stretching of the term, could be called positions of authority.

(In a rare instance, a black mine laborer would be promoted to motor-man on a mantrip train, used to carry men into the mines and also to carry the coal out of the mines. His brakeman or triprider would always be a black. Under no circumstances would you find a black motorman and a white brakeman, although the reverse was frequently true.)

Uncle Frank gasped for breath. "My chest feels a bit tight and sore from that black phlegm I just coughed up. Excuse me. I'm going out on the front porch for some air." The others stared after him in silence.

Uncle Elliott turned to Uncle Ben. "Would you let your children follow you into the mines, the way you followed your father?"

Uncle Ben coughed and drank a water glass half full of whiskey in one gulp to clear the old coal dust from his lungs and throat. "Hell, no! I wouldn't put my children in a cage to go down five hundred feet under the ground to take the punishment and abuse I took from those redneck crackers they brought in from Mississippi, Alabama, and Georgia to supervise the McRobert Mine operation. Those mines were a grave for the living. We only differed from the dead in that we were regurgitated back to the earth's surface every afternoon, only to be reswallowed into its bowels again the next morning."

"So why have you stayed in the mines for twenty years?" Uncle Elliott asked.

"I'm trapped," Uncle Ben answered. "What else can a black man do here?"

Uncle Elliott's laugh was hard. "Nigger! You aren't trapped, you're enslaved. You're enslaved to the company landlord for your shack. You're enslaved to the company store for your food. You're enslaved to the company hospital for your medical care. You're enslaved to the company clothing store for your wife's underwear and your babies' shoes. The corporate master owns you the same as he owns the town you live in, the shack you sleep in, the stores that you buy in, the hospital that you die in, and the graveyard that you'll be buried in."

Uncle Elliott laughed again and looked up as Uncle Frank came back into the room.

"I remember one day in the Edgewater mines when the boss wanted me to be careful and not let a loose rock fall on the mule," Elliott said, his humorous eyes on Frank. "I said 'Yes, sah! But what about me?' He said, 'I can always hire another nigger, but I would have to buy another mule.'"

Uncle Frank echoed Elliott's grin. "That philosophy is a hangover from the antebellum South, when the mine operators and the railroad builders found it more economical to hire slaves by the day or week from the local plantation owners rather than to own them."

At that point my mother called me into the adjoining room and said: "Your father is going to disown us if we don't catch that six-thirty train back to Chicago."

I had a lot to think about as our train made its way to the North again.

CHAPTER 9

DuSable High, Class of '39

THERE WERE FOUR OF US IN DON'S POOL HALL ON THE SOUTH Side one Monday morning—Gene Vine, Slim Rose, Eddie Davis, and me. We had cut Spanish class to listen to records on the penny vendor: each was to pay for and play five records at a penny a tune.

It was my turn to choose, and I picked Earl Hines' "Rosetta."

Gene's ambition was to be a professional dancer, and he had the agility and style of a natural born tap dancer. All he lacked was the kind of discipline that would have made him practice three or four hours a day. Gene started tapping in rhythm with the song, and the rest of us started clapping to the off beat. Gene kept on tapping to our hand beat after the record was finished, and everybody in the pool hall stopped to watch.

"Man, that was groovy and solid," I said, when he ended his routine. "You ought to try out for the Regal Theatre Amateur Nite or Major Edward Bowes' Radio Amateur Hour."

"You're better than a lot of professional tap dancers," Eddie said.

"Man, I'm not that good," Gene said.

"Come on," I said. "You could be the next Bill 'Bojangles' Robinson if you wanted to."

Gene looked at me out of his sleepy eyes. "Bojangles, ha," he said. He went to the other side of the pool hall and sat down.

The rest of us stood up and stretched luxuriously. It didn't worry us that we were cutting class. We did that a lot. Plenty of times we'd take most of the day off, especially if Gene's mother, a day worker who earned two dollars a day plus fourteen cents streetcar fare, was working.

On those days we'd go over to Gene's apartment and goof off. I would play the piano, and Gene would tap.

We were freshmen at the new Wendell Phillips High School on South Wabash. It was the first new high school to be built in an all-black community in the history of the city, but that didn't impress us. Even at its opening, when I came into the brand new building to find decorators still putting up light green paint in the corridors, the school was jammed. It had been planned to accommodate 2,500 students, but when I started in February 1935, I was one of 1,300 freshmen in a total enrollment of 3,548 students—all blacks except for one female white student.

The extraordinarily large enrollment at the new school had been caused by an early morning fire at the old Wendell Phillips High School on East Pershing in January. School authorities closed down the old facility and transferred the entire staff, faculty, records, trophies, students, and tradition into a new high school that had no books or supplies. The new three million dollar facility hadn't been scheduled to open until September 1935.

The absence of books and supplies gave me the excuse I wanted to hang out at Nick and Angel's Hamburger Grill and the school supply store at 4859 South State Street. That's where I took up with Gene and Slim and Eddie. My new friends weren't troublemakers. They just shared with me a general indifference to school.

Slim Rose's highest ambition, for example, was to be able to afford twenty-two cents a day for two packs of Camel cigarettes so he wouldn't have to bum drags or go searching for long butts along the street gutters. He also wanted to have ten cents to get into the Warwick Hall on East 47th Street every Sunday afternoon to do the "jelly," a slow drag with a stomach roll and bear hug, to the music of Nat Cole (the "King" was added six years later) and his Twelve Royal Dukes, or Tony Fambro and his Jungle Rhythm Orchestra. The "jelly" was performed best to the slow beat of Duke Ellington's "Mood Indigo," "Solitude," or Hoagy Carmichael's immortal "Stardust."

It was at DuSable that I made up my mind I was going to be a professional musician. And DuSable offered me some opportunities to learn, though they didn't all have to do with classes. Nat Cole, for instance, was a classmate—he was enrolled in the Spanish class we were all cutting, until he signed a contract with promoter Malcolm B. Smith to take his first band on the road in March 1935. I did, however, take Dr. Mildred Bryant Jones' harmony classes seriously. They introduced me to counterpoint and music composition.

Gene was still sitting down, recovering from his exertions, when Slim said, "Clapping my hands and watching you dance has made me hungry. Let's go down to Nick and Angel's and get two sou (nickel) hamburgers with chili sauce and split them four ways."

"I got a deece (dime) for a malted milk shake with four straws," I said.

The others agreed and we headed for the pool hall exit.

Looking west across State Street from Don's front door, we could see the rear of the two-story frame house on 50th and Dearborn where three black men were killed in the street by some white Chicago policemen in 1931 while they were trying to put a seventy-one-year-old woman's furniture back into the apartment from which she had been evicted for being three months behind in her rent.

We strolled the two blocks from 51st Street to Nick and Angel's. The west side of State Street was taken up by two-story brick structures that lacked any socially redeemable character, intermixed with a few frame buildings that looked like they had been nailed together by a bored carpenter lacking plans. The block also had five-story brick walk-ups with faces that had been masked with wrought iron fire escapes to provide a quick exit from the crowded structures.

Down in the 4900 block on the west side of State, there were eighteen two-story frame structures built before 1900. They were in varying stages of deterioration. Some stood erect, proudly painted in an effort to retain the appearance of their lost youth; others had begun to lean, unmasking their advanced stages of deterioration.

Scattered in between the frame buildings were six vacant lots, weed- and rubble-filled gaps once occupied by buildings whose owners had either ceased to care for them or had simply lacked the funds to keep them nice neighbors. The ground floors of the other buildings routinely housed small school supply and candy stores, with the exception of Sam's Grocery and Meat Market at 4960 South State Street and a black-owned eat shop called the D & C Lunchroom at 1904 South State.

As we walked along, Gene and Slim fell into a violent argument about who had the lightest complexion. Eddie and I tried to stay out of it, keeping our eyes on the sidewalk as we walked along. It seemed a silly argument to me, since we all knew that black female slaves' involuntary contact with both white and red men had given blacks a million variations in skin color. Some very dark blacks have a reddish hue to their complexion, while others, equally dark, have slight tone mixtures that range from a blue tinge to a brown cast. You might have said Gene was light black and Slim was medium black. But what did it matter? I kept thinking. And do to this day.

They were still going on about it when we got to Nick and Angel's. But the place was jammed with students and drop-outs eating hamburgers and hot dogs, drinking pop and smoking cigarettes, so we crossed the street to the D & C Lunchroom, where they specialized in hot tamales and chili.

While the owners, Frank Davis and Samuel Collins, were getting food for us, we continued the discussion about skin color. It had all started the previous day, when we had gone to see the movie *Imitation of Life*, starring Fredi Washington, Louise Beavers, and Claudette Colbert at the Metropolitan Theater at 46th and South Parkway. Fredi Washington was a fair-skinned, blue-eyed black woman who played the role of a young black woman named Peola, who wanted to pass for a white. The co-star, Louise Beavers, was both fat and dark-skinned. Her character was Aunt Delilah, the mother who was rejected by her light-skinned daughter.

White folks found the picture both sensational and comforting, because it ended with the implication that any black who tried to pass for a white would ultimately be conscience-stricken. The picture was also a box office success in the black community because it was the first time that the color caste system among blacks had been examined in a movie.

Slim and Gene were rehashing the color caste system, not because either of them would ever be able to pass for white, but because they felt that a light-complexioned black might have some cultural and economic advantage over a dark-complexioned black. The argument drew the attention of the owners of the shop. Both men were college graduates. Davis had finished Morehouse College in Atlanta, Georgia. He was light-skinned, with straight black hair. Collins was a coffee-and-cream color and had wooly, dark red hair. He had a liberal arts degree from Howard University in Washington, D.C.

"Light-complexioned blacks have had economic advantages dating back to the earliest days of slavery," Davis said. "Particularly if they have been identified and accepted by the slave master as his offspring in some surreptitious manner."

"Yeah, but a very dark child, the color of Gene or Slim, wouldn't get such recognition even if the master slept with his mother every night," Collins said.

"So I think it's silly for you two guys to be squabbling over the smell of the pork chop, as opposed to the pork chop itself."

He went on with a laugh. "That kind of argument is about as productive as bleaching cream. Have you ever thought about the thousands of black women in Chicago who go to bed every night after applying Palmer's Skin Whitener to their faces only to check the mirror the next morning and find out they're as black as they were the night before?"

We laughed with him.

"Those who subscribe to the teachings of Marcus Garvey don't have to keep looking for the elusive emulsified escape that is offered in those cans," Collins said.

"And what were Garvey's teachings on skin color?" Slim asked.

"Garvey did not believe we should make a distinction among ourselves based on a color caste system," Collins told him gravely. "He believed that such a system was evil and worked a great harm to our racial solidarity. He accused one of our major civil rights groups of advocating advancement just for those who were as near to white as possible. He was opposed to anything that resembled a 'blue-vein' aristocracy among blacks, or what we might call from that movie you boys are discussing a 'Peola' class system."

"What's that about blue veins?" Eddie said.

"There are clubs and churches in Chicago that will not accept as members any black person, no matter what his accomplishments, unless he is light enough so you can see the blueness of their veins through their skin."

"Yes," Frank Davis added. "Let me show you a picture from the society section of last week's *Chicago Defender*. Do you see any dark or brown-skinned girls in that group?" We checked out the picture of young girl debutantes in long dresses. Every one of them had light skin and hair carefully arranged to imitate the loose curls white women were wearing then. "You can safely assume they have all established themselves as 'blue veins' or 'Peolas,'" Davis said.

"But Chicago's blue-vein society is really subtle when compared to the one in Washington, D.C," Collins said. "The way it's flaunted there, in the public schools, private universities, hiring and promotional policies in private business, and in both municipal and federal government jobs is incomprehensible. Your civil service score may get you in the door, but you can forget about a substantial promotion unless you're the right shade of black. And the right shade of black is yellow.

"If you're white, you're all right; if you're yellow, you're mellow; if you're brown, stick around; but if you're black, get back," Collins said. "The owner of the Morris Perfect Eat Shop once told me he is partial to real light-skinned girls with 'good' hair, because they make a good appearance and attract the big spenders to his place. That kind of philosophy is shared by a lot of people who hire secretaries, nurses, typists, receptionists. The utility companies have just begun to hire Negroes, and you can bet what kind of looks will get you the job."

"That ain't all," his partner said. "Those color-conscious bastards are perpetuating that propaganda through their children. If a kid wants to marry somebody who is not the right shade, he or she is usually rejected by the whole family. Occasionally a gross difference is acceptable if the prospect happens to be a black professional with both high status and big money. There might also be an exception of the prospective spouse has some other Caucasian feature: if not color, then hair, or if not hair, then maybe blue eyes will be an acceptable substitute."

We studied each others' faces while we munched the last of our food. Then Gene jumped up. "Man," he said, staring at his watch. "I've got to run home and mop the kitchen and make up my bed before my mother gets home."

Later on, I was to regret the hours I stole from school to spend with my friends in this fashion. But at the time I believed my destiny was to be a musician and that the education I was picking up outside of school was superior to anything available in the classroom.

In sharp contrast to my attitude was that of a well-dressed upperclassman I observed in the school. He always seemed to be rushing to some unknown destination, his eyes focused straight ahead. That was John H. Johnson, now president of Johnson Publishing Company, which produces *Ebony, Jet,* and *Ebony, Jr.* magazines. He is also president of Radio Station WJPC in Chicago and Fashion Fair Cosmetics.

In April 1936, the Chicago Board of Education voted to change the name of Wendell Phillips High School to Jean Baptiste Pointe DuSable High School, after the black man who first settled on the land that would later be known as Chicago. The name had been chosen in a poll by the *Chicago Defender*. Second choice had been Alexander Pushkin, the Russian poet and author who was a descendant of a West African adventurer. John H. Johnson was the president of the first class to graduate after the name had been changed.

My own ambitions were taking other directions, though. In Captain Walter Dyett's band and orchestra in room 345, I was getting to listen to performances by such great piano artists as Nat Cole, Dorothy Donegan, Thomas Rigsby, Martha Davis, Rudy Martin, and John Young.

Music as a profession offered glamour, travel, and contacts. And it was a hell of a lot of fun. I can't think of any other business where you can have your cake and eat it too. The price for that is a very high mortality rate among young talented jazz musicians.

At age fifteen, my talents were hardly being sought after by established band leaders, so I decided to organize the best available musical talent in Chicago and start my own group. I learned years later that this was a very sound business principle. I found I had a good nose for sniffing out high-paying gigs, and enough personality—some called it cockiness—to persuade the owner or promoter to give me and my boys the job.

By early fall of 1935 my band was gigging at least three nights a week. That work record was very good when you consider that the country was in the midst of the Depression. Older and more talented artists were sitting on their hands, talking about the good old days of the 1920s. As a matter of fact, I was working so regularly that Harry W. Gray, the business agent for the Musicians Protective Union Local 208 of the American Federation of Musicians, would come on my jobs and threaten to pull the band off the stand because I was not a card-carrying union musician. In one instance, the band was actually pulled from the stage for playing in a union hall because there was a nonunion musician in the group. That one person without a union card was me, the orchestra leader.

On Christmas night, 1935, Gray called me off the bandstand in a loud and crusty voice. The look on his face was both solemn and mean when he asked, "Young man, why are you causing me so many problems?"

"All I want to do, Mr. Gray, is play music," I replied.

"Why in the hell don't you join the union?"

"I tried," I said.

With a flash of anger in his eyes, Gray growled, "What the hell do you mean you tried?"

"Just that," I retorted. "Mr. Musco C. Buckner, the financial secretary and treasurer of the union, told me that I would not be eligible for membership until I had reached my sixteenth birthday."

Gray's expression softened slightly. "When will you be sixteen?"

"Three months from today, on February twenty-fifth," I answered.

Gray smiled and said, "I will see you at the local at three p.m. on the twenty-fifth."

He made a note in his little black book, then turned quickly and walked out of the dance hall.

On my sixteenth birthday, I joined the union and became the youngest band leader in Local 208. The union card was my admission to adulthood; most of my music associates were five to twenty-five years my senior. This accelerated social aging caused my mother some serious concerns, but my father let it be known that he thought I could handle myself. Time proved him right, because he never found it necessary to put any restrictions on the hours I came home. He understood the life of a musician since he had made several attempts himself at making music a career. My father's only requirement of me was that I call home and give my whereabouts anytime I thought I would have to be out past the time the gig would ordinarily require.

Dad would always say, "I don't want you to call home for my sake, but for your mother's sake. She has a tendency to worry about your late hours."

Late hours became morning and even daylight hours as musicians would congregate for "jam sessions" (an event where musicians from various bands would try to out-blow or out-solo each other) at a different club every morning after work. For example, I saw Duke Ellington, Earl Hines, Cassino Simpson, and Art Tatum in a piano-playing contest at the Annex Cafe, located at 2300 South State, that lasted three and a half hours.

This kind of action was very common at the Three Deuces, located at 222 North State, particularly when Roy Eldridge (trumpet) with side men like Dave Young (tenor sax), Johnny Collins (guitar), Scoops Carry (alto sax), Zutty Singleton (drums), and Truck Parkham (bass) were on the stand. White musicians such as Benny Goodman, Tommy Dorsey, Paul Whiteman, and Artie Shaw would pack the place with their side men every night they were in town, seeking an opportunity to jam and learn what that old black magic called jazz was all about.

Plotnick's Arcadia at 4800 South Cottage Grove Avenue would have a breakfast dance and jam session every Tuesday morning from four a.m. until they poured the last person into a cab. The Mid-Nite Club at 3140 South Indiana held the same kind of session on Saturday morning. The Panama Cafe

Nite Club at 207 East 58th put on four floor shows nightly, complete with a chorus line, and featured Eddie Cole's band with Nat King Cole at the piano. So did the Dreamland Cafe at 4700 South State and the Cafe Montclare at 2903 South State Street where they put on a red hot floor show, plus a special breakfast dance every Thursday morning.

The classy night spots on the South Side during that period included the Grand Terrace at 3955 South Parkway, where Earl Hines and his NBC Orchestra played seven nights a week for eight hours. The evening would start with a half-hour dance set followed by a fifteen-minute intermission. The band would come back and play another short dance set and then begin playing the first part of the stage show, which was in three segments, each lasting one to one and a half hours.

The show would include a dozen beautifully costumed "high yellow" chorus girls who would make three to six garment changes per show. In addition, the show would contain top-flight dance teams such as the Nicholas Brothers and the Four Step Brothers, or singles like Bill "Bojangles" Robinson, along with torch and blues singers on a par with Ethel Waters or Lena Horne, plus comedians equivalent to Redd Foxx or Flip Wilson. (These types of productions have not been staged any place in the country, including Las Vegas, in the past thirty years.)

Dave's Cafe at 343 East Garfield and the old Club Delisa at 5512–16 South State featured the band of Albert Ammons (piano) and his Rhythm Kings. (Ammons was the father of Gene Ammons, a tenor saxophone player, and Bishop Edsel Ammons, both former DuSable students.) Both Dave's and Delisa had above average entertainment that attracted a lot of white folks to the South Side, as did the Grand Terrace. This is only a small sampling of clubs on the South Side of Chicago in the 1930s.

All the clubs had one thing in common, and that was a Jim Crow seating policy in the heart of the ghetto. The best tables in the house were always reserved for whites. It was a common sight to walk into any of the class South Side clubs and see white folks hogging the ringside seats while blacks sat on the side and in the rear. If it serves as any consolation, Chicago was still one step ahead of New York's Cotton Club, which was located in black Harlem but did not admit any blacks unless they were celebrities.

Many a morning, I would get home just in time to change from a tuxedo into school clothing. The fact that I finished high school after such early exposure to show business is attributed to my family indoctrinating me with the need for a high school diploma. (Unfortunately, we believed that a diploma, a degree, and education were synonymous.)

Mrs. Mary Herrick, my civics teacher, would occasionally stop me in the corridor and ask, "What do you plan to make out of yourself, Dempsey?"

My reply was always the same, "A musician."

She would smile and say, "Don't you want to back your music up with another career choice in case you change your mind about music as a total lifestyle?"

The bell rang and I went to class without answering that question for Mrs. Herrick, or for myself. The next time we met in the hall, I remember telling Mrs. Herrick that I had the opportunity to meet the ex-heavyweight champion, Jack Johnson, at the new night club he had opened at 3831 South Michigan. She looked surprised, but did not comment.

Mrs. Herrick was one of the few teachers during the entire time I was in public school who actually showed an interest in my activities both inside and outside of the school building. For this reason, I have found it necessary to give her an oral report card on my activities at irregular intervals over a period that has now passed its forty-fourth year.

Nineteen thirty-seven was my best year, financially, in the music business. In addition to a brand new 1937 Buick, it afforded me the kind of clothing I felt a young band leader needed. (The first car I owned was a 1934 Graham Page, which my father gave me in 1936.)

A Jewish boy from the West Side of Chicago—Benny Goodman—was directly responsible for my success in 1937 because he made black jazz legitimate by calling it "swing" and playing it before mass white audiences. Swing was nothing more than warmed-over 1920 New Orleans–Chicago style jazz as played by Louis Armstrong, King Oliver, Johnny Dodds, Erskine Tate, Earl Hines, and other blacks two decades earlier. Benny Goodman took jazz out of her "cat house" environment and put her in a white virginal lace gown and she was received in her country with wild enthusiasm. The *New York Times* solemnly suggested that the craze was getting out of hand, quoting a psychologist on the "dangerously hypnotic influence of swing, cunningly devised to a faster tempo than seventy-two bars to the minute—faster than the human pulse."

My pulse rate must have doubled on the evening of June 22, 1937, because it was liberation night for blacks throughout the world. My music prosperity permitted me to spend $27.50 (two weeks' salary for a family man working under the Public Works Administration) for a ringside seat at Comiskey Park to see the 23-year-old, 197-and-a-half pound Joe Louis deck the 197-pound James J. Braddock for the heavyweight championship of the world.

When Joe Louis knocked James Braddock d.o.a. (dead on his ass) in the eighth round, my head reeled. Even in that state of great excitement, I wondered what my Uncle Otis, the great Jack Johnson fan, would have thought when they raised Joe Louis' hand and announced that he was the new heavyweight champion of the world. I did not have to wonder what the black community thought because the South Side had gone totally berserk, with black people running up and down streets shouting, crying, laughing, and singing as if the millennium had come.

Streetcars could not move because the streets were filled with people from curb to curb. Taxicabs were trying to get through 35th Street by honking their horns and moving slowly down the sidewalks. Whiskey and beer bottles appeared in many hands, seemingly by magic. Huge bonfires were started on street corners, not because black hands were cold, but because black hearts were warm with the feeling of liberation.

The condition of the street would not permit me to liberate my car; I walked from Comiskey Park to the Eighth Regiment Armory at 35th and Giles where the Roy Eldridge and Benny Goodman orchestras were appearing in a "Battle of Swing." When I reached the armory door, I could see Dave Young blowing one of his tenor choruses of "Lady Be Good."

There must have been two thousand people in the hall when I arrived. I worked my way through the crowd to the bandstand to greet Roy, Dave, Zutty, Scoops, and other members of the band. Within an hour after I arrived, five thousand people had entered the armory. The police had to close the doors and stop the band from playing because people were literally hanging from the ceiling. The crowd later went through the ceiling when Benny Goodman's band opened their set with "King Porter Stomp" and followed it with "Big John Special."

The drive of Gene Krupa's drums and the screams of Harry James' trumpet rocked the foundation of the solidly built armory. Those white boys were playing black music like it had never been heard before. The Goodman formula for this swing with a beat was that he had some of the best-trained white musicians in the country playing the musical arrangements of two of the best black arrangers in the nation, namely, Fletcher Henderson and Jimmy Mundy. The Goodman sound was Black America speaking through a white ambassador of swing.

Wendell Phillips High School and its successor, DuSable, literally bubbled over with swingers without portfolio. Major H. Clark Smith, musical director at Wendell Phillips, trained some of America's most talented swingers in the persons of Ray Nance (trumpet and violin with Duke Ellington), Willie Randall (saxophones and arranger for Earl Hines), Milton Hinton (bass violin with Cab Calloway), Charlie Allen (trumpet with Duke Ellington), Quinn Wilson (bass and arranger for Earl Hines), and Lionel Hampton (drummer with Louis Armstrong and vibra harp with Benny Goodman).

Goodman first heard Hampton play in Los Angeles at the Paradise Cafe in an after-hours jam session. The musical success of the Goodman Quartet that included Hampton, Teddy Wilson on piano, Gene Krupa on drums, and Goodman on clarinet is legendary.

Major Clark's successor, Captain Walter Dyett, retained the legend with DuSable swingers who became movie, radio, and television stars, such as Red (Redd Foxx) Sanford, who appeared in the DuSable Hi-Jinks of 1939; Austin Powell and his Cats and the Fiddle (Powell was both singer and composer); the immortal Nat "King" Cole; and Dorothy Donegan, the jazz piano genius and star of radio, movies, television, and night clubs.

Many talented DuSable swingers' and singers' musical careers were eclipsed by the racist policies prevailing in show business that mirrored white America during the 1930s; those policies manifest only slight modification today. A few of the eclipsed musical talents were Savannah Strong (standing ovation for "At My Beck and Call"); Elizabeth Hunt Moutoussamy (memorable rendition of George Gershwin's "Summertime"); and Bessie Sutton (show stopper of the 1936 Hi-Jinks singing Duke Ellington's "I Let a Song Go Out of My Heart").

The musical and economic mix within the DuSable student body of the 1930s gave it a high educational aspiration level that ceased to exist after the homeowner population living west of State Street was displaced for a public housing community. Prior to the building of the Robert Taylor Homes housing project in the 1960s, there were 312 black homeowners living between 47th and 55th Streets, west of State and east of Federal Street. After the Robert Taylor Homes were completed, the homeowner population had been reduced to 23, according to the 1970 census. The difference was noticeable.

CHAPTER 10

My Street of Broken Dreams

IN THE WEEKS BEFORE OUR GRADUATION IN JUNE 1939, THE DuSable High School seniors did a lot of talking about the dismal job picture for blacks. We knew well enough that there were few "clean" jobs for us, other than clerking at the post office or being Pullman porters. There were no black bus drivers or conductors, no black streetcar operators, no black elevated motormen. No blacks were working in responsible positions in neighborhood banks or in black ghetto branches of life insurance companies or major retail stores. Blacks weren't even able to get jobs as cashiers in the Bronzeville drugstore chains.

We knew all that—it was inescapable. We saw the "White Only" job ads for the industrial positions the war had opened up, and we read the "White Help Wanted" signs on the factory gates and hiring halls. The situation was so bad that some of my contemporaries at school even failed courses in order to delay joining that weary march from factory gate to factory gate in search of jobs that did not exist.

I shook my head with the others. But the truth was that I somehow thought it was going to turn out differently for me. Hadn't I been working for years on my music? Didn't I have a skill to sell? I knew that by 1939 jobs for black musicians were drying up, that the craze for "black jazz" had turned to a craze for "white swing" and hundreds of talented black musicians were living off the Federal Arts Project, practicing their craft for an average salary of fifty-five dollars a month. But what did statistics matter to me, when all I needed was just one job?

My father looked at me with a solemn stare when I talked like this, but he knew he would have to let me face reality for myself this time. By September, I had worn the soles off several pairs of shoes, trudging from one agency to another in search of that full-time job as a musician. My father grew more and more silent as I told him the stories of my many disappointments.

Then on a Tuesday morning in September, he came into my room and woke me up.

"Boy, if you're going to get a job, you have to be the first one in line at the employment office," he said.

"What?"

"Get up," he said. He watched as I stumbled out of bed and reached for my clothes. "This is how it's going to be," he said. "You can't drive your car until you find a job. I'm going to give you fourteen cents for streetcar fare every day, and fifty cents for lunch money. You understand?"

"Yes, sir," I said.

"Don't spend the lunch money unless you get a job."

"Yes, sir," I said.

Dad had a cousin who worked at the Armour Soap Works at 31st and Bensen and a friend at the starch factory in the 2900 block on Archer Avenue. They were three blocks apart, so Dad had settled it in his mind that I would visit both places on this first day of serious job hunting.

I walked to 51st and Indiana to catch the streetcar and rode the Indiana car to 31st and transferred to a westbound trolley. The riders were all blacks talking loudly; some wore blue denim overalls, others wore their Sunday best. When we reached Wentworth, oddly dressed white folks speaking with foreign accents and smelling of garlic started to fill the trolley. In the six blocks from Wentworth to Halsted, "Big Red" collected an overflow clientele causing both men and women to hang off the rear steps of the trolley and hold the door's center bar and side handles for support.

The air around the Armour Soap Works was pungent, but not as overwhelming as the smell from the stockyards to the south of 39th Street. Following my father's instructions, I did not go directly to the Armour employment office but walked over the South branch of the Chicago River to the starch factory and waited outside the entrance door. After about an hour, a tall, blond man in white overalls came to the door with a cold expression on his face. "Boy! We ain't hiring today."

I left the starch factory feeling worthless and went back across the bridge to the Armour employment office in a one-story red-faced brick building with about a thirty by seventy feet interior. A middle-aged white man sat at a desk behind a three-foot railing. Facing him were ten rows of wooden benches filled with black and white men, both young and old. The men sitting erect with their eyes focused on the man at the front desk appeared to be new in the job market or just recently laid-off. But others sat in a hopeless leaning position, looking alternately at the floor, the walls, the ceiling, and seldom focusing their attention on the man at the front desk. Occasionally the phone would ring and everyone would look up. The desk man would beckon one or two of the bench warmers. Usually they were sent directly to the plant to work without work clothes or rubber boots. I learned that these jobs would only last a half day or sometimes a week, if you were lucky.

I repeated my trips daily to both the starch factory and the soap works for sixty-nine straight days, including Saturdays. Job hunting was one of the coldest, loneliest, and most dehumanizing experiences that I had ever encountered. Each day ended as it started except that the soles of my shoes and the seat of my pants became thinner.

My father finally decided my only chance was to buy a job. He was right. I went to the Factory Employment Agency on East Van Buren between Wabash and State. For ten dollars, I got a job as a porter for the Apex Box Company located at 2509 West Cermak Road. The job paid twenty-eight cents per hour or eleven dollars and twenty cents per week.

There was only one black working at Apex. His name was Art and he was a freight elevator operator and order filler. Art had a coffee-brown complexion, and a quick smile that displayed his straight pearly teeth. Art was respected by both the bosses and employees alike because of his business-like, no-nonsense attitude. The other employees were either Polish or Italian, mostly Polish women, and the plant owners were German Jews.

With Art's assistance, I made the necessary mental adjustments to perform my portering duties with dispatch. My tasks included cleaning and mopping four two-stall washrooms and sweeping the plant floors continuously throughout the day. After one month on the job, I was commended by my supervisors and subsequently by the vice president of the company for performing my portering chores with both pride and enthusiasm.

My father had taught me early in life not to accept money for any assignment that I did not intend to do well. A laborer at Wilson & Co., he made pulling hams out of vats in a cold room sound like an important and exciting activity.

"I pulled two more vats of hams today than Polock Joe and Mexican Frank who was not even in the running," he would sometimes say.

So positive did my Dad make my attitude about work that he would make me quit paper routes and other odd jobs as a means of punishment for misconduct.

Drawing a weekly paycheck from Apex gave me a very secure feeling and enabled me to make a regular contribution to the family treasurer, Mother. She balanced the housing and food budget, she deposited 25 percent of the combined salaries in a joint savings account, and she was the judge of how much Dad and I would be permitted to spend foolishly on the weekends. We both respected her ability to manage our incomes. She was so debt-conscious that she felt that the rent was delinquent if it was not paid seven days before it was due.

My days at Apex went without conflict until Saturday, March 9, 1940. Early that February I had received a call from Zinky Cohn, the business agent for Local 208, the black musicians' union, to put together a seven-piece band for a job at a dance hall. I was overjoyed about the opportunity and the fact that the three-hour gig paid six dollars to each side man and ten dollars to the leader, me. That would almost double my income that week.

All was well that evening until the band started playing "Sunny Side of the Street" and I looked down from the bandstand and saw four white girls from the Apex Box Company smiling and waving. I practically fell off the piano bench, because I knew that Travis the porter could never explain Jack Travis the band leader to those "ofays." Other blacks, of course, understood the dual role Negroes had to play in the American scheme of things, but somehow I couldn't bear the idea of explaining that dilemma to whites.

I could accept my menial job as a porter as long as I kept it separated from my "real" life as a musician, but this sudden collision of the two roles made me feel confused and ashamed. I did not return to my portering position at Apex.

The Apex job was the price I paid for my pride and principle. In retrospect, I think the price was small even though it meant joining 200,000 jobless

Chicagoans. I was on the streets two days before I decided I would use the ten dollars I made on the music gig to buy another job.

This time the factory employment agency sent me to the Quality Wet Wash Laundry. The plant superintendent, Emil Gunther, spoke in a heavy Germanic accent as his saucer-shaped blue eyes surveyed me meticulously.

"Can you read and write?" he asked.

"Yes, sir. I am a graduate of DuSable High School," I said.

"Good, did you bring any work clothes?"

"No, sir," I answered, "but I am prepared to work in the clothes that I have on."

After another quick glance he said, "Come with me." We walked through the wet steamy laundry room past the men working at the washer, the wringers, and then into the dry section where both black men and women were standing in small booths sorting dirty clothes. Some sorters wore homemade masks over their noses and mouths to cut down on the odor of the soiled clothes and the dust. When we reached the drying tumbler at the rear of the building he stopped and introduced me to the operator.

"I want you to teach this young man how to be a bundle boy," Gunther said.

"Come with me, schoolboy," the operator said, turning off the drying machine. ("Schoolboy" was a name that followed me the entire time I remained at the "Big Q.")

I followed Griffin to the bundle racks, where he explained my duties. "There are thirty-nine truck drivers, and it is your job to see that the bags of wet wash and the packages of finished clothes are placed on the proper racks for them to load on their trucks in the morning and again in the afternoon."

Joe Quinn, a former Notre Dame football star under the legendary coach Knute Rockne, was the supervisor of the truck drivers and the husband of Mary Quinn, my former English teacher at DuSable High. He was a tall, muscular, dark-haired man with a large, oblong head that was set four inches above his broad shoulders. He walked with a fast, wide gait and whenever he came down from his second floor office to check out a complaint about a lost bundle of clothes, he would ask me to accompany him on the search through the laundry racks.

On these excursions I began to attempt to convince Joe Quinn that he should make me a truckdriver.

One afternoon, after I had raised the question for an uncountable number of times, he turned to me and said sadly, "Travis, I wish you would try to understand that if I had the power to hire you as a driver, all of the other drivers would quit."

"All the drivers like me," I said. "I can't remember a single day since I started working here that at least two or three of them have not invited me to join them at the coke machine or offered me a bar of candy."

"Travis, I am sure they all like you as a 'colored bundle boy;' but I am equally sure that they would hate you as a colored driver," Quinn said.

"Why, Mr. Quinn?" I asked. The answer was quick in coming: "Seventy-five percent of our laundry routes are in the colored community and your presence as a driver would be a threat to what is now considered a well-paying 'white man's job,'" he said. He looked at me briefly and then reached out his hand. "I'm sorry," he said. He turned and walked out.

At that moment, I literally could not breathe. I knew then I could never be content with just making an hourly wage of thirty-three cents or thirteen dollars and twenty cents per week while white laundry drivers in the green uniforms with the big red "Q" on the back of their jackets made thirty-five to fifty dollars per week for a lot less work.

On January 15, 1941, A. Philip Randolph, president of the Brotherhood of Sleeping Car Porters, issued a newspaper release suggesting that 10,000 blacks march on Washington D.C., to demand the right to work and fight for "our country." Randolph believed that this action was necessary because in the fall of 1940, when the national defense program was moving into its second year, over 90 percent of the holders of defense contracts either employed no blacks at all or confined them to unskilled labor or custodial jobs. There were less than 5,000 blacks among the 175,000 trainees in defense vocational programs.

The "March on Washington Movement" was tantamount to hitting the "American Mule" on the head. It was the first time that a black leader got President Roosevelt to focus his attention on the need to abolish discrimination in the defense industry and in government employment. By the end of May, Randolph was promising that not 10,000, but 100,000 blacks would join the march. The idea was spreading like a Southern California forest fire in mid-August.

The White House was not just simply impressed, it was alarmed. It was so alarmed at the thought of 100,000 blacks marching through the streets of

Washington, D.C., the citadel of "Jim Crow," that President Roosevelt signed Executive Order 8802 on June 25, 1941, just a few days before the march was to have taken place.

The order was prefaced with a general statement to the effect that there would be no discrimination in the employment of workers in defense industries or in government because of "race, creed, color, or national origin." The order also confirmed that there should be no discrimination in defense training programs.

I felt that defense training would be the gateway to the millennium for millions of blacks. At least I hoped it would be for me. Executive Order 8802 seemed too good to be true.

Sixty-five defense plants were listed in the want ad section of the daily newspapers but only two companies even allowed me to fill out applications. The rest said that they had filled their trainee quota and suggested, frequently with a smile, that I try again next week, next month, or next year. By this time I was wearing my heart on the bottom of my feet, and each step I took started a rhythmic "there ain't no hope" feeling pulsing from the soles of my feet to the crown of my head.

The weight of my heart made my shoes so heavy that I had to share my burden with both my father and mother. In spite of our closeness as a family, my parents had not realized how seriously I was taking my inability to get more than menial employment. It was then Dad suggested I go to see Alderman Earl B. Dickerson.

Dickerson, now an alert ninety year old, was then at the height of his political career and had just been appointed by President Franklin D. Roosevelt to the newly formed Fair Employment Practice Committee. I went down to his office at 3507 South Parkway without an appointment late one afternoon and after an hour wait, I was invited into the inner office. "What can I do for you, young man?" he said.

"I would like to be an aviation engineer or mechanic."

"Have you had any training or experience in either field?" Dickerson snapped.

I described my job experience and told him of my eagerness to have a job.

"Son, your feelings about the subject are not enough. You need training or experience, and it is helpful to have both," he said.

I told Alderman Dickerson about my experience looking for jobs at the defense plants while he made some notes.

"My committee is investigating hundreds of complaints like yours. I am going to suggest that in the meantime you go over to the Armour Institute at 3300 South Federal Street (formerly Armour Avenue) and see if they are offering any aviation programs in which you might enroll," he said.

Following his suggestion, I went over to the Armour Institute of Technology, which had merged with Lewis Institute the year before, to form the Illinois Institute of Technology, but found it did not offer courses in aviation defense work. However, a small white-haired gentleman said, "I understand there are some being offered at the Wendell Phillips High School."

I went directly to Phillips and enrolled in a four-month, forty-hour-per-week, government-sponsored aviation mechanic program. The instructor, a very attractive bronze-colored aviatrix named Mrs. Willa Brown, was part owner of the Coffey School of Aeronautics, the school that issued the completion certificate upon my graduation from the course.

When I received the aviation mechanic certificate on a Friday afternoon, I knew I had my hand on a direct passport into the defense industry. The thought of becoming a defense worker filled me with so much hope that I could not sleep more than two hours per night for the next three nights.

Monday morning I got up and was fully dressed by three a.m. In the process of releasing the burglar latch on the front door, I awakened my father, who turned on his bedroom light, looked at the clock and shouted, "Boy! ...don't you know it's just five minutes after three?"

"Yes, sir!" I answered.

"Where are you going this early?" he muttered.

"To get a job. I want to be the first in line at the defense plant employment office."

"Good luck," he said and turned out the light.

At high noon, my employment world was still dark. The bright rays of hope that my aviation mechanic certificate gave me gradually dimmed with each job rejection.

"We ain't hiring no boys today." "We won't need any mechanic trainee for at least nine months." "You are over-qualified for our present position opening." "We already got one colored fellow working here as a washroom attendant." That comment had a familiar ring.

When I returned home after dinnertime that evening, my father was sitting on the front steps smoking one of his favorite three-for-ten-cents El Producto cigars. As he exhaled the smoke from the cigar he smiled and asked, "How did things go today?"

"No good, Dad," I replied. "The same old three-six-nine." (The phrase comes from the policy "dream book" and means "shit.")

Reflecting a look of understanding, Dad said gently, "Sit down, son. I heard some good news at the stockyards today. They're hiring new men in my section of the Sweet Pickle Department and also on the beef-killing floor at Wilson's. I understand they are also hiring at both Swift and Armour."

"God Almighty," I said. "That means I can go to work with you in the morning."

"Nope!" Dad said. "I don't want you working at Wilson & Co. As a matter of fact, I didn't want you working in the stockyards, period. But since the yards appear to be your only option, you should go to the Armour & Company employment office at 43rd & Packer first, and then go down the street about a half a block to Swift & Company."

The next morning my feet hit the floor when Dad's Big Ben clock alarmed at five o'clock. Mother was already in the kitchen fixing breakfast and preparing brown bag lunches for both Dad and myself. I was excited because I was about to become part of the Packingtown (stockyards) that my Dad, Uncle Otis, and Uncle Joe always talked about.

On a hot summer day, an east wind would cause a diluted version of the foul smell and brown mist from the fertilizer plant to descend upon Chicago like a smog from downtown to Morgan Park and from Ashland Avenue to Lake Michigan. My father warned me not to accept a job in the fertilizer plant because I would not be able to get the odor out of the pores of my skin. The permanent body stench would cause one to become a social leper like Dad's friends "Stinky" Davis and "Funky" Mose. The odor was so terrible that these men had become outcasts and Dad never saw them anymore. In spite of the very real handicaps of these jobs, black workers were sometimes forced to take them because they were all that was available to them.

The fertilizer fumes were dominant among the many smells crowding my nostrils as I walked through the stockyards, along with the sounds and smells of the thousands of hogs and cows being herded into the killing rooms through the overhead runways, crisscrossing the brick-paved Packingtown streets. In addition, there was the scent from the rancid blood of dead animals along with that of the animals' waste, added to the rank flavor from dirty and sweat-stained clothes worn by the work gangs.

Animal cries from the area made Packingtown both ugly and somber on the brightest of the sunniest days.

At the Armour Employment Office, I found at least one hundred men, both black and white, waiting for the employment manager to open the door.

Finally, a broad-shouldered, big-faced old Irishman stepped outside of the door. It seemed that more than half the fellows knew the Irishman and many of them started shouting "Big Mac" and waving their arms to get his attention. He stood there for several minutes looking over the human herd before he started beckoning for those individuals he intended to employ that day. Although I was almost at the rear of the crowd he beckoned for me (I attribute my luck that day to my six-foot height).

"What kind of work can you do?" he asked me when I reached the front. "Any kind," I replied.

He gave me a yellow slip and directed me through the door behind him to the doctor's office where I was checked for heart trouble, tuberculosis, hernia, and venereal disease.

Then I reported to the time-keeper's office in the Sweet Pickle Department in my high-top rubber boots and brand new blue denim overalls, with fifteen other black laborers. A short, reddish-skinned man in a dingy gray smock stepped out of the time-keeper's office and motioned for us to encircle him for instructions. "Mexican" Frank was his name and he introduced himself as the assistant foreman. Assistant foreman was the lowest official supervisory position in the plant. (No blacks had achieved even this lowly rank in the stockyards' seventy-five-year history, although blacks did sometimes act in an unofficial capacity as a gang "strawboss.")

Our gang was assigned to pull floating, half-frozen bacon bellies out of a long tank and then load them into pushtrucks. This job was cold and wet. How my dad performed this task with enthusiasm for forty years was beyond me then—and is now.

My Dad and Uncle Joe once explained the routine for black work assignments in Packingtown, saying, "Black folks cannot be permitted to work with finished meat products." Aunt Mary, naturally, asked, "Why not?"

Plant visitors and foreign guests come to the room where bacon is being handled for packaging and they would be offended if they saw black hands touch something they might eat, was the reply.

"That's ridiculous," Aunt Mary said. "Black folks have been handling food for white folks as long as I can remember."

"I understand how you feel, Mary," Uncle Joe said. "But I overheard a superintendent in a long white frock say to an assistant superintendent, 'We must be scrupulous along sanitary lines, and only white hands are fit to touch the meat. We could hire Negro women, but their hands would have to be washed almost every hour and we would have to manicure them.'

"Mary, I could not believe my ears," he laughed.

Dad interrupted: "The oleo [margarine] department barred Negro women although no hand touched the butterine in the course of packing. At the same time, Negro men pack pails of the same butterine, which not only is shoveled into the receptacles, but must often be molded by black hands into a workable mass. This is allowed because the white public does not see this action. The walls in the butterine room are painted white and the workers are clad in white, and the public relations men thought that the plant image would be prettier if the workers were white."

With my eyes still blinking from all the whiteness, I said, "What chance does a black man or woman have of getting one of those clean jobs wearing a white uniform or frock?"

Dad answered calmly, "None! Unless there is a strike or a war."

That conversation took place just fifteen days before the Japanese bombed Pearl Harbor on December 7, 1941.

CHAPTER 11

World War II

"THE COLORED FOLKS HAVE BOMBED PEARL HARBOR! THE colored folks have bombed Pearl Harbor!" yelled Willie "Pretty Stockyard" Cole as he rushed through the front door of Nelson Sykes' Brass Rail Saloon at 329 East 47th Street.

For several seconds everyone in the barroom was silent; then Frank Williams, who had just finished swallowing his shot glass of Canadian Club whiskey, said in a loud guttural voice: "Nigger! What the hell you been smoking?"

That question tore up the barflies and guys who responded with everything from a tee-hee to a belly laugh. Everyone, that is, except "Pretty Willie," who was standing in the middle of the floor waving his arms for attention and shouting, "I'm serious as a barrel of rattlesnakes. Look! I'm crossin' my heart on my mother's grave. The Japanese have just bombed a place near California called Pearl Harbor."

A drunk named "Broke" Hunter standing at the end of the bar interrupted Willie's shouting with, "I know the white folks are going to give me a steady job now."

"Amen," replied "Fat" Clark. "I recall my father tellin' me how much overtime money colored people made during the last big war."

By this time Nelson Sykes had turned the table model Zenith radio up full blast and the voice of President Franklin D. Roosevelt was heard saying, "On December 7, 1941, a date which will live in infamy—the United States of America was suddenly and deliberately attacked by naval and air forces of the Empire of Japan. Very many American lives have been lost. As Commander in

Chief of the Army and Navy, I have directed that all measures be taken for our defense. Always will we remember the character of the onslaught against us...."

In the summer of 1941, as the Japanese were invading the French colonies of Indochina, the United States drew the line and embargoed first scrap iron, and then oil. Pearl Harbor was inevitable and its timetable predictable. The Japanese would have to go to war before they ran out of gasoline.

"Baby the Pimp" Bell distracted our attention from President Roosevelt's radio speech when he shouted, "Bartender, I'm buying two rounds of drinks for everybody in the house." Bell then raised a water glass of VO 90 proof whiskey above his head and said in a very slow and solemn tone, "Remember Pearl Harbor."

The freeloaders' immediate response to Bell's drinks on the house was drowned out by the roar of the Englewood "El" express train thundering overhead on its nonstop route past 43rd, 47th, and 55th Streets en route to its stop at the 58th Street elevated station. The smothered acknowledgements to "Baby" Bell's toast were certainly not unanimous. Some blacks experienced a vicarious pleasure from the thought that "Charlie" was getting his ass kicked by some "colored" people. (There was a small black sect on the South Side known as "the Moors" who were actually pro-Japanese.)

Three days after Pearl Harbor, Germany and Italy came to the aid of Japan and declared war on the United States. On December 19th, the Congress of the United States extended military conscription to include men between the ages of twenty and forty-four. Thousands of white men had begun to volunteer for service in the Air Corps, the Marines, the Navy, and the Army the day after Pearl Harbor. Black men were not permitted to volunteer for any duty except the Army and kitchen (mess) duty in the Navy.

At the same time, American industry responded to the call by literally opening up thousands of new plants overnight. These factories ranged from huge shipbuilding yards employing masses of people to tiny one-man operations in the basements of private homes. Many of the plants in the union stockyards were on triple shifts. The magnates of industry and big business were recruiting whites for the clean, new, high-paying war jobs, while the dirty, low-paying stockyard and steel mill jobs were being offered to blacks. Low-paying or otherwise, there now existed a thirst for black laborers that had not been paralleled since World War I. And as white men and women left the cleaner jobs in the stockyards for positions in the defense industry, blacks were pulled in as their replacements at Armour & Company, as well as in other industries.

Although I had worked at Armour & Company only a little more than a month, I was transferred from the Sweet Pickle Department to the Canning Department. This assignment was considered a cleaner and steadier job. The symbolic significance of the departmental transfer was that I was instructed to dispose of my blue denim overalls and wear white denims because I would be handling sealed cans of processed meats that would ultimately reach Army and civilian markets. Handling canned meats had a side benefit because I was soon introduced to an old timer in the department named "Kiddo" Hamilton. One day at lunch, Kiddo said, "Why do you bring a cold lunch from home every day when you can have a hot one on the house?"

"What do you mean?"

"Kid, buy yourself a five-cent loaf of bread and I will show you how to eat well for a week."

The next day at lunch Kiddo took me over to the south end of the department where there were some hot pipes running along the wall. Kiddo had tied ham, sausage, and Spam to the pipes earlier in the day so that at lunch time the meat would be red hot and juicy.

The delicious times lasted for about a month before I began to have problems with my sexual drive. Needless to say, I had suffered some embarrassment and I was in a dilemma about my love life. I first shared my delicacy with an older lady friend who guaranteed she had a cure for my distress. However, before trying her remedy, I reluctantly told my father about my recent experience. He literally fell out of his chair laughing and said, "Boy, are you trying to tell me you are all used up at age twenty-one?"

I looked at Dad without replying. He then seemed to recognize that I was serious and stopped laughing.

"What have you been drinking?" he asked.

"An occasional bottle of beer,"

He pondered with a serious look on his face and asked, "Has anybody been cooking for you other than your mother?"

"No!"

"Your problem must be related to something that you are eating or drinking," Dad persisted. "Think, boy! What have you been eating or drinking within the past month that is different than your diet of three months ago?"

"Oh! Oh!"

"Oh! Oh! What?"

"I have been eating stockyard meat with Kiddo Hamilton every day."

"What kind?"

"Canned Army-ration Spam and sausage."

Dad broke into hysterical laughter that was so extensive I thought he was having a convulsion. Finally he stopped laughing and wiped the tears from his eyes and said, "Boy, don't you know that they put saltpeter [potassium nitrate] in that soldier meat so they won't have no nature, and that is the answer to your problem?" Dad began to laugh again and this time I joined him.

"Son, there ain't no such thing as a free lunch," Dad said between laughs, "and I am going to suggest that you 'brown bag' it from now on, the same way I do."

I followed Dad's suggestion and my delicacy straightened up in a little less than a week. I stopped hanging out with Kiddo at lunch after I quit the Armour meat diet. I started "brown-bagging" it and sitting out on the curbstone. When the weather wouldn't permit, I'd sit in the locker room and eat. One day, to my surprise, I saw a middle-aged man who looked just like Erskine Tate, the great band leader of the 1920s and '30s, sitting in front of a locker about ten feet from mine. The gentleman looked both unfriendly and ill tempered. His partially bald head was large enough to accommodate a seven and three quarter inch hat. He had a strong Indian-red complexion and his face was filled with hundreds of small pockmarks (possibly the product of some childhood illness). His eyes were large and piercing. Several days passed before I asked John "Stormy Monday" Ransom who that sour-looking fellow was who had the locker down from mine. John came over and cautiously whispered, "Man! That's Erskine Tate, one of the finest band leaders Chicago ever produced!"

I couldn't believe my ears. Why would a man who had reached his summit in music be working as a laborer at Armour & Company? You would not have to be Duke Ellington to know that racism afflicts all black musicians. The good ones and the mediocre ones suffer in one black kettle of Jim Crow. Without further hesitation, I walked over and introduced myself to Tate. He didn't appear pleased at all to meet me until I told him I had attended Willard Elementary School with both his daughter, Evelyn, and his nephew, Emmett, and also, that I was a member of Local 208 of the Musician's Union. That broke the ice. He smiled and invited me to sit down on the bench beside him in front of his locker. I had hardly sat down when the lunch whistle blew for us to return to work. As I left, Tate said, "Come around at noon tomorrow and we'll talk about music."

The next day we ate and I had an opportunity to tell Tate that my mother had taken me to the Vendome Theater at 31st and State to hear his band accompany such great blues singers as Mamie Smith, Bessie Smith, Ethel Waters, and Mae Alix. Tate appeared delighted and said, "I believe I had one of my greatest bands during that period because both Louis Armstrong and Earl 'Fatha' Hines were side men in that orchestra. There are others who will tell you my best band was the one I took into the Metropolitan Theater at 46th and South Parkway."

I simply nodded to Tate's statements because between the ages of eight and ten, when I saw him at both theatres, I was not equipped to make a musical judgment on the merits of either band. (Live bands were used in the theatre pits to set the mood for various scene changes in the old silent movies. The band would be given a new music script with each film. There would be several themes, eight to sixteen bars long. If the band leader held up one finger, the band would play the love theme, two fingers would signal the villain theme. Most theatres in black ghettos had a lone piano player.) Tate and I became daily lunch companions for the next several months that I worked at the yards.

On Friday afternoon, August 7, 1942, when I arrived home, my mother told me she had put a letter on the dresser for me.

"Who would be writing me a letter?"

"Since I didn't open it, I would suggest that you read it and see."

I opened the envelope and the first word I saw in bold type was "GREET-INGS." The letter continued, "You are hereby notified that you have been selected for training and service therein. This local board will furnish transportation to an induction... You will there be examined, and, if accepted...you will be inducted into the land or naval forces. Failure to report subjects the violator to fine and imprisonment."

As I sat on the bed staring at the letter, mother yelled from the kitchen, "Who was the letter from?"

"The draft board."

"The who?"

"The Army, Mama."

Mother rushed into the bedroom and snatched the letter from my hand. She read the letter twice and said, in an utterance that sounded like a prayer, "I know Uncle Sam is not going to take my only child. I know Uncle Sam is not going to take my only child."

"Mama, the 'man' wants some cannon fodder and he ain't making no exceptions."

My world came to an abrupt end when I reported to the induction center, where I passed the physical examination. I was then ordered by my draft board to report back on September 9, 1942, to be transported from the board to the Illinois Central Station at 12th and Michigan Avenue, where I would board a train for Fort Custer in Michigan.

The last ten days before I left for the Army were spent partying with my friends. The best times consisted of "joint hopping" from the Keyhole Lounge at 39th and King Drive to the Red Moon Lounge at 61st Street, four doors west of South Park, and the Wonder Bar on 63rd, three doors east of South Park. Sometimes we would cover as many as fifteen taverns in one night. The night before I was to leave, Claude Jenkins gave a party in my honor at his mother's home at 59th and Prairie. He had invited about twenty fellows who included Charlie Murray, Joe Simmons, "Jelly" Martin, and Milton Turner. The party broke up about four a.m. and several of my friends had to walk me home.

I had only been in bed an hour when Dad awakened me to wish me good luck and to ask me to write. An hour later, Mother shook my bed and said, "It's time for you to get up and go to the draft board."

I didn't realize it immediately, but my mother's face looked as if she had been crying all night. At that moment, she was putting up a brave front. She had packed a big suitcase for me. 1 looked at her and said: "All I need, Ma, according to the instructions, are a few personal items such as a toothbrush, a comb, and a change of underclothes."

She responded in a soft, tearful voice, "You have got to have two pairs of pajamas." Mother reluctantly began to unpack the suitcase. She lifted each piece from the bag as gingerly as she would have lifted a baby. As she touched each garment, she would repeat: "Why do they have to take my only child? Why do they have to take my only child?" At this point she started shaking and screaming: "Why, Lord? Why are they taking my only child?"

I said, "Mother, I don't know," and started crying myself, uncontrollably. Without saying goodbye, I dashed out of the kitchen door and down the back stairs, sobbing loudly and screaming, "Mama! I don't want to go! Mama! I don't want to go."

At eight a.m. sharp the draftee bus was loaded and ready to go—with or without me. The thirty-five-minute bus ride from the draft board on Garfield Boulevard (55th Street) north down Michigan Avenue to the 12th Street train station mentally took less than five minutes. My mind was absorbed in the past. It was not until I boarded the train an hour later with a group of about one hundred draftees that I began to feel like a cow among a herd of stockyard cattle being led to slaughter by a belled goat. (The stockyards used trained goats to lead herds of cows to the slaughter house. The goat would then return to the cattle pen to lead another herd. A single goat would lead several thousand cows to their deaths daily.) The herd instinct helped deliver the cows to the killing floor. What was delivering me? Was it loyalty? Was it fear? Was it propaganda? Was it the opportunity to become a first-class American?

"Battle Creek! Battle Creek!" yelled the conductor.

"Follow me," shouted our group leader as he waved his arms toward the front of the train. After we got off the train we were instructed to jump into the Army trucks that were lined up to take us into Fort Custer. Within twenty minutes, I was standing in the street in the company area of the 1,609th Service Unit. The "old" soldiers (three days in service) were laughing and shouting, "Shorty got your gal and gone" from the balcony and windows of the type of double-deck barracks that would be my home for the next four years. We were left standing in the streets for about ten minutes before a tall, slim, shifty-eyed man came out of the barracks and for several minutes looked through the draftees as if they were transparent.

He then said: "I am 1st Sgt. Hammond. We are going to process you through this reception center within three or four days and then you will be shipped to another camp for your basic training."

At this point he was distracted by a draftee who was talking. He said to the recruit, "What's your name, soldier?"

"John Rose," the recruit replied.

The sergeant wrote his name down and said: "Soldier, if I catch you with your big trap open again, I am going to make you think hell is paradise." Hammond gave Rose a hard stare and then turned and walked back to the center column where he announced that Buck Sgt. Willie Moore would be in charge of taking us to the warehouse for our G.I. (government issue) clothes and then to the dispensary for immunization shots.

We had just returned to the barracks with two duffel bags of Army gear when Moore blew his whistle for us to fall in formation in the street directly in front of the barracks for the retreat, a ceremony signaling the lowering of the flag at sundown. At the end of the ten-minute ritual, we were told to fall out for chow (withdraw from formation to eat). The "old" recruits ran to be the first in line at the mess hall. When I found out what was happening, I was about two hundredth in a line of three hundred and fifty men waiting to eat. A young soldier standing in front of me fell to the ground. Luckily, someone standing nearby recognized that it was an epileptic seizure and rapidly placed a stick in his mouth to prevent the disabled soldier from biting his tongue.

The first meal and the first night in the Army were uneventful except that I almost fell off the top of a double-deck bunk as I turned in my sleep. The next morning I was awakened by a thundering voice on the loud speaker: "Ha, ha, ha, ha, I am the Shadow. Since the Shadow sees all and knows all, the Shadow can see you laying there on your big, black ass. Ha, ha, ha, get up! Get up! Get up! Every swinging dick let your feet hit the floor and your ass hit the door for reveille."

That afternoon, as we stood at attention for retreat, Hammond, accompanying Major Peterson, did an inspection of the troops. When they reached me, the major stopped and asked me: "What's your name, soldier?"

"Private Dempsey J. Travis," I replied.

Hammond interrupted, reprimanding me: "Goddammit, soldier, you always say 'sir' when you are speaking to an officer."

I replied, "Yes, sir!"

Peterson then asked: "What did you do for a living as a civilian?"

"I was a musician, sir!"

"Did you get this soldier's name, Sergeant?" the major inquired.

Hammond replied: "I did, sir." And they both stepped briskly down to the center of the parade ground to take their position in front of the troops for retreat. The next day I was called to the orderly room and told by Hammond: "Soldier, you have been selected to be a member of the permanent personnel of the 1,609 Service Unit."

That was my first break, in that it meant that I would be stationed at Fort Custer and that I could go home every weekend after I finished my twelve-week basic training. My second break came when I was asked to organize an orchestra to play for the Friday and Saturday night U.S.O. dances in

Battle Creek. The gig paid three dollars a night per man. Everything was going smoothly until one Sunday Hammond asked me: "What did you bring me from your last trip to town?"

"What?"

Hammond responded in a harsh tone, "You heard me."

I asked, "What was I supposed to have brought you?"

"A pint of Grand Dad every time you play a dance."

That meant that I would be giving Hammond one-third of my salary for the privilege of playing music. That was, as my father used to say, "Too much sugar for a dime." My pride and conscience would not permit me to swallow Hammond's strong-arm tactics. I immediately made the top of Hammond's "people-to-make-miserable" list. For instance, if the last train for Chicago left at 9:45 p.m., he would issue my pass to commence at midnight. On Thanksgiving, a girlfriend came to visit me from Chicago, and Hammond refused to let me leave the camp until midnight when everything in town was closed. He further restricted the pass to a 5 a.m. return for reveille. Hammond was such a son-of-a-bitch that I was forced to take refuge on several occasions in the non-commissioned officer's room and literally weep. The other alternative would simply be to illegally destroy Hammond.

The legal destruction of Private Travis was on the top of Hammond's May agenda. When I returned to camp from a weekend pass in Chicago on Monday, May 10, 1943, Hammond had executed his most fiendish scheme—I was put under house arrest the moment I entered the barracks.

"Guards, you have made a mistake," I pleaded. "I am not late. I wasn't due back in camp until 0700." The two guards simply shook their heads and kept their hands on their guns.

After about an hour, Hammond walked into the barracks with a sardonic grin and said, "I have orders in my hand to ship you to a port of embarkation."

All my feathers fell. I knew Hammond had the noose around my neck and was about to pull the trap door. Hammond then gave the guards the following instructions: "Keep this soldier under close surveillance and don't consider this assignment complete until Private Travis is placed on the troop train, and the train is out of your sight."

"Attention!" the guard shouted. "Right face, forward march." The three of us marched off to the train in cadence. En route, soldiers on the street stopped and stared at me as if I were a common criminal.

The troop train that I was placed on was loaded with black men who had just been released from the stockade (Army prison). Most of them had been convicted for AWOL (absent without leave), desertion, and other military offenses. Sending soldiers overseas prematurely was one method of controlling and punishing the incorrigibles.

I had never even missed bed check. But getting on Sgt. Hammond's list was enough to make me an incorrigible. He had nailed me to the cross.

CHAPTER 12

Camp Shenango

THE EXTENT OF SEGREGATION AND DISCRIMINATION IN THE armed forces through World War II is something that has been conveniently left out of the history books. And the full viciousness of the situation was something I had disregarded during my relatively privileged time at Fort Custer.

Comparing Fort Custer to Camp Shenango, Pennsylvania, is like comparing the high-rise public housing complex of Cabrini-Green to Lake Shore Drive's rows of luxury high rises on Chicago's lakefront.

From the moment I stepped off the train with the others at Camp Shenango, it was borne in on me that as a black man, I had no status, no rights, no dignity, no claim to human treatment. For a lot of us, the hellishness of Camp Shenango was symbolized by the mud that engulfed our feet and ankles as we got off the train. It was a slimy mud, it was a smelly mud, it was a mud that consumed you mentally without incarcerating you physically. It was a mud that could drive men mad.

Maybe 10 percent of the soldiers at Camp Shenango, a huge installation where thousands of soldiers were being processed to be shipped overseas, were blacks. They kept us out of the way as much as possible. The blacks' barracks, about a mile and a half from the main gate, over by the woods, was like a separate little Jim Crow ghetto on the post. Though conditions at the post were bad for all the soldiers, black and white, for blacks they were simply unspeakable.

We could not use the white PX—the only PX—or the white recreational facilities. For us there were no roads, no movie theatre. It was as if I had suddenly been thrust into one of my relatives' stories about the Old South: blacks were supposed to efface themselves, to wait around for whites, not to get in the way, to literally get to the back of the bus.

Later on, I became aware that Shenango had some German prisoners of war, and they were treated better than black American soldiers. They were allowed to use facilities we could not. It was as if it was we who were the enemy aliens.

Other unofficial "enemy aliens" had their own troubles during these sad times.

One hundred and twenty thousand men, women, and children of Japanese ancestry, seventy thousand of them American citizens, were confined to internment camps for varying amounts of time during World War II. Yet, more than a million persons of German and Italian ancestry living in the U.S. at that time remained free, although a few were also incarcerated. Throughout the course of the war, no Japanese Americans residing in the U.S. were ever charged with espionage or sabotage. Reparations for these persons, hustled out of their homes, businesses, and family lives with as little as a day's notice and able to take only two suitcases of belongings with them, is a topic now being debated at hearings held in various places of the country in late 1981. Forty years—to the year—after the bombing of Pearl Harbor.

But back to Shenango.

The food was bad. Army food is bad, of course, but this was no joke; it wasn't possible to eat it. Bad meat, undercooked, or watery "shit on a shingle"—it seemed like every meal was a new outrage.

I remember on the third night I was there I went to the mess hall—a separate mess hall for blacks, of course—and found men jumping up and down on the tables, stomping the food in their trays into the table tops. I had been sent to a madhouse, and I knew then that I was going to have to think carefully about ways to retain my sanity. I couldn't escape through a movie or a 3.2 (alcohol content) beer in the post exchange, because there were no such things in the "colored" section of the camp. And blacks were not permitted in the white area except on official daytime business.

Even if you needed medical attention, you were suspect if you showed your face on "their" side of the camp. Once I was sent to the hospital because I had hurt my foot in obstacle course training. A white, middle-aged doctor with full colonel rank asked me, without a smile or an examination, "Boy— what's your problem?"

"My right leg and foot are in pain."

"Your what?"

"My leg and foot have been hurt, sir."

"Where is the blood, nigger?" the doctor said.

"The injury is internal and didn't break the skin, sir."

"Boy!" he snarled, glaring at me. "A nigger's feet are supposed to hurt. Don't you show your black face in this hospital again trying to goldbrick unless you're bleeding."

By the fourth week of my time at Camp Shenango, the authorities, worried by the presence of the large number of black soldiers being shipped in daily, opened a makeshift post exchange in a one-story barrack and a small theater for black troops. We had to attend the tiny movie house in shifts.

But by that time, there was a mood of simmering resentment on the post. We didn't know at the time, but that was true at camps all over the country. During the spring and summer of 1943, outbreaks of racial violence between black and white soldiers occurred at at least nineteen camps across the country, from Mississippi to New Jersey, from North Carolina to California. In addition, soldiers on leave in several cities were involved in racial violence. The exact number of soldiers involved in these incidents was never recorded; in fact, the Army did its best at the time to keep the incidents out of the papers. By all accounts, the outbreak I was to witness at Shenango was one of the bloodiest.

At camps all over the country, blacks were experiencing the same kind of treatment I was. Years later, Mrs. Mary Herrick, my old teacher from DuSable High, would share with me some letters from classmates of mine, written during the war.

"Oh, yes, about that incident you heard over the radio," James Armand wrote from Camp Van Doren in Mississippi. "One of the boys down here in the Infantry went into town and got shot by a town policeman. It has quiet[ed] down now. They talk about shipping all the North boys back up North. I hope so, but I doubt it." The soldier added a footnote: "P.S. You don't have to worry about me fooling with these crackers down here in Mississippi. They are crazy as hell."

James Norman wrote from Greensboro, North Carolina: "Do you know I entered a drug store (Walgreen's) in Greensboro, and they refused to serve me. I naturally have heard of discrimination but I didn't think that applied to soldiers. It makes you stop and wonder sometimes why we are fighting."

James W. Hopson had his eyes opened when he left his station at Camp LeJeune, North Carolina, for a day trip into Washington, D.C.: "The cafeteria in the Capitol building has a unique way of discriminating. The signs on the doors read 'Senators and Employees,' but our guide told us that it was a public restaurant and that the signs were put there for other reasons. We, of darker hue in the group, knew what that reason was. After leaving the Capitol we visited the United Nations Service Center across the street from the Washington Terminal. We must have been the first Negroes to ever go in there, for we met wild-eyed stares and even the Negro employees seemed to be surprised.

"However, everyone was very cordial afterwards. I have termed Washington as the dividing line of the nation. South of it one enters a strange world with Middle Age customs. North of it one sees a nation struggling to make the meaning of freedom a reality."

The immediate cause of concern to the Camp Shenango authorities was that blacks were trying to receive services at the white post exchange and to gain entry at the white movie theaters. These young men needed something to do besides playing blackjack or poker all night and day.

Some black soldiers shot craps on doubled blankets spread out over the latrine floor within an arm's reach of men using the latrines. Sometimes the gamblers would shout in chorus, "Roll those dice, baby needs a new pair of shoes, and daddy needs some money to make honey with Bonnie." Sometimes a kneeling crap shooter would look up at a soldier sitting on the toilet and growl, "Cut it short and mix some water with that shit."

The morning of July 14, 1943, was hot and dusty. I said to "Kansas," my upper bunkmate who hailed from that great state, "Let's stay in the barracks and play cards until it's time for the movie."

"Okay," he said, "if the game is draw poker with five cents as the limit."

Kansas was in good spirits that day and talked non-stop about his plans as we played cards. He had an undergraduate degree from an Eastern college and planned to go to medical school when he got out of the Army. Kansas maintained his cheerful manner in spite of all the miseries of life at Camp Shenango. The only thing I ever heard him complain about was the commanding officer—white, of course—who refused to select him for an Army special training program, which would have allowed him to enter medical school while still in the Army.

The hours passed quickly, and we didn't stop to go to lunch because we had heard that they were serving a dish fondly called "dear old Billy goat." At five-thirty we hit the chow line and then went directly to the theater that had been set up for blacks. The line was already too long for us to catch the first show, and we started to change our plans and head into a small town, Sharon, Pennsylvania, about twenty miles from the camp. But Kansas was against it. "Let's wait until Saturday and go into Youngstown, Ohio, where we can ball," he said. So we waited around to catch the second show.

When we came out, there was a large group of blacks milling around in front of the theatre. We went over to see what was going on.

"A black soldier just got both eyes kicked out because he tried to buy a cold beer in the white post exchange," someone in the group told us.

Another black soldier screamed, "Let's go down there and get those cracker bastards!"

Kansas and I were staring at each other, wondering what we should do, when six open Army trucks pulled up, filled with white military police carrying M-1 rifles and double-barreled shotguns aimed directly at us. On signal the whites turned out all the lights on the east end of the post and opened fire on the unarmed blacks standing in the middle of the street. We all tried to break for cover, but it was too late. The screams and cries of those who had been shot pierced the hot July night air.

I was knocked to the ground by a blunt force. I saw Kansas lying near me. I didn't realize I had been shot until I felt a warm, sticky substance soaking my pants leg and shoulder. There was noise and confusion all around me, and then silence.

The Army ambulances pulled up within a half hour. Medics with flashlights stepped over the wounded bodies, lying on the ground as thick as flies, trying to decide who was dead, who was alive, who warranted a trip to the hospital or the morgue. When they reached me and Kansas, they motioned for the stretcher bearers with their flashlights.

"Can you walk?" a medic asked me.

I tried, but I was too numb to move. The medic turned me over and said to another medic, "This nigger has been shot three times." Then they turned their flashlights on Kansas. "They got this one in the head, but he'll be all right."

What did they mean? Did they mean he would be all right but I wouldn't? As I lay there preparing to die, my thoughts were not of heaven or hell, but of hate. I was cursing the darkness, and I was bleeding with hate.

On the way to the hospital, I heard the ambulance driver say to the medic, "Why the hell do we shoot our own men?"

"Who said they were men?" the medic said. "We shoot niggers like rabbits where I come from."

At the hospital, Kansas was rolled into a small room and I was left on a cart in the corridor. After a few minutes a doctor rushed into the little room. I could see him lift my friend's eyelids. He put a stethoscope to his chest, and the last thing he did was try to straighten his legs, which were in a bent position. They wouldn't straighten out. He put out the lights and closed the door.

Kansas was dead.

I came out of sedation at daybreak, amidst the groaning of a ward full of young soldiers who had been wounded the night before in the Camp Shenango riot. I learned later that the violence was still going on—it lasted three days, with soldiers breaking into the supply dump to get guns and ammunition.

In the bed to my left was an eighteen-year-old kid whimpering for his mother, his doctor, anybody. I tried to get out of bed, but the lower part of my body was paralyzed. I joined his cries, by screaming, "Help me! Help me! I can't move!"

Two orderlies rushed over and checked my pulse.

"Don't worry," one said. "Your legs will be all right."

He was pushed aside by an important-looking man in a dark blue serge civilian suit.

"Excuse yourself for a few minutes," the man said. "I want to talk with this soldier."

He leaned over my bed and asked, in a soft voice, "How are you feeling this morning, young man?"

"Awful."

"Who shot you?" he said. He pulled a small black book from his pocket and made several notations in it.

"What?" I asked.

"Did you have a gun?"

I didn't answer. I turned my head away in disgust. The man leaned closer. "Soldier, I'm here from Washington to help you," he whispered. "You must cooperate."

I turned my head back to look him straight in his saucer-shaped hazel eyes and said, "How?"

"I thought you might help me catch the radical Communist troublemakers," he said in serious tones—and with a straight face.

"They were all white fascists dressed in the United States Army's green fatigues," I whispered. "Both the fascists and their guns spoke with a Southern accent."

The man gave me a puzzled glance and made a few more notes. Then he walked away.

Later on I was awakened from a nap by the voices of a team of doctors discussing my condition at the foot of my bed. Without saying anything to me, the physician in charge pulled down the sheet, turned me on my stomach, and began jabbing his fingers in the center of my back just above the buttocks.

"Do you feel anything?"

"Yes!"

That response must have coincided with his diagnosis, because he turned and said to the others, "He'll walk again."

The Camp Shenango riot didn't make the newspapers in Chicago. The only way my parents found out what had happened to me was through the Red Cross. On Wednesday, they were walking down the corridor toward me. Dad was wearing his important facial expression, the one that complemented his million-dollar stride. When Mother spotted me her face beamed like a well-lit Christmas tree.

I was literally choking in an effort to hold back the tears. Mingled with the tears of joy at seeing my parents again were some tears of grief for my friend, Kansas, whose body was lying on a white table in the hospital morgue waiting to be shipped in a flag-draped pine box to his family.

I had a rough convalescense after that. My temperature rose until I was shipped in an ambulance over bumpy roads to the Veterans General Hospital in Butler, Pennsylvania, a fifty-mile drive. I was to have an operation there, and I was given a private room on the top floor of the hospital. But the first person to visit me was not a doctor, but the blue-suited man I had met earlier at the base hospital in Shenango.

"I hope your trip was comfortable, and I'm sure you'll find this private room an improvement over the crowded ward back at the base hospital," he said.

I nodded.

"Don't discuss the Shenango situation with anyone in the hospital. Do you understand?"

I nodded again. He raised his right hand, parted his first and second fingers in a Winston Churchill "V for Victory" sign, said, "Good luck," and left the room.

My surgeon, Lt. Col. Richard Babcock, was a ruddy-faced, partially bald man with a very infectious and charming personality. Within a few days after I entered the hospital, he had me feeling as if he and I were in an undeclared war against the world. Col. Babcock knew my private room was not a privilege, but a prison in which to keep me quarantined to prevent the spread of a contagious virus called "niggeritis." He also knew that my operation could not be performed until the Red Cross was able to locate enough Negro Type A blood plasma in their segregated blood banks.

Moreover, the colonel was wise enough to know if I were ever able to escape from my hospital room, I would be treated as an untouchable by the white patients.

"Don't take any books or papers in that room, Mary. They put a coon in there yesterday who can't read or write," I heard a white woman hospital employee outside my partially closed room door say one day. Several days later I caught a little white lady in a Red Cross cap peeking into my room.

"Hello, there!" I said. "Won't you come in?"

She blushed, smiled sheepishly and stepped into the room, extending her hand.

"I'm Mary. I came up to see if we could do anything for you."

"I don't know, but I would certainly like to get out of this bed."

After lunch the next day, Mary came up with a wheelchair that had been ordered by Dr. Babcock and offered to take me for a ride. But out in the corridor we got such stares of hatred and gasps of disapproval that I said, "Let's go back to the room."

Mary was only five feet tall and weighed less than one hundred pounds, but she had a lot of guts, and she arrived daily for my ride after that. The stares continued until one day she rolled my chair down to the hospital auditorium, and I played a couple of jazz numbers on the piano during the recreation hour. After that I started to have some friends, and some of the white soldiers even began offering to replace Mary as my wheelchair pilot.

One day we were within two hundred feet of my room when a tall, grim-faced soldier in a purple robe and white pajamas jumped into the wheelchair's path with both arms stretched out like a traffic cop. The man grabbed the arms of the wheelchair, and both Mary and I were about to panic. He burst into a loud laugh. "My buddies and me have decided to take turns chauffeuring the piano player around," he said. The big soldier introduced himself as Pfc. James Messina from Newark, New Jersey. Mary, recovered by this time, thanked him for his offer, but her face flushed as she added sharply, "Soldier, you could have offered your services in a fashion that would have been less threatening."

Jim, one of eight children of an Italian family, had completed his junior year at Rutgers University a month before he was drafted into the Army. Sometimes he would try to equate the prejudice against Italians with that against blacks, but I kept telling him, "Jim, you can get that monkey off your back if you remove the vowel 'a' from the end of your name and change your church. Man, that would make you an instant WASP."

"Travis, you got the right name and the right church. The only thing wrong with you is your color," he said.

"Some of you Italians are dark enough to pass for colored," I would say when Jim tried to get too hip. And I teased him that that might be because Hannibal and his Carthaginian troops from North Africa had occupied Italy for fifteen years from 218 B.C. to 203 B.C.

I had two successful operations, but the third was postponed several times. Lt. Col. Babcock and the other surgeon, Col. Cohen, disagreed over the risk involved in removing the bullet fragments from the lower part of my back. Babcock thought such an operation would cripple me permanently. Cohen disagreed. Babcock resigned from the case, and Col. Cohen went ahead and performed the operation—successfully.

I had a thirty-day leave in Chicago—which my mother and I spent writing letters to the President, U.S. Rep. William T. Dawson, and U.S. Senators Scott W. Lucas (Dem.) and C. Wayland Brooks (Rep.) from Illinois to try to get me discharged.

Back at the hospital in Butler, I was told I had been reassigned to Camp Shenango. I protested to Col. Cohen that I was still having trouble walking. He looked at me piercingly. "Soldier, that limp you have attempted to perfect in your right leg is a fake."

"Sir!" I protested. "It's excruciating for me to have to walk on this leg."

"Don't worry, soldier," he said. "With your I.Q., you aren't going to have to stand. We're going to arrange for you to sit for the duration."

It didn't work out quite like that, but it was close. When I got back to Shenango, I found that some changes had been made. The official name of the post had been changed to Camp Reynolds, and a large service club had sprouted in the black area of the camp. Further, the color bars had been lowered, and blacks were allowed to attend the main movie theatre in the white area. All this was done to cleanse the air of the racist stench that had hovered over the place after the riot.

In June 1944, having given up all attempts to get discharged from the Army, I was shipped to Camp Lee, Virginia.

The train had a three-hour layover in Washington, D.C., and I had a good opportunity to witness Jim Crow with no clothes on. Everything was racially separated, from water fountains to soda fountains. Even the taxicabs were separate. Blacks could only ride in cabs owned or driven by other blacks, and black cabs weren't permitted to enter the horseshoe curve in front of Union Station. Women, men, and children had to carry their luggage a block to get to transportation.

Racism was so contagious in the District of Columbia that black people were practicing it on each other. On the Capital Transit, a circular advertising rooms for "light-colored folks only" was distributed.

Roy Eldridge, the black trumpet star with the Gene Krupa Orchestra, received double pay for not appearing with the band at Lowe's Theater in Washington. The Howard Theater on Florida Avenue was the only movie house with live, top-flight black stage shows. They featured such bands as Jimmie Lunceford, Claude Hopkins, Baron Lee, Lucky Millinder, Duke Ellington, Andy Kirk, Erskine Hawkin, and Count Basie. I saw most of the same name bands with the U.S.O. shows during my tour at Camp Lee.

After the Washington exposure, I didn't find Confederate Virginia as bad as I had expected. My survival mechanism made quick adjustments to a less subtle form of American apartheid. I found the seats at the back of the bus and the "for colored only" waiting rooms in the train stations offensive, but not unbearable.

Back at the post, the black Army's heavily shod feet marched left-right, left-right, in the hot Virginia sun. The drill sergeant would lead the platoon in an ad lib lyric to a World War I melody:

Virginia is a helluva state,
Parlez-vous;

Virginia is a helluva state,
Parlez-vous;
Virginia is a helluva state,
The asshole of the forty-eight,
Hinky, dinky parlez-vous.

As we continued our march, we would sing:

They say this is a white man's war,
Parlez-vous;
They say this is a white man's war,
Parlez-vous;
They say this is a white man's war,
Well, what the hell are we fighting for?
Hinky, dinky parlez-vous.

The exhilaration of marching was preparing a positive feeling of esprit de corps for when we went overseas. But I wasn't going. My I.Q. score got me selected out to attend the Quartermaster School for Administrators. I was sent to Aberdeen Proving Ground in Maryland, over my protests, with the company commander telling me, "I received a special order from Washington stating that you are to be sent to Maryland for the duration of the war, not overseas."

Major Sloan, the company commander at Aberdeen, asked me to organize a band for the company. I accepted with genuine joy.

"Good," he said, in his booming Texas accent. "You can do that in your spare time. Right now, I want you to type."

"Sorry, sir, I don't know how to type."

"Private Travis, you can learn." Major Sloan reached into his bottom desk drawer, pulled out a typing book, and handed it to me. Then he told his company clerk to give me a desk and a typewriter. Within thirty days I had become a self-taught fifty-words-a-minute typist.

Major Sloan made me assistant manager of the colored post exchange, then manager, and finally I became area manager over three post exchanges, including the first large integrated post exchange at Aberdeen. In that position, I won the first-prize weekly award for the best-operated post exchange. I continued to win the weekly contest for two straight years. The Army took my picture, but did not run it in the post newspaper as was usually done. The executive officer in charge of post exchanges told me, "Travis, we just can't afford to print this. It would offend too many people. I hope you'll understand."

So my Army career ended in relative prosperity: I got a promotion to Technical Sgt. Fourth Grade, and, along with the bi-weekly salary I received as exchange manager, I was making double my sergeant's pay. My father was a great lover of cigars, and I used to send him at least two boxes of the best smokes each month.

I liked to think about him back in Chicago, smoking my cigars and bragging to the neighbors about his son. I liked to think about that, and about how it was going to be when I went home.

I had adopted New York's Harlem as my new neighborhood on most of my weekend passes. Each of more than one hundred train rides into New York City always revealed something new. Harlem was New York's most visible neighborhood from the train because the railroad tracks were not covered. New York City's political power brokers in the 1930s decided to cover the railroad tracks in the white communities out of funds from the New Deal Westside Improvement Program; however, they did not feel such an amenity was necessary in Black Harlem. Uncovered tracks meant that Harlem's blacks living between 125th and 155th Streets near the railroad had to endure the never-ending sound of clashing steel from the conjugating railroad cars. The intermittent moans and squeals of the cows and pigs being railroaded to the killing floor punctuated their Harlem days and nights. Floating through every open window were latent cases of silicosis germinating from the railroads' constant spewing of soot, smoke, grit, and grime. Harlem was the coal mine of New York City.

The economic deprivation that prevailed in the Harlem mine, in spite of the war boom, caused thousands of black women to line up six mornings a week in the "slave markets" of mid-town Manhattan and the upper Bronx. White housewives were bidding for their services in 1944 at auction prices ranging between twenty-five and thirty cents per hour with the cost of the noon meal deducted. White trade unions made sure blacks would have to work for such slave wages by denying them union cards, thus adding to their handicap to compete for better jobs.

The economically depressed noon-day Harlem transformed into a free-spending, glittering showplace each night under the Harlem moon before the clock struck twelve. Downtown white folks came uptown nightly to slum, get high, and sometimes fly. Every night, the Savoy Ballroom, 133rd and Lenox Avenue, Smalls' Paradise Cabaret, 135th Street and 7th Avenue, and the Elks

Rendezvous, 133rd Street and Lenox, were loaded with white folks who wanted to see or learn to do the latest dance crazes, such as Peckin, Trucking, or the old Lindy Hop. Harlem at night in the 1940s was very reminiscent of the night life on the South Side of Chicago during the 1920s and '30s. Harlem's Apollo Theatre's 1890 architecture was not comparable to the Louis XIV castle appearance of Chicago's Regal Theatre. But the talent at both theatres was the same. Black entertainers rotated from black ghetto to ghetto in the fashion of the old Circuit Court judges.

My desire to return to Chicago was often forgotten when I saw talented former DuSable High School entertainers such as Ray Sneed, Jr. performing his famous exotic dance at Smalls' Paradise, or got a wave of recognition from John Young, the pianist, as he played "Foggy Bottom" with the Andy Kirk band on the stage of the Apollo Theatre, or encountered the famous pianist, Dorothy Donegan, as I caught her act at the Howard Theater in Washington, in concert at the Walnut Theatre in Philadelphia, or backstage at New York's Zanzibar Cabaret when she appeared there in the Cab Calloway Cotton Club Review.

Mid-Manhattan's thirty-six legitimate theatres afforded me the opportunity to balance my jazz interest against the best in live theatre. During the 1944 theatrical season, I caught Paul Robeson, the original genius for all seasons, in his powerful and poetic performance in the title role of Shakespeare's *Othello* at the Shubert Theatre on 44th Street west of Broadway. *Carmen Jones*, Billy Rose's black version of George Bizet's opera, was the best musical on Broadway that year and I saw it at a Saturday matinee for the grand price of two dollars. *Anna Lucasta* was presented by the American Negro Theatre at the Library Theatre located in Harlem at 103 West 135th Street for a subscription price of seventy-five cents per seat. *Anna* is the story of a Polish family written by a white playwright. The tragedy, the comedy, and the drama of the black experience in Harlem, as expressed by Langston Hughes, Claude McKay, and James Weldon Johnson, had not penetrated the Broadway stage by 1944. (Richard Wright's *Native Son*, a Chicago-based novel with a stinging social commentary, reached Broadway in 1941.)

"Black folks are happy folks and that's why they are not seen in serious roles in the movies or on the stage," said Art Mills as he leaned on the clover-shaped bar at Smalls' Paradise.

"Bullshit," I responded. "How can you be happy when the man is constantly kicking your ass?"

Art retorted, "Haven't you ever seen a white man kicking a nigger's ass and the nigger was laughing?"

After a brief reflection, I responded, "Yes! I have on more than a few occasions. However, none of them were laughing because it was funny. They laughed in self-defense. A laugh was sometimes the only weapon the nigger had to save his pride. Particularly, if it meant the end of his job or his life."

At this point I walked over to the jukebox and put in a nickel to hear the Mills Brothers and Ella Fitzgerald's rendition of "Into Each Life Some Rain Must Fall." I played that song twenty-three times and Art said, "Man, aren't you tired of hearing that song?"

I replied, "For some unknown reason I can't stop playing it."

Art said, "Are you having trouble with your old lady?"

"Nope!" I replied, "but I think I will call my mother. I haven't talked to her for two months."

I placed a collect call to Chicago and the first thing my mother said was, "Where are you? I have been calling Aberdeen trying to reach you for two days to tell you we had to rush your father to the County Hospital."

I hung up the phone abruptly and called Sgt. Morris Brown for a special pass to go to Chicago. He told me I could go directly from New York and that he would mail my furlough papers directly to my home. I caught the New York Central's "Pacemaker" that afternoon and arrived in Chicago on Saturday morning, December 16, 1944.

I went directly from the train station to the County Hospital. Dad's fear of the County Hospital and its alleged "black bottle" for colored folks meant he had to have been critically ill to consent to going there. My arrival at Dad's bedside confirmed my suspicions. They had tubes hooked into his arms and his nose. I had been in the ward for more than an hour when Dad opened his eyes, beckoned for me to come closer, then touched the sergeant's stripes on my Army uniform, smiled without saying a word and closed his eyes again.

Since Dad was on the critical list the intern permitted me to sit by his bed throughout the night. The only sound Dad made all night came from a heavy roaring in his chest. At 5:48 a.m. Sunday morning he opened his eyes and said, "I didn't think you would get here in time." I didn't respond. I simply touched his hand and smiled. Dad looked at me through his weak, watery eyes and said in a soft but audible voice, "Boy! Take care of your mother." Seconds after he spoke those words his eyes seemed to reel back into his head, and his mouth snapped open as if his jawbone had become unhinged. My father was pronounced dead at 6:03 a.m. Sunday, December 17, 1944.

My Aunt Willie invited Mother and me over to her home at 5336 South Wabash after the funeral. We stayed through the Christmas holiday. Christmas without Dad was a bust. Aunt Willie's excellently prepared meals fell flat on my taste buds. Her expensive imported whiskies did not even give me a buzz. My spirit was so low that a street curb seemed high.

Aunt Willie's son, Frank, said, "Man, you are going to grieve yourself to death. Uncle Louis [my father] would not dig your mood at all. Let's get the hell out of the house and go and drink with Daddy-O Daylie, the rhyming bartender, down at the DuSable Lounge. Hey! We can also check out Floyd 'Guitar Blues' Smith's Trio." (The DuSable was located on Oakland Boulevard, about one hundred feet west of Cottage Grove in the basement of the DuSable Hotel.)

To our disappointment, we found that Daddy-O had moved his talents to Charlie Coles' El Grotto Supper Club at 6400 South Cottage Grove in the basement of the Pershing Hotel. The twenty-five block trip South to hear Daddy-O's rhymes and to see him do tricks with the ice cubes gave me the first real laugh I had during my furlough in Chicago.

The next day we decided to go downtown to see the World's Champion Joe Louis' wife, Marva Louis, the new singing sensation. She was accompanied by my friend Zinky Cohn, the piano wizard, on the stage of the Rialto Theater at State and Van Buren. (The Rialto was a famous burlesque theatre that changed its policy from strip tease to all black stage shows in the fall of 1944.) Thursday, December 28, 1944, marked the first time in my twenty-plus years of visiting the Loop and its theatres that I had ever seen such a large army of blacks outside the boundary lines of our South Side black ghetto.

Our Allied armies had pulled up along the German Siegfried line in December, 1944, when Hitler launched his last fanatical counter-offensive of the war. So effective was the Germans' offensive that all the troops were forced back some fifty miles, almost to the sea.

The tides turned in January, 1945, when the Allies retaliated with a renewed offensive. The Soviets had also begun a winter offensive. By the end of February, the Soviet Allied troops had moved westward within thirty miles of Berlin. The American and British troops were advancing eastward. Victory for the Allied troops was in the air when President Franklin D. Roosevelt died suddenly on April 12, 1945, in Warm Springs, Georgia. Although most blacks had been denied the right to cast a vote for Roosevelt in the four times he was elected president, they reacted to his death as one would react to the loss of a close friend or relative. (Roosevelt served less than three months in his fourth term.)

I arrived in Washington, D.C. from Aberdeen, Maryland, on Saturday, April 14, to visit with relatives over the weekend. The train station was jammed with dignitaries of all types awaiting the 10:30 a.m. arrival of the Roosevelt funeral train. Black and white folks stood integrated on both sides of the streets, sidewalk deep, from the train station to the Capitol. Many of them were openly weeping. The hot and humid Potomac weather made waiting for the funeral procession onerous. It was heartbreaking to stand there among a throng of blacks and whites who had become unified in tears over a fallen leader. The vibrations of my heartbeat seemed louder than the clop, clop from the hoofs of the six white horses that pulled the caisson carrying President Roosevelt's flag-covered coffin. The moans from the crowd as the coffin passed were subdued by the drone of planes overhead, and the humming from the motors of the slow moving black limousines.

The war moved swiftly in the next twenty-five days. The German government surrendered unconditionally at General Eisenhower's headquarters on May 7, and May 8, 1945, was declared as V-E (Victory in Europe) Day. Less than 120 days after Roosevelt's death, President Harry S. Truman issued an ultimatum to the Japanese to surrender or face "prompt and utter destruction." Truman waited a week and on August 6, 1945, his promise of destruction fell out of the sky in the epoch-making form of an atomic bomb over the city of Hiroshima in Japan. The city was obliterated: 75,000 to 80,000 people were killed, and thousands more permanently injured. On August 14, Japan agreed to surrender. One hundred and fifty days later, on February 2, 1946, I surrendered my uniform at Indian Town Gap, Pennsylvania. The captain at the "Gap" separation center told us that we had thirty days to get out of uniform and into civilian clothes. Within thirty hours after I left the "Gap" I was back in Chicago standing on the corner of 47th and South Parkway in a ready-made double-breasted cocoa brown suit. The real world that I was about to grapple with was unlike the civilian utopia I dreamed about during my forty months and twenty-three days in the Army.

CHAPTER 13

Facing Facts

"BLACK BOY! YOU CAN'T READ, YOU CAN'T WRITE, AND YOU CAN'T do arithmetic. All you can hope to do is succeed as a common laborer, at some task that requires a strong back and a weak mind."

Those were not the exact words in the letters I had received from Roosevelt, DePaul, and Northwestern Universities, but they might as well have been. They all meant the same thing: I was being rejected. I could tell myself that I knew I had talents, that I had even managed to experience success in that unlikely setting, the segregated U.S. Army, but none of it mattered. I felt utterly destroyed.

It didn't seem to help to reflect that my rejection might have more to do with my color than with my potential. After all, I knew that DePaul and Northwestern had strict quotas for both blacks and Jews. But my anguish and shame at being rejected by Roosevelt was far greater.

Roosevelt was quota-free. It had emerged on April 17, 1945, spawned by protests over the bigotry of the Central YMCA College. That was after Dr. Edward J. Sparling, president of the YMCA College, had refused to give the board of trustees a black head count, since that would have meant establishing quotas for the education-hungry black veterans returning from the war. At that time, tuition fees for all students at the college were the same, but blacks could not use the YMCA swimming pool or other athletic facilities in the Association Building at 19 South LaSalle Street.

In February 1946, however, Roosevelt represented hope for black veterans, and many of my buddies were heading downtown to attend.

I was left out. In spite of all my ambitions and the new sense of adulthood that I had brought with me from the Army experience, I was too dumb to attend. My feelings can best be described in a blues lyric I composed:

If you don't believe I am dead, baby,
Just try calling me on the phone.
The man done buried my mind,
And my body is all alone.

Those notices from the university authorities convinced me I was a dead-head, since I had flunked their exams. I took it all very seriously, and I went back to my pre-war job at Armour. I was rehired with veterans' preference as a "Georgia mule." The preference helped, because 30,000 members of the United Packing House Workers' Union had just returned from a strike called on January 16, 1946, against post-war cutbacks in jobs, hours, and wages.

A "mule" unloaded the boned hams from the end of a conveyer into a two-wheeled "Georgia buggy" and then pulled the buggy, in the manner of a harnessed animal, to a scale a hundred feet away. The work was hard, demeaning, and boring, and my unhappiness grew. Only the lunchbreaks provided any mental stimulation at all, as twenty or so other "mules" and I would gather around to talk about black issues. I liked to talk about what I was already calling my "Negro Agenda."

For example, there was the question of black folks who had lived around 61st and 62nd Streets and Calumet since the early 1930s but who still weren't permitted to go to the White City Roller Rink at 63rd and Calumet until 1946. It took picket lines, bloodied heads, and many arrests before they were let in.

We talked about the incident when Cab Calloway, the internationally famous band leader, was beaten over the head and had a finger broken when he tried to see Lionel Hampton and his orchestra at the "white only" Pla-Mor Ballroom in Kansas City, Missouri. The Stevens (later the Hilton), the Sherman House, and the Congress Hotels in downtown Chicago refused to accommodate the National Negro Museum and Historical Foundation for a planned celebration of "Negro History Week." The downtown hotels in Chicago, and most restaurants, did not allow blacks to sit and eat, either.

One day I hauled my "Georgia buggy" over to the scale. The white man, in a white frock, wrote down the weight on a white piece of paper and slapped it on top of the load of dead hams in the buggy, just like he always did.

"Pull that load to the Sweet Pickle Department and rush right back and get another one," he said.

As I was chugging along following the orders, the department superintendent stopped me.

"If you don't quit, we are going to fire you in two weeks. Your noontime discussions with the men are causing morale problems in the department," he said.

"What are you talking about?" I asked.

"You know," he said, and he walked away.

I quit the stockyards in March 1946. I knew that kind of work held no hope for me. Instead, I decided to take a chance on self-employment. I had taken an accounting correspondence course during my army years, and now I decided to set up as a tax consultant, filling out tax returns for the members of Rev. Victoria Pitts' storefront church at 2216 South State Street.

That work brought about a change in my self-image. It gave me so much confidence that I enrolled in two courses at Englewood Evening Junior College, where there were no entrance requirements and the registration fee was only five dollars. With the help of my high school friend, Dustalear Cook, who had become a Chicago schoolteacher, I passed both courses with better than a "B" average.

That summer I tried a more ambitious venture. I leased the Pershing Ballroom in the Pershing Hotel at 64th and Cottage Grove for four separate dance dates. I booked a popular recording act, the "Cats and the Fiddle," headed by Austin Powell, for the first date.

It was a flop. I had a partner, a man I had admired because he had a college degree. But only 420 people attended. I had personally sold 390 tickets, and my college-educated partner had sold thirty. We assigned our three remaining dates to the Adams Brothers, two local dance promoters, and dissolved our partnership.

By then I was even more determined to get an education, I took the placement examination at Wilson Junior College and was told I would have to take remedial reading and English. Not understanding just what I was letting myself in for, I stopped at the next table and registered for American Literature 117.

While I was standing there, I overheard two teachers in a heated discussion over who was going to share an office with a new appointee to the English department. A bespectacled male teacher was telling a redheaded woman teacher, "Okay, I'll share my office with her. I learned to understand them through my military experience in World War I." The woman gave a sigh of relief. It became clear as I listened that the "them" they were talking about was Henrietta L. McMillen, Ph.D., the first black appointed to the English department in the Chicago Junior College system. She later became head of the English department for both Wilson Junior and the Chicago Teachers' College.

Oh, those "thems," I thought. It was a word that curdled the human sensibilities of all those blacks who made history by being "firsts" and then had to suffer the curse of being thought of always as exceptions to the "thems."

In the remedial reading class, on the first day, the instructor paced back and forth in front of us and then delivered a little speech that has echoed in my mind ever since.

"Now, I think I should start this class by telling you that if you have gone this far in life and still have to be assigned to this remedial reading class, you'd just better face the fact that you're not going to make it. The cards of academic life have been stacked against you. My statistics show that only one out of every two hundred people who are enrolled in this class graduate from college with an undergraduate degree. Eighty-five percent of you present today will not survive your first college year."

Dr. Witney E. Smith's statement set my brain whirling with mad promises to myself that I would be that one out of the two hundred to graduate from college. But the promises didn't seem at all realistic when I was brought up sharply against a terrible and unexpected obstacle: I could not read. Oh, sure, I could work my way through application forms and letters and so forth, but as far as doing more sophisticated reading, the type of thing I had to do if I was to have any hope of staying in college, I was floundering. And I hadn't even understood, when I graduated from high school, how handicapped I was.

In the remedial reading course, I struggled painfully through high-school-level texts, reading every page one word at a time. But in the "Lit" class, for which I had so casually signed up, I was required to read one book each week and write a comprehensive report about what I read. I quickly discovered that this was far beyond me. I spent ten to twenty minutes on a single page, staying up until early in the morning.

"Why don't you go to bed, boy, and get some sleep?" my mother would call.

"Mama, there is no time to sleep. I have got to learn to read."

"You're ruining your health."

"Mama, how can I have a healthy body with a hungry mind?"

"Suit yourself," she would answer as I returned to wrestling with Hawthorne or Thoreau or Sinclair Lewis.

When Dr. Ernest Ernst read my first book report, he threatened to throw me out of the class. He thought it was a joke. I protested that it was not and told him I was willing to do it over and over until it was acceptable to him. He let me stay in the class provided I came to his counseling office on Mondays, Wednesdays, and Fridays to review my work.

"Dr. Ernst, what did I do wrong?"

He shook his head. "Well, you just didn't understand what you read. Why don't you try again?"

I had no resentment. I just kept trying.

About the eighth week into the semester, it paid off. I was inching through a book by Theodore Dreiser, one word and one phrase at a time, when suddenly it clicked! It became clear—it all fell into place. The phrases rolled together into sentences, and the sentences rolled into paragraphs of thoughts and ideas.

I let out a loud yelp, and my mother tumbled out of her bed and came running—she must have thought I had injured myself somehow.

"Great God A'mighty, Mama, I can read!" I said.

Not long after that, I had a similar spontaneous experience in writing. It had been almost impossible for me to express myself on paper in a logical fashion. If you cannot grasp ideas logically when you read them, you certainly cannot explain and recreate them. If Dempsey couldn't read, you can be certain he would not be able to write.

In December of 1946, I was trying to put together a letter to the Veterans Administration, complaining about the fact that I had never received a disability check for my service-connected disabilities. Like magic, I discovered I had written eight full pages in less than an hour, describing, giving reasons, and drawing conclusions. Before that time, it would have taken me that long to compose two poorly constructed paragraphs. I had learned to read, and now I had learned to write! I was twenty-six years old, and at that age discovering the written page was a euphoric experience. Unearthing the potential of a mature mind is a powerful instrument for change.

My studies suddenly became easier. In spite of the facts of the negative society around me, I was able to keep the spirit to fight past my obstacles.

Other students in the remedial reading class did not, and they succumbed in the first academic year, as Dr. Witney E. Smith had predicted.

But I knew you had to keep the spirit, even in the face of incidents like the one that occurred when Thomas Leonard tried to buy a small can of aspirin for a headache in Sam's Tap Room at 1034 East 43rd Street. Thomas was refused service and was subsequently shot in the stomach by a member of an anti-black Oakland-Kenwood area mob. Three of his friends were brutally beaten by a white mob of forty men. The blacks were all arrested and taken before Judge Charles Daugherty on January 3, 1947, in felony court and held on counts of assault with intent to kill.

It was spirit that propelled Jackie Robinson to run the bases of liberation for Black America when he was called to play in the major leagues on April 9, 1947. And it was spirit that rocketed me through Wilson Junior College in sixteen months instead of the usual twenty-four. I received my diploma on January 30, 1948.

My Wilson diploma was a quick passport to Roosevelt University, the fountainhead of democracy in higher education. Of course, Roosevelt didn't have much competition. In 1948, the spirit of brotherhood that permeated the walls of the university was unlike anything I had ever experienced. Every morning when I stepped inside the university's walls I was enveloped with a feeling of hope for black people in America. However, each afternoon when I stepped outside the university's doors onto Michigan Avenue, I was jarred back to the realization that Roosevelt University did not mirror the real world.

Daily, as I walked north on Michigan to catch the bus going south, I looked at the tall, white-owned office buildings and said, "Those buildings don't even have black smoke coming out of the chimney." I knew that blacks did not have a "toenail hold" on the financial fortunes of America, and I decided I was going to work for change since the status quo was simply unacceptable to me. At the time I believed that I could best work for change through classes in law and politics.

In my classes at Roosevelt I met some brilliant young blacks. There was Gus Savage; Harold Washington; Oscar Brown, Jr., writer, actor, producer, and singer; Robert L. Kimbrough, now a dentist; Frank London Brown, author of *Trumbull Park*; Mark Jones, Circuit Court Judge, Cook County, Illinois; and Clarence Towns, also a dentist.

Savage, Washington, Oscar Brown, Jr., Frank Brown, Bennett Johnson, and I were all sitting on the floor in a temporary housing trailer project at 57th and Perry, the home of Gus and Eunice Savage, when we all agreed, after much debate, on a single "Black Agenda." One of the planks in the Agenda was that both Gus Savage and Harold Washington should run for Congress. Gus agreed to run from a West Side district and Harold agreed to run from the South Side.

It has taken thirty-two years to fulfill a commitment that sounded like a "pork dieter's" dream. The six men who sat on the floor that night were dreamers all right, dreamers who have continued to support each other financially and spiritually over the years—in days of both feast and famine. Unfortunately, there was an abundance of famine and very little feast. Both Gus and Harold took their seats in Congress in January 1981, representing the 1st and 2nd Congressional Districts in Illinois. Both the 1st and 2nd Congressional Districts are expansions of the restrictive covenant areas occupied by blacks prior to 1948.

What Congress refused to achieve legislatively, the United States Supreme Court did—when it ruled in *Shelley vs. Kraemer* on Monday, May 3, 1948, that racial restrictive convenants were unenforceable.

The next morning Mr. Richard Hill, Jr., lawyer and the former president of the first black-owned national bank in Illinois, the Douglas National Bank at 36th and State Streets, gave me and his son, Oscar, who became an attorney, a ride to Roosevelt University. Mr. Hill turned around in the driver's seat and held up the *Chicago Tribune* that he had just bought from the newsstand at Garfield and Michigan, asking "What does this headline on restrictive covenants mean to you and Oscar?"

Both Oscar and I gave vague answers about Jim Crow housing that did not satisfy Mr. Hill. As Mr. Hill drove north on Michigan Boulevard he explained: "Colored people can live in the 61st block on Rhodes with the full sanction of the law. The covenant suit pending against Mary A. Green at 6439 S. Maryland, brought by Vivian McCormick, 6435 Maryland, and Bessie McGray, 6417 S. Maryland, to enforce a covenant against Negroes living in that block will be dismissed.

"As a matter of fact," he continued, "all race restrictions in every state of the Union and in the District of Columbia have been struck down as a result of the Supreme Court decision. Every race restriction recorded against real estate in Cook County is now meaningless. They can be tossed out as scraps of paper." Neither Oscar nor I said a word until Mr. Hill stopped the car at Roosevelt University, where we thanked him for the ride.

I was thinking hard about the decision and what it would mean to black people. I had always been more or less aware of housing and the problems it presented and the human toll that segregation had taken in Chicago. In spite of my failure to be aware of the case as it went through the courts, I understood its importance. And, of course, I was well aware that the postwar period had been one of acute housing shortage, with a resulting acceleration in tension between blacks and whites in many areas of the city.

By April of 1949, for example, a simmering situation burst into violence in Park Manor. Jesse Howell's home at 6958 South Prairie was burned; a Ku Klux Klan cross was planted on the lawn of Ruth Minor's house at 215 East 70th Street; and a roving gang of white hoodlums smashed windows at the home of Mrs. A. Carter at 7023 South Vernon.

Both the Federal Housing Administration and the Veterans Administration supported the racist climate for years after the 1948 Supreme Court decision on restrictive covenants by refusing mortgages to blacks moving into white areas such as Park Manor, Chatham, South Shore, Kenwood, and Hyde Park. The Veterans Administration made funds available through the G.I. Bill to educate black minds, but under the same bill it was working, in practice, to exclude blacks from needed housing, most spectacularly in the suburbs. These kinds of governmental inconsistencies kept pushing me toward a career in law.

Quite by accident, I launched a career in the field of housing, instead of law. At the home of Theodore McNeal, Jr., at 4640 South Michigan Avenue, in the Rosenwald Building, I started talking about housing during dinner one night with Moselynne E. Hardwick, my fiancée from Cleveland, Tennessee; Mae Robinson, McNeal's mother; and Eugene N. Robinson, his stepfather. Mrs. Robinson said, "I understand you plan to enter law school this fall after you graduate from Roosevelt University?" I told her I had been accepted at the Chicago Kent College of Law.

"I guess you will go into criminal law?" she said in a less than enthusiastic tone. "I think your personality is more suited to dealing with happier situations," she said.

"Like what?" I asked.

"In the field of real estate, you would be dealing with families buying homes or possibly young couples renting their first apartments. You must admit that people in those categories create a better working environment than someone who might be on his way to breaking into a jailhouse."

Moselynne and I discussed Mrs. Robinson's suggestion extensively after we left the dinner party. Mrs. Robinson had put something on my mind, and I enrolled in a real estate principles course at Roosevelt the following week as a career hedge to supplement the income from my G.I. bill while in law school.

In August 1949, three major events took place. I asked Moselynne to marry me; I received my bachelor of arts degree from Roosevelt University (thirty-two months from the day after I entered Wilson Junior College); and I passed the real estate broker's exam.

I formally opened my first real estate office when I proudly hung my real estate license in a third floor bedroom on August 17, 1949, at 5428 South Indiana, where I lived with my mother. September was just as eventful because at high noon on September 17, 1949, Mose and I were married. One week later I entered law school. In 1949, I had achieved my 1946 three-year projection. I finished college, married a beautiful, loving girl, and entered a profession.

CHAPTER 14

Don't Stop Me Now

I HAD CHOSEN THE 1949 RECESSION AS A TIME TO GO INTO BUSI-
ness, and things were tough. For a while I shared an office in the afternoons, since I was attending law school in the morning, with an attorney
named William Hughes, over the old State Theater at 3509 South State. The
agreement was that I wouldn't have to pay my half of the rent until I earned
my first real estate commission. Three months later, I had not earned a single
commission, and few prospects were fighting for my attention. Then Hughes,
who worked full time at the post office at night, moved across the street into
the Binga Arcade building at 3460 South State to share offices with several
other part-time lawyers.

Since he had taken the desk, chairs, telephone, and telephone directory,
for several months I used an orange crate for a desk and a tin scrub bucket
for a chair. On the rare occasions when I had appointments with clients with
wallets intact, Attorney Horace Galloway, who leased the suite, would let me
use his front office.

One day Dr. Allen L. Wright, M.D., a 1939 DuSable classmate who now
practices medicine in Chicago, paid me a surprise visit. He found Travis, the
real estate broker, sitting on a pail behind a wooden box. His face did not
reveal any surprise at what must have been an incongruous sight.

"What do you have to sell in Douglas Park?" he said.

"I have a deluxe yellow brick three-flat, with three six-room apartments
with two baths in each unit, at 1641 South Drake Avenue."

"That sounds like something I might be interested in. When can I see it?"

"Any time you want. But we'll have to take the streetcar, because I don't own a car."

Dr. Wright drove me over to see the property. A few days later we saw it again with his wife, Alyce. They bought it. It was my first sale. The commission was $1,240, which was more money than I had ever had in my life at one time.

When Moselynne came home from work that evening I had placed the big check in the middle of the bed, where she couldn't miss it.

"Baby! You can quit your job now and come home and take care of our business," I said.

Moselynne's typing ability proved a real asset to our enterprise. She would type twenty or more letters every day to property owners in the Douglas Park area, soliciting property for sale. Then she would type an equal number of letters to the 3,416 owners and tenants being displaced by urban renewal on the 100-acre Lake Meadows development site, from 31st to 35th Streets, from King Drive to the Lake. Douglas Park properties were attractive to these displaced families, because the $3,000 to $5,000 in equity they received from urban renewal represented a good down payment for West Side properties, providing the buyers weren't too old to qualify for a mortgage.

I got to be very good at matching South Side people with West Side housing. Many blacks chose Douglas Park because the West Side Jewish residents being displaced by black South Side immigrants never reacted violently, as did the Irish and Poles on the Southeast and Southwest Sides. The Jewish homeowners in Douglas Park were so cordial toward me that I would sometimes get up enough nerve to ask them why they were moving.

"We're moving west to California," they always said.

I thought it was strange that so many people from the same area would be moving to the West Coast. Later on a Jewish friend told me that Skokie, Illinois, and California were synonymous. In the west area of Hyde Park, the Jewish sellers would always tell me they were moving south to Florida, when they were in fact moving north, to Lake Shore Drive or Highland Park, or Chicago's very, very white North Shore.

Searching out mortgages for blacks displaced by urban renewal in 1950 and 1951 was more exhausting than driving a 1923 Model T Ford non-stop from Chicago to California. The Ford would ultimately reach its destination, but the displaced family frequently would not find its mortgage. Major white Loop banks and savings and loan associations were not interested in making loans to black borrowers. The two very small black-owned savings and loan associations didn't have enough money to meet the demand. And angry whites were wildly demonstrating at City Hall against seven sites in white neighborhoods that were being proposed for subsidized housing for low-income displaced blacks.

But at the same time, white speculators were having no trouble getting mortgage money from life insurance companies and savings and loan associations to exploit black home buyers through contract sales. It was common for blacks to buy homes on contract from speculators at prices that had been marked up 200 to 300 percent. Contract selling was a common practice in Chicago into the early 1970s. A successful lawsuit filed by both the Westside and the Southside Contract Buyers' Leagues slowed the practice. The land contract is intrinsically a good document. It was the white speculators' exploitive use of the instrument which gave it a slaveship stench.

Human exploitation in any form is vicious. Exploiting an economically and culturally disadvantaged people in their efforts to seek basic shelter is vile. I starved the first nine months I was in the real estate business because I refused to become a "bird dog" for white speculators and their white and black lending sponsors who were plundering the black housing market with land contracts.

I had been a licensed broker on a bare survival diet for almost a year before I met Henry Banach, a man of Polish ancestry, and another named August Saldukus. Through Banach, I was able to get loans for blacks through the Polish-controlled Universal Savings and Loan Association on the city's Near South Side. Saldukus was president of the Midland Savings and Loan Association. During my first years in the business, these two institutions made 99 percent of my loans. I was delighted with the arrangement, because ultimately all my people were able to get deeds instead of contracts. Both institutions charged a 5 percent service fee plus 6 percent interest annually. These prices were bargains, since the other money available demanded a 10 percent cash service fee up front, plus 6 percent per annum.

The magnitude of the discrimination in the mortgage market was—and is—obvious when you consider that the average white buyer in that period was paying a 1 percent or less service charge, with an interest rate hovering just above 5 percent. Some institutions were paying brokers a 1 percent finders fee for every white borrower who qualified for a mortgage.

That discrimination, and the oppressive effect of the land contract on the black community, made it evident to me that the only way a black man could survive in real estate and serve his people was by creating a source within the black community to use some of that community's own wealth. So I began to dream about what was to become the Sivart Mortgage Corporation, the conduit needed to achieve that objective.

Sivart, as a mortgage banking institution with its roots, purposes—and dreams—in the black community, could tap the billions in black savings being held by white institutions in the form of pension funds, insurance premiums, time deposits, and savings certificates. But there were many obstacles that had to be surmounted, and finally getting the thing underway was to take years.

In 1951, Chicago was a city deeply divided by the most overt racist practices, so much so that when I spoke of my Sivart dream to people like my mother, they shook their heads and said I was hopelessly out of step. Black lives in Chicago at that time were still clouded by one report after another of outbreaks of racial violence.

On June 8, 1951, Harvey Clark Jr. ventured into the white suburb of Cicero, the most vehemently defended bastion of white racism in the Chicago metropolitan area. Clark and Maurice Scott, Sr., who owned the moving van that was carrying Clark's belongings, were greeted by several members of the Cicero Police Department when they arrived at 6139 19th Court in Cicero, where Clark had rented a third-floor apartment.

"You niggers have no moving permit, and you can't move your nigger junk into this building," was their "welcome wagon" salute.

In the middle of the afternoon, George C. Adams, Harvey Clark's attorney, who was a Creole of black, French, and Indian ancestry, received a telephone call from the janitor at the Cicero building. The janitor told him the police had halted Clark's move-in. Adams got hold of Maurice Scott, Jr., the son of the moving van owner, and the two sped off to Cicero in Adams' car.

When the car pulled up at the address, Scott saw a policeman holding a gun at the back of his father's head and kneeing him forward, Scott ran over to them, and another Cicero cop put a gun to his head, while white women crowded around to deluge his face with layers of thick, frothy spit.

Clark and his lawyer, with the aid of two attorneys for the National Association for the Advancement of Colored People (NAACP), Ulysses S. Key and George M. Leighton, obtained an injunction against the Cicero police from U.S. Federal Judge John P. Barnes. The injunction allowed Clark to move his furniture into the apartment a month later, on July 10, but it did not abate the racist rage in the breast of the Cicero mob.

Only a small knot of whites watched the move-in, but by 9:30 the following night, the pack had grown to a growling mob of some 5,000 people, more than half of them women. The family never was allowed to occupy the apartment. During the night, teenage hoodlums broke into the building and threw Clark's furniture, clothing, and other personal property out of the third-floor windows. Each time a window was broken or an object was hurled out, the mob would roar in delight. The roars amplified to a frenzy when the Cicero rioters began to lynch the Clark family—symbolically—by setting fire to the furniture and clothing that had been thrown to the ground.

By the second night, the atmosphere in Cicero was one of a raw carnival without masks, a mob in search of a collective orgasm of racial hatred. The mob was still there, howling and jeering, on the third night, but that was the night Police Chief Konovsky and his men went home, leaving the Clark family's possessions to the mercy of the good white citizens of Cicero. Law and order for Black America had failed.

Finally, at the urging of Alderman Archibald Carey and the Cook County sheriff, Governor Adlai Stevenson sent in the National Guard to quell the disorder. It took 500 bayonet-wielding Guardsmen to end the incident. It was the first time since the bloody Chicago riot of 1919 that a Governor had to send troops into Cook County. A $200,000 lawsuit was filed in federal court against Cicero's town officials for violating the Constitutional civil rights of the Scotts, Edwards, and the Clark family.

The protective legal umbrella the NAACP put over the Clark's civil rights case was one of the reasons that I became a paid-up life member of that organization in the fall of 1952. Paying out a lump sum of $500 for a civil rights membership in those dark economic days was not a small thing for me—or for the NAACP. The organization had only 88 fully paid life members nationally and 133 subscribing life members in 1953, compared with 20,000 fully paid life members and 33,000 subscribing life members in 1975, according to Beatrice Steele, Chicago NAACP life membership chair.

So a new life member in those days was very important, so important that the executive secretary, the legendary Walter White, would fly from New York City to the city of the donor to personally present him with a life membership plaque. I will never forget my own presentation. The Life Membership Committee of the Chicago Branch of the NAACP arranged a meeting for the occasion in the Wendell Phillips High School Assembly Hall. At the last minute, Walter White was called to Washington D.C., and he sent in his place his assistant, Roy Wilkins.

I found it curiously hard to speak before this friendly and expectant audience about my conviction that civil rights and my own life and quest for economic success were inextricably intertwined. I had been working out my ideas on this for years, ever since I first began to listen to my father and his brothers talk about the situation of blacks in America around our dining room table. Nevertheless, my voice quavered as I spoke.

In contrast, the whites who crashed bricks through the front window of Donald Howard's apartment at 10630 South Beasley on August 6, 1953, were having no such difficulty in expressing themselves. They weren't saying, "Welcome to the National Association for the Advancement of Colored People," nor were they saying, "Welcome to Trumbull Park Homes." They were shouting:

"Coon, coon, you came too soon,

"You and your kind should go to the moon."

The siege of Trumbull Park was the longest and most costly racial incident in Chicago history. In the late summer and fall of 1953, as many as 1,200 policemen patrolled the area around the 427-unit Trumbull Park project on some days.

My friend and fellow Roosevelt University alumnus, the late Frank London Brown, was a tenant in Trumbull Park. I lived his terrors daily. He would call and tell me that he was coming to visit if he could get the "Black Mariah" to pick him up. Blacks leaving Trumbull Park for any purpose had to be transported out of the area, for their own protection, in a dingy, black patrol wagon that reeked with strong, offensive odors left over from its usual function of ferrying drunks and criminals. The police would give their passengers the option of being dropped off at 95th and State Streets or 95th and Cottage Grove, which were the southern boundaries of the "Black Belt" in 1953. To get back into Trumbull Park, Frank would have to call Essex 5-5910, and the paddy wagon would pick him up again at one of those two points within twenty to thirty minutes—maybe. Not surprisingly, visiting among blacks in Trumbull Park was discouraged by the Chicago police.

Nearly thirty years later, I could not trace the exact route of the "Black Mariahs" when I visited the area, because expressway construction had eliminated some of the streets. But I found that in addition to blacks living in the project, others had bought private homes on the east side of the 106th block on Beasley. I talked to a white man, about sixty-five years old, who told me, "The doctor said I had high blood pressure and a bad heart, and I would have to live with these ailments the rest of my life. The way I look at it is, if the good Negroes in this project don't try to marry my granddaughter or molest my wife, I'm resigned to live with them as neighbors as long as there is breath in my body."

CHAPTER 15

Civil Rights Struggle—Northern Style

I N 1954, A LOT OF THINGS WERE BEGINNING—JUST BEGINNING—
to change for blacks. And I had my problems too.

I was hospitalized with a mysterious disease for four months. The
doctors, although they admitted they did not know what was wrong with me,
recommended surgery. I insisted they confer with me first. So, one morning,
two cheerful young surgeons appeared in my room carrying a large anatomy
chart and explained in lay language how they were going to proceed.

"What do you expect to find after you open my stomach?" I asked.

They looked at each other and then at me. "We're not sure."

"Then it's an exploratory operation," I said.

"Yes. But it's the only way we can find out exactly what is wrong with you."

I asked them to give me a half hour to make a decision. When they returned, I had called my wife and mother to come to the hospital to help me
dress and check out.

The doctors were shocked. They warned me I was making a mistake and
that I would never be readmitted to Billings Hospital, the prestigious University of Chicago hospital on Chicago's South Side. The threat didn't disturb
me, because it sounded to me like such a readmission would give me a quick
entry into the cemetery.

I was at home for two weeks, physically sinking, when I got a letter from
the head of internal medicine at Billings, asking that I call him. I was readmitted as an outpatient, and a young internist finally found the cause of the
trouble, diagnosing it as "obstructive jaundice." The symptoms had not been
produced by cancer, as they had thought.

"Boy, are you lucky," my wife said when I told her the news.

"Baby, I'm lucky in more ways than one," I said. "I'm lucky in having you as my wife, and I'm lucky that God gave me an opportunity to reexamine my life and the world around me during the four months I've been on my back."

It was unfortunate that I had to go through such a crisis before I saw the fineness of life clearly: that is, that time for Dempsey was not eternal. As simple as that observation might appear, most of us seldom confront those realities in the earlier years, or we would not misuse our time and our bodies in the ways we do.

Most young blacks shy away from thinking about the effective use of time in accomplishing career goals. As a matter of fact, many of my friends attributed my illness to overwork. They kept reminding me that I had worked hard—too hard, they said—in organizing the Travis Realty Corp. in 1949, the Travis Insurance Agency in 1950, and the Sivart Mortgage Corp. in 1953. I had overtaxed my body by age thirty-four, they said.

Nonsense!

But there were more things to think about other than the personal problems of Dempsey Travis. Too much was changing for blacks during those months.

The May 17, 1954, Supreme Court public school desegregation ruling in *Brown v. Board of Education* monopolized my attention during my hospital stay. Was it possible, I wondered, that the old "separate but equal" principle the Court had enshrined in the 1886 *Plessy v. Ferguson* decision, but had now been overturned, could be dismantled? Could it be done for education in a housing market that was, as I well knew, intensively segregated? I did not see how it could. I thought that the housing issue should have been dealt with first, or at least simultaneously, with the public school issue. If there had been a mobile black housing market in the 1950s, when there was a great desire among blacks to integrate, it's obvious that there could have been blacks in every neighborhood school without the devastating drawn-out problems that have plagued American education ever since the 1954 decision.

The desire to integrate and to bury the black identity was very strong in the 1950s. For example, the board of directors of the National Negro Business League at its 1954 convention at the Parkway Ballroom in Chicago seriously considered deleting the word "Negro" from its title. The Chicago Negro Chamber of Commerce later changed its name to the Cosmopolitan

Chamber of Commerce, and the national organization dropped the word "Negro" from its title. Both organizations lost members because of strong minority opposition, and the Chicago Chamber split into two separate bodies, the Cosmopolitan and the Negro Chamber of Commerce.

Black organizations, in their search for a new identity, were receiving their signals of change in the civil rights struggle from two geographically and culturally separate locations: the United States government in Washington, D.C., and the movie industry out in Hollywood.

From Washington, the winds of change were measured in three U.S. Supreme Court desegregation decisions: housing in 1948, railway dining cars in 1950, and schools in 1954. And, in 1949, Truman's Army integration policy was implemented—and subsequently followed by both the Navy and the Air Force.

Out in California, the "Black Sambo" and "Farina" images were finally under attack in the Hollywood Hills. The Clarence Brown adaptation of William Faulkner's *Intruder in the Dust*, starring Juano Hernandez, shot on location in Oxford, Mississippi, showed the black American in a new positive image—one that had never been seen on an American screen. *Dust* was followed in 1956 by *Young Man with a Horn*, which co-starred Juano Hernandez with Kirk Douglas. Then came a series of Sidney Poitier movies that appeared to indicate that America was finally ready to integrate.

In many ways it seemed a time of hope, yet the steady drumbeat of flare-ups of racial violence continued to backlash those hopes.

On Sunday, August 28, 1955, Emmett Louis Till, a fourteen-year-old Chicago boy, was kidnapped at pistol point from his uncle's home in Money, Mississippi, and then murdered. The child was kidnapped by Roy Bryant and his half brother, J. W. Milam, for making a "wolf whistle" at Mrs. Bryant, an incident that the two men alleged had taken place four days earlier. Till's water-swollen body, with one side of his face beaten to a pulp, a bullet hole in his head, and a cotton gin fan lashed to his feet, was fished out of the Tallahatchie River near Greenwood, Mississippi, three days after he was kidnapped. Till was the 575th recorded lynching victim in Mississippi since 1882.

The all-white Mississippi jury manifested no higher thought for a black boy's life than for a rabbit's life when they acquitted Roy Bryant and J. W. Milam of the Till murder and kidnapping, even though the half brothers had admitted taking the boy from his uncle's home. Deputy U.S. Attorney

William P. Rogers said in a television interview, "We just have no authority to step into a state if we think there is a failure in the administration of justice."

It was the knowledge of that kind of failure of justice that made Rosa Parks' refusal to move to the back of a Montgomery, Alabama, bus on December 1, 1955, more than a matter of risking going to jail. By defying a white bus driver in the cradle of the Confederacy, Mrs. Parks had said that she was willing to die.

It was a time when even the smallest acts of everyday living could call upon a black person's deepest reserves of courage and heroism. Even a man like Dempsey Travis, real estate broker on the South Side of Chicago, who dealt with such mundane matters as mortgages and real estate closings, had to draw courage from such figures as Dr. Martin Luther King, Jr. Dr. King's effective and moving oratory generated the adrenaline that thousands of blacks needed to make an early commitment to protest passively but to work actively for civil rights.

The civil rights revolution that grew after Mrs. Parks' arrest changed America's open violence toward blacks into a more subtle form of racism. But in the struggle against Jim Crow, Dr. King and many of his followers paid the full price for their commitment. That price was violent death. They gave their lives so little black girls and boys, in the North and South, would never have to raise the question asked in the poem of my late friend, Langston Hughes:

> *Where is the Jim Crow section*
> *On this merry-go-round*
> *Mister, cause I want to ride?*
> *Down South where I come from*
> *White and colored*
> *Can't sit side by side.*
> *Down South on the train,*
> *There's a Jim Crow car.*
> *On the bus we're put in the back*
> *But there ain't no back*
> *To a merry-go-round!*
> *Where's the horse*
> *For a kid that's black?*

Fighting Jim Crow housing in 1955 could best be described as a grim merry-go-round. I scrambled around the clock seven days a week in an effort to remove the obstacles between the black community and a mortgage market anchored in racism.

I felt myself very alone in my fight until I met George S. Harris, president of the National Association of Real Estate Brokers, a black real estate organization known as Realtist and a counterpart to the National Association of Real Estate Boards, which excluded blacks from membership at that time.

"Travis," Harris told me in the fall of 1955, "your efforts are like a minnow trying to change the tide of the ocean. I'll show you how we can lick this problem if you join NAREB and become a part of an organized effort that's fighting for democracy in housing."

I accepted Harris' invitation and went to New York that year to a NAREB convention. There I met many successful young black realtors, such as Q.V. Williamson of Atlanta, Georgia, who became the first black elected to the Atlanta Board of Aldermen since Reconstruction; William Harps of Washington, D.C., the first black member of the American Institute of Real Estate Appraisers and later its president; and S.B. Odell of Oakland, California, a wealthy real estate developer and broker. We all shared the same goals. And George Harris proved to be a master parliamentarian and orator. Seeing him in action was an inspiration. He became my mentor and friend until his death in September, 1980, at the age of eighty-two.

I came back from New York fired by the idea of working with the Dearborn Real Estate Board, the Chicago affiliate of the NAREB, as a powerful voice for black housing in the Chicago metropolitan area. But I was impatient. The slow parliamentary pace of the group irritated me, because I couldn't help thinking that Chicago could burn down—it seemed to have a knack for it—while we were exercising ourselves over Robert's Rules of Order.

I felt we needed new leadership and an active plan to deal with racism in housing. But the group was very much bound to tradition and the way things had always been done. For instance, it was a tradition that the first vice president should succeed to the presidency of the Dearborn Board.

The day before the election, I polled the "young Turks" in the group for support for my own candidacy for the presidency. The old guard was surprised and displeased when I won by two votes. They considered my move both rude and rash. I considered that rudeness and rashness are sometimes necessary when confronting vicious and pervasive problems like racism in the housing market.

My first five months in office were hell. Some members threatened to re-
sign from the board. There was no staff. I had to use my own staff and financial
resources, not exactly those of a Rockefeller at the time. The tide turned in
May 1958, when four of my "young Turk" allies and I packed the Parkway
Ballroom with more than 700 people for my installation banquet. It was at
this point that I began to get the attention of the white and black press in
Chicago and my presidency of the Dearborn Real Estate Board allowed me to
make some noise about the serious issue of Jim Crow in insurance.

"Quarantine the niggers" was a gentleman's agreement within the insurance industry that had become 90.5 percent effective by late 1959. January
1960 found black people who lived on the South and West Sides of Chicago
being red-lined by 285 of the 310 casualty and fire insurance companies operating in the State of Illinois.

Black homeowners and tenants living within the "off limits" area were
slapped with fire and automobile insurance rates that sometimes exceeded 700
percent of the amount charged whites living in identical housing and driving
identical cars in other sections of the city. Black markets for high-rated, sub-
standard insurance policies were created by mass cancellation of the standard-
rated insurance policies held by those living in the "black-lined" areas.

Prominence in the black community did not immunize one against
discrimination by the insurance industry. Among my insurance clients who
were affected by the mass cancellations were Earl B. Dickerson, president of
Supreme Liberty Life Insurance Company; Dr. N. O. Galloway, president of
the Chicago Urban League and, also, president of the Medical Associates; Kit
Baldwin, president of Baldwin Ice Cream Company; and Irving Mollison, a
South Side resident and a Federal Claims Court Judge in New York.

The underwriting practices that permitted insurance companies to cancel
or reject insurance policies based upon the color of one's skin as opposed to the
merit of the individual risk made me furious. As a young businessman, I took a
fighting position on the side of the black community rather than the "go along
and get along" attitude adopted by many of my business contemporaries. My
stand-up posture did not enhance my business with blacks or endear me with
the white insurance establishment. The only bottom line compensation that I
received from fighting against injustices was the ability to look in the mirror
each morning while shaving a face that reflected a feeling of contentment for
having been on the right side of blacks' struggle for civil rights.

My presidency of the Dearborn Real Estate Board is best described in a book titled *Negro Politics: The Search for Leadership* (1960, The Free Press), by Dr. James Q. Wilson and Henry Lee Shaltuck, professor of government at Harvard University. Dr. Wilson said:

> *Dempsey J. Travis, a real estate broker, is a young and energetic businessman who has sought to organize Negro real estate and insurance men into a campaign to alter a policy of fire insurance companies that results in an inability to insure properties in Negro areas against fire losses. His energy has carried him to the presidency of the Dearborn Real Estate Board, a professional association of Negro real estate brokers, and to the vice-presidency of the Chicago Insurance Brokers Association, a group of Negro insurance men. Efforts by Negroes to halt and reverse the series of fire insurance cancellations on the South Side of the city brought Travis to the forefront as an organizer and spokesman. The stake of the Negro businessmen in the issue was clearly a tangible one, since property and insurance sales are severely hampered by this inability to obtain fire coverage at a figure near the manual rates . . . . Travis, with a few others, held a series of meetings among interested parties in the Negro community, and then met in conference with the Mayor and the state director of insurance, attended by insurance company representatives. The issue was quickly seen by Negro leaders such as Travis as a racial one, and he alleged in a newspaper interview that "290 insurance companies are practicing Jim Crow."*

My first term as president ended successfully and I was reelected to a second term without opposition. In 1970, I was drafted to serve a third term as president. I became the first person other than the founder and first president, the late Elmore Baker, to serve as the president for more than two years in the Dearborn Board's forty-year history.

CHAPTER 16

Front Lines

THE CHICAGO BRANCH OF THE NAACP HAD MORE THAN 50,000 dues-paying members in 1959, and it was the largest branch in the country. The presidency of the branch carried a lot of national prestige and responsibility, and it was a highly coveted office.

Yet to serve as president of a professional or civil rights organization required both a personal commitment and a great financial sacrifice. And sacrifice was what some fellow members of the Chicago Branch of the NAACP were asking me to do when they urged me to run in the election of October 1959.

I refused to consider the initial request because I did not feel I could afford to be away from my fledgling business for an additional year, having just completed two years as president of the Dearborn Real Estate Board. Moreover, I had recently been elected to the first vice presidency of the NAREB (National Association of Real Estate Brokers) at their convention in New York.

However, in the interim, I met Dr. Martin Luther King, Jr., and Daisey Bates, the pillar behind her late husband, L.C. Bates, who was the key black leader in the 1957 desegregation battle at the Central High School in Little Rock, Arkansas.

The sacrifice I was being asked to make was miniscule compared to the way Dr. King and Daisey Bates were laying their lives on the line. It was with them in mind that I agreed to accept the nomination and run against the late Gerald Bullock, a schoolteacher and civil rights organizer.

The election contest that year was hard-fought and very political. On the night of the election in December 1959, the Dunbar High School auditorium was jam-packed with 3,400 paid-up members, both blacks and whites, and an additional 2,000 people overflowed into the street. Ballots were cast after nominating speeches were made. I will never forget the "Blue Stocking Candidate" label that the late State Rep. William Robinson hung on me in his powerful address for my opponent.

The ballots were hand-counted all night, and I did not know until late morning the following day that I had been elected president of the largest and most powerful NAACP branch in the country.

My election to the presidency of the Chicago Branch of the NAACP gave me a broader base from which to continue the struggle I had begun as president of the Dearborn Real Estate Board against the practice of insurance "Jim Crowism" in hearings before the State Senate Committee, the State House Insurance Committee, and in the offices of both Mayor Richard M. Daley and Joseph S. Gerber, the state insurance director. In the struggle with the insurance giants I sometimes felt like a small boy crying in the wilderness. However, I learned that if people cry long enough, their eyes will ultimately clear, and they will see that the solution is not in crying but in fighting back.

Never had a black social club responded to the financial needs of a civil rights organization as did the Winsomettes, headed by Bernadine Washington, who presented a check in the sum of $3,000 to the NAACP in May 1960. The following month, the Chicago Branch of the NAACP, sparked by the new consciousness of black oppression in both the North and South, had the most successful Freedom Fund Dinner in its history, netting the organization $31,000. Thurgood Marshall, NAACP chief legal counsel and currently United States Supreme Court Justice, was the speaker for the event, which was held on June 17, 1960, in the Morrison Hotel. Marshall told his listeners, who included Chicago Mayor Richard J. Daley, "If we are going to fight segregation in housing in Georgia, we are going to fight it in Chicago."

The fight for freedom in Chicago became a reality to me when I received the following message by telegram from America's two foremost civil rights leaders:

WE ARE REQUESTING YOUR COOPERATION IN
AN IMPORTANT UNDERTAKING. WE BELIEVE

A MIGHTY VOICE MUST BE HEARD AT FORTH-COMING POLITICAL CONVENTIONS DEMANDING ELEMENTARY JUSTICE FOR THE NEGRO. WE PLAN TO COME TO CONVENTION AND NEED YOUR HELP. EACH PARTY MUST REPUDIATE SEGREGATIONISTS WITHIN ITS RANKS. CHICAGO HAS HISTORICAL OPPORTUNITY TO UNIQUE CONTRIBUTION TO CIVIL RIGHTS. COURAGEOUS SOUTHERN STUDENTS AND MILLIONS OF DISENFRANCHISED NEGROES LOOK TO PEOPLE OF YOUR CITY TO REPRESENT THEM BEFORE CONVENTION. WE URGE YOU AND OTHER COMMUNITY LEADERS TO COOPERATE WITH US, IN ORGANIZATION OF NON-VIOLENT "MARCH ON THE CONVENTIONS MOVEMENT FOR FREEDOM NOW." LOS ANGELES LEADERS BEING CALLED UPON FOR SIMILAR ACTION. JOAN SUALT, HUNTER ODELL, AND NORMAN HILL IN CHICAGO AS OUR REPRESENTATIVES TO ASSIST YOU IN CONVENING COMMUNITY COMMITTEE TO IMPLEMENT OUR SHARED OBJECTIVES. PLEASE WIRE READINESS TO SERVE ON COMMITTEE TO COOPERATE WITH US AND REPRESENTATIVES IN ACHIEVING OBJECTIVES OF THIS PROJECT.

A. PHILIP RANDOLPH& MARTIN LUTHER KING JR.

The initial meeting of the Chicago March on Conventions Committee assembled in the Blue Room of the Parkway Ballroom and was called to order on June 21, 1960, at 3:55 p.m. by Bayard Rustin, executive assistant to A. Philip Randolph. Some Chicago leaders attended. Rustin expressed appreciation for the presence on the part of those community leaders in the hall and introduced A. Philip Randolph.

In his remarks, Randolph, often called the father of the modern civil rights march, discussed both the purpose and program of the "March on the Conventions Movement for Freedom Now." He stressed the importance of the march in Chicago and in Los Angeles as a demonstration on the part of black people and their supporters in the labor movement and liberal movements for a strong civil rights platform for each of the two conventions.

"This demonstration shall be a protest against the conspiracy of silence on civil rights and the piecemealness which characterizes both the Republican and Democratic parties," said Randolph. Randolph, who had been called the most dangerous man in America by President Woodrow Wilson, said the "March on Conventions Movement" would emphasize the need for a presidential executive order to implement court decisions ending segregation in housing and the guaranteeing of the right to vote. He wanted the march in Chicago to be a huge, mass demonstration that would leave no doubt that black people stood firmly behind their leaders in the demand for an end to equivocation on the civil rights question.

In addition to the insurance "Jim Crow," there was job "Jim Crow," housing "Jim Crow," and graveyard "Jim Crow," as evidenced by the sign, "For Caucasians Only," on the gate of the Oakwood Cemetery at 67th and Cottage Grove. I believed that the solution to the insurance "Jim Crow" could be reached through housing integration.

At an NAACP Board meeting in January 1960, three days after I was installed as president, I outlined a plan for integrating suburban housing. The Board approved my integration idea, and invitations were extended to 127 suburban village officials in Cook, Kane, McHenry, Lake, Will, and Du-Page Counties to attend a one-day conference to be held in April, entitled, "A Blueprint for Democracy in Housing." Cooperating organizations for the conference were the American Friends Service Committee, the Chicago Urban League, and the Union of American Hebrew Congregations. Members of these same organizations joined me in the cold north winds of February on the picket lines in support of a national boycott against F. W. Woolworth, S.S. Kresge, S.H. Kress, and W.T. Grant stores for continuing their policy of refusing to practice "Democracy in Eating" at the lunch counters in their Southern stores.

The morning session on "Democracy in Housing" was held at Roosevelt University, and the luncheon and afternoon sessions were held in the Blackstone Hotel. Both sessions were packed with people who did not need the lesson: 350 white and black liberals who were closely identified with the Civil Rights Movement. Only eight of the 127 village officials who were invited attended.

The meeting, the first of its kind to be held in Chicago, was a monetary success but a media flop in terms of getting the integration message into the right ears. The messages were many, coming from such authorities as Dr. Louis Laurenti, a professor from the University of California who discussed his new book, *Race and Housing Values*; Dr. Curtis D. MacDougall, professor of journalism at Northwestern University's Medill School of Journalism, who talked on "Exploring the Race Myth;" Dr. George Grier, of the research division of New York State's Commission Against Discrimination, who expounded on his book, *Property Values and Race*; and Dr. Dietrich C. Reitzes, of George Williams College, who gave a dissertation on "Changing the Climate on Integrated Housing." In addition, there were many other national authorities present who spoke supportively for ethnically mixed housing.

The suburban refusal to respond to our effort told me again that white folks generally did not want to hear anything about living next door to black folks. Deerfield, Illinois, typified the 1960 suburban racial mind-set when they voted to have a green park rather a dark-skinned neighbor.

Civil rights for blacks in Chicago in 1960 were still in the Dark Ages. Racial flare-ups were constantly taking place in at least a dozen public high schools. Bands of white teenage hoodlums were waging a campaign of harassment in the schools and in the streets.

Private business schools in the Loop did not have a race problem like the public schools, because they simply did not admit blacks. Mary L. Jackson, of 400 South Hamlin, and Mrs. Rachel Hawkins, of 2124 South Drake, who were both employed as secretaries at the Navy Pier University of Illinois Campus, were denied admission to the Moser Evening School on East Jackson Boulevard because they were blacks. The reason for denying blacks admission was given by Mrs. Paul Moser, president of the school, who politely said, "We never have."

But there were some happy notes in a sour time.

Rustin, Randolph's heir apparent and the architect of the 200,000-plus-person march on Washington in August, 1963, explained the importance of a large demonstration in Chicago to follow the demonstration in Los Angeles at the Democratic Convention. The Los Angeles committee was planning a demonstration of 5,000 to 10,000 people, and we were urged to set similar goals for Chicago, lest the implication be left that the black leadership was concentrating on the Democratic Party and endorsing the Republican Party.

"'The March on the Conventions Movement' is a demonstration against the do nothingness of both parties," said Rustin.

In the question and answer period, Randolph, with characteristic quiet dignity, made clear that the march movement welcomed and solicited the cooperation of black Republicans in Chicago, especially those who would be delegates to the Republican National Convention. As to future plans by the march movement, Randolph said, "We will cross that bridge when we get to it." For the entire period leading up to the Convention, the emphasis was to be on mobilizing the maximum number of people to take part in the demonstration.

Nominations for additional co-chairmen for the Chicago Organizing Committee were made from the floor. Twenty-four nominees were accepted, representing a cross-section of groups and organizations in Chicago. The meeting decided that ten additional co-chairmen would be nominated at the meeting of co-chairmen scheduled for the following week.

In his deep, Harvard-accented baritone voice, cultivated during his many years of orating on the street corners of Harlem, Randolph urged the selection of a coordinator to centralize the responsibility for the overall march. It was the consensus of the meeting that at the co-chairmen's meeting the following week, a coordinator would be selected, and that presently an interim convener of the co-chairmen's meeting should be selected. Upon nomination by the Rev. Owen Pelt, I was unanimously elected as the interim convener, and next was unanimously elected as general march coordinator.

Thousands of sign-up cards were printed to get people to pledge their support and participation in the rally and demonstration. The job performed during the next seventeen days by a small staff of five, which included Timuel D. Black, Norman Hill, Bennett Johnson, Joan Suall, and Carl Fuqua, executive secretary of the Chicago Branch of the NAACP, in bringing together support groups for the rally and march was monumental.

The afternoon pre-convention "March for Freedom Now" rally held Sunday, July 24, 1960, in the Liberty Baptist Church at 4853 South Park, packed the church and then spilled over into the streets. Some 5,000 supporters heard remarks by Roy Wilkins, New York Governor Nelson Rockefeller, and A. Philip Randolph. And nearly 4,000 supporters attended the West Side evening rally held at Stone Temple Baptist Church at 3622 Douglas Boulevard and heard both Dr. Martin Luther King, Jr. and Randolph.

At 4:00 p.m., July 25, 1960, the demonstrators assembled in front of Rev. Louis Rawls' Tabernacle Baptist Church, 4130 South Indiana Avenue. At 5:10 p.m.—sharp—more than 10,000 marchers, by a police count, stepped off proudly en route to the Amphitheatre at Root and Halsted, the site of the G.O.P. Convention.

Sharing the front line of the march were Dr. Martin Luther King, Jr., A. Philip Randolph, Ralph Abernathy, and Dempsey J. Travis. Right behind us were the student sit-in leaders: Diane Nash, Bernard Lee, and Marion Barry, now mayor of Washington, D.C. The Chicago march was the largest of its kind ever held in the country. We marched north on Indiana and west on 39th Street singing to the tune of "I've Been Working on the Railroad:"

We've been marching on the vigil
All the live long day.
And we'll be marching on the vigil
Till Americans change their ways.
Can't you hear our plea for freedom?
Rise up so early in the morn.
Can't you hear our plea for freedom?
Put Civil Rights in your platform!

That fine hour faded quickly on Sunday afternoon, August 29, when I was called by a Chicago newspaper reporter and told about a wade-in by the NAACP Youth Council, which included forty black and ten white sympathizers, at Rainbow Beach, between 75th and 77th Streets and the lake. Blacks had previously refrained from using this beach because over the years they had been unrelentingly molested by both lifeguards and white bathers. The black youths' objective was to prove that Chicago had a chance not to earn the title of the most segregated city in the nation, and also that Chicago must permit its black citizens to wade in the blue waters of Lake Michigan. But the NAACP could not prevent the violence that was to follow when twenty-one-year-old Velma Murphy, of 9216 South Parnell, was hit with a rock. Gangs of white youths, some armed with stones, despite the presence of ninety-six policemen, followed the autos of the demonstrators who left the beach at 77th Street to as far west as 79th and Stony Island.

My civil rights objectives had not been accomplished when I decided not to seek reelection for a second term as NAACP president. I had been a truant from Travis Realty Company, Sivart Mortgage Corporation, and the Travis

Insurance Agency for three years, two as president of the Dearborn Board and one with the NAACP. I felt a longer absence would destroy my small business enterprise.

Unattended businesses generally go into a holding pattern before they fold up and disappear. Black businesses too often just instantly self-destruct. My business had neither self-destructed nor disappeared, but it was fading fast. Sales volume at Travis Realty Company for the year 1960 dropped 40 percent from the previous year. Sivart did not receive an authorization from the Federal Housing Administration to act as loan correspondent mortgagee for the Chicago Metropolitan Mutual Assurance Company until August 1, 1960, which meant few, if any, FHA loans could be generated and closed before January 1, 1961.

My insurance sales suffered the same disastrous results as the real estate sales. The price I paid for participating in the civil rights movement came within a hairline of destroying my business career.

The white establishments called me a demagogue, and my black business peers privately called me a fool, a fool for investing my time in what they considered unrelated black problems.

To this day, I cannot differentiate between economic problems and civil rights problems—they are irrevocably saddled with each other, more so in this country than anywhere else on Planet Earth.

CHAPTER 17

Raising the "Cotton Curtain"

I N THE 1960S, JOHN FITZGERALD KENNEDY TURNED ON THE LIGHT
at the end of the housing corridor for black Americans. Lyndon Johnson
kept it burning but Richard Milhous Nixon turned it off in the 1970s.

The 1960s marked the real beginning for black participation in the housing market without most of the traditional restraints that had been imposed
by both the private and public sectors. Black home ownership in Chicago
increased from 36,667 in 1960 to 74,219 in 1970, a staggering 103 percent in
one decade. The executive order for equal opportunity housing signed by President Kennedy on November 20, 1962, was a proclamation to both friend and
foe that all federal agencies were directed to prevent discrimination because of
race, creed, or national origin in federally assisted or federally owned housing.

The precedents for fair housing, which had been ineffective, included:
The Civil Rights Act of 1866 ("All citizens of the U.S. shall have the same
right in every state and territory, as is enjoyed by white citizens thereof, to
inherit, purchase, lease, sell, hold, and convey real and personal property.");
the 1917 U. S. Supreme Court (*Buchanan v. Warley*) which held racial zoning
ordinances invalid; the 1948 Supreme Court Decision (*Shelly v. Kraemer*)
which held racial restrictive covenants judicially unenforceable; the Housing
Act of 1949, whereby Congress made the National Housing Policy Declara-
tion: "to realize as soon as possible the goal of a decent home and a suitable
living environment for every American family."

Upon signing his executive order, President Kennedy made this statement:

> *It is neither proper nor equitable that Americans should be denied the benefits of housing owned by the Federal Government or financed through Federal assistance on the basis of their race, color, creed, or national origin. Our national policy is equal opportunity for all and the Federal Government will continue to take such legal and proper steps as it may to achieve the realization of that goal.*

The order called for an end to discrimination in the rental or sale or use of government-owned and operated housing and of housing provided, after November 20, 1962, with the aid of federal loans, advances, grants, or contributions, or with the assistance of loans insured, guaranteed, or otherwise secured by the credit of the federal government. That order was, of course, designed to open up a large segment of the housing market to minority group home-seekers and turn a pressing need into an effective demand.

At the time the order was issued, openly voiced dismay and fearful projections of imminent social and economic catastrophes were plentiful. But the dire circumstances did not materialize.

Home building did not collapse, and builders and lenders did not panic. They went right on building and financing homes at one of the highest rates in history. Those who had hoped for some kind of social revolution were equally without satisfaction.

There were results, however. In the week ending November 30, 1962, the first full week in which the order was effective, the FHA department of the Housing and Home Finance Agency (one of HUD's predecessors) said it received new-home mortgage applications at a rate of about 199,000.

More revealing are some totals available from the spring of 1964. Under the various federally assisted programs, including the VA, some 600,000 units were either completed or approved; about 800 urban renewal projects were underway or in planning.

New housing subject to the order included: FHA mortgage insurance applications for new units as of November, 1963, totaling 282,500 units, of which 191,700 were single-family and 90,800 multi-family; in addition, the FHA held 70,000 units acquired through foreclosure for sale or rental on the newly opened market. The VA, during this period, reported requests for 100,000 units subject to the Equal Opportunity Order.

And then President Kennedy was assassinated.

The Housing Proclamation of the New Frontier was implemented and expanded with the legislative skills of President Lyndon Baines Johnson's Great Society.

The United Mortgage Bankers of America Inc. (UMBA) was organized in Chicago in 1962 because blacks were not admitted to membership in either the Mortgage Bankers Association of America or any of its local subsidiaries. The history of UMBA parallels the Kennedy and Johnson administration, because prior to the Kennedy election and the appointment of Robert C. Weaver as the first black Federal Housing Administrator, there were no black mortgage bankers. As a matter of fact, blacks could not enroll in mortgage banker courses that were limited to members of the white trade association.

Mortgage banking is the primary vehicle for channeling FHA and VA housing investment dollars from major insurance companies and pension funds into the black community. The need for blacks to participate became obvious when one considers that between 1947 and 1960 the government insured more than one million mortgage loans for veterans in suburban areas, and 800,000 for veterans in the cities; 99.5 percent of all mortgage loans approved for northern cities were for white veterans. The VA and FHA loans made to blacks in the city were a direct byproduct of a campaign initiated in 1953 by the National Association of Real Estate Brokers (NAREB) entitled "Democracy In Housing."

NAREB was pushing for legislation to enable FHA and VA to make direct loans to black home buyers in as much as all other lending avenues were closed. The local Dearborn Real Estate Board, under the presidency of Robert N. Landrum, set up a series of meetings and workshops advocating and supporting the national position.

Out of this dual action came a compromise called the Voluntary Home Mortgage Credit Program (VHMCP) enacted as part of the Housing Act of 1954, which marked the first formal governmental recognition that minority citizens needed special assistance to equalize their opportunity to obtain home financing.

Although President Dwight Eisenhower supported the VHMCP concept and brought attention in his housing message to Congress on January 24, 1954, to the fact that "many members of minority groups, regardless of their income or economic status, have had the least opportunity of all citizens to acquire good homes," the VHMCP was a flop because it had to depend on the same lenders who had denied blacks loans through the regular sources.

Mechanically the program worked as follows: a black home buyer had to be humiliated and rejected by three lending institutions. Once this had been achieved, he could file an application in the Regional VHMCP office, which was located in the old Federal Court Building on Clark and Adams. The regional office would in turn circulate his application among lenders who had agreed to participate in the program. This ritual (by my experience) could take from six months to a year to find out you had been rejected.

Having sent ten black families through this burning-sands experience, Travis Realty Company dropped out of the program. It was after this experience that the Travis Realty sales force decided to organize the Sivart Mortgage Corporation in order to circumvent this mortgage bottleneck. We did not achieve our objective, because the Federal Housing Administration would not approve an application for a black mortgage banking company in 1954.

Access to capital was in 1962, and remains today, the primary thrust of UMBA. During its first years, the members of UMBA conducted door-to-door campaigns in their own communities, and conducted an extensive survey nationally in search of economic input for their black communities through mortgage financing. Speaking before church and civic organizations throughout the nation, the first members used strategy that ranged from street picketing and conference room confrontations to legal action.

Results began to surface, when in February 1963, a ten-million-dollar commitment was made to three of UMBA's member companies by the International Ladies Garment Workers Union, headquartered in New York City. Prior to this major breakthrough, the sole source of funds for black mortgage bankers was from black life insurance companies.

In rather rapid succession, a total of fifty million dollars was made available that year for mortgage money from banks and savings and loan associations based in New York City. Visits to sixty-three banks, forty-eight life insurance companies, and ten savings and loan associations in New York City and in Washington, D.C., made by some forty black mortgage bankers and real estate representatives, added impetus.

UMBA used what I described as "quiet persuasion." It urged white-owned financial institutions to consider these facts: 85 percent of the savings of blacks were in major white financial institutions; some 38 percent of black families, as compared to 62 percent of white families, were homeowners; the number of black households with more than $5,000 income a year rose almost twenty-fold between 1950 and 1960 from 43,000 to 766,000, and yet the majority of black households were still substandard dwellings although the owners could afford reasonably priced houses.

An additional stimulus to the minority housing market came in 1967, when the insurance industry launched its unprecedented two-billion-dollar urban investment program. At the same time FHA changed its policies and announced its intention to insure single family mortgages in blighted areas. With these major innovations and policy changes, UMBA realized what in actuality would have been a wild dream seven years earlier.

In 1969, the Federal National Mortgage Association (FNMA) appointed nine blacks and one Spanish-speaking mortgage correspondent, thus giving a big thrust to the black mortgage banking industry. However, at the same time, national priorities shifted and the alliance between HUD and the insurance industry faded with the change of administrations. Although the nation was still sorely in need of low and moderate cost housing, President Nixon refocused his commitments and priorities toward black capitalism and moving disadvantaged blacks to the suburbs. In 1969, when Nixon took office, there were five black mortgage banking companies in Chicago. In 1981, Sivart Mortgage is the only one left in this city. Nationally, the liquidations of black mortgage bankers have been equally disastrous, with their number having been reduced from fifty to seven.

While all this progress was helpful, there were still many blanks to fill in. As always, it helped to backtrack and reevaluate the past in order to proceed forward.

The need for a black-controlled mortgage company was evident when you consider that in 1960 more than 3,200 Chicago families, mostly black, were displaced by urban renewal and the city was given a quota of 2,000 Section 221 government loans. Only three such loans were made for homes within the city during 1960, according to the Community Conservation Board, the issuers of the loan certificates. John L. Waner, area director of FHA in Chicago, commented, "Unless the lenders liberalize their practices in making loans to the minorities, there is a strong possibility that the government itself will move in."

I knew that a government that had not permitted a black mortgage banking company to squeak through its racist-laden bureaucracy until 1960 would not intervene in the mortgage market on behalf of minorities. Hence, Sivart Mortgage Corporation became the vehicle for opening the doors wider to the FHA mortgage market.

The Sivart mortgage banking presence in Chicago not only raised the "cotton curtain" between the black community and the FHA, it also created jobs for blacks within the mortgage banking industry in "lily-white" companies that had never previously considered a black either for a job or a mortgage application. The John F. Kennedy "New Frontier" philosophy, and the appointment of Robert C. Weaver, created a political climate that permitted Sivart Mortgage Corporation to exist.

The Washington political climate of FHA was six years ahead of the national mortgage banking industry in accepting blacks among its ranks. In 1960 it was impossible for a black man or woman to gain membership in either the Mortgage Bankers of America or any of its local chapters. A denial of membership was also a denial of the right to participate in the only educational programs in mortgage banking being offered in the country.

Recognizing that I could not survive in the mortgage banking field without black support, I suggested to Charles L. Warden, president of the National Association of Real Estate Brokers, during its annual meeting in Boston, Massachusetts, on August 20, 1961, that a committee be formed for the purpose of surveying the lending practices of the life insurance industry, whose premium proceeds were regularly invested for use by mortgage bankers. A survey of some twenty-five major life insurance companies was completed and a report was made at the next annual convention, which was held in Dallas, Texas, in August, 1962. The survey would become a meaningless stack of papers if we did not create an institutional vehicle to follow through and implement our findings. Therefore, on August 14, 1962, I made a plea before five hundred real estate men and women at the Dallas convention to join me in setting up a black mortgage banking association that would be an arm of NAREB. A formal breakfast meeting of twenty real estate brokers was called on the morning of August 15, 1962, for the purpose of discussing the preliminary organizational structure of the new mortgage banking association. I was selected temporary chairman.

The next meeting of UMBA was held October 13, 1962, in Chicago at the Sherman Hotel. At that meeting I was elected both president and chairman of the board. It was decided that a survey be made of lending institutions in New York City in February, 1963 in order to determine their lending practices toward minorities. Two hundred questionnaires were mailed out, and the ninety-three institutions that replied and agreed to an interview included fifty-five savings banks, thirty life insurance companies, seven savings and loan associations, and one pension fund. Four hundred million dollars in oral commitments were made by the savings and loan industry, but none materialized. The life insurance industry made no promises, and thus had no commitments to keep. This was also true of the mutual savings institutions.

To get commercial banks to finance a FHA mortgage commitment from a black life insurance company was almost a hopeless task. The unwillingness had to be racial, since the principal of a FHA loan is fully insured by the U.S. government. The 100 percent guarantee did not carry much weight with Jerome M. Sax, executive vice president of the Exchange National Bank of Chicago, who stated in a letter dated July 14, 1960: "After reviewing the report of the Sivart Corporation and your own personal statement, we are agreeable to interim financing on your FHA mortgage loans up to $15,000. These loans would be thirty to sixty day loans and would be personally endorsed by yourself and Mrs. Travis."

Sax's letter takes on more significance when you consider the fact that the Sivart Corporation statement reflected a liquid net worth in excess of $100,000 and yet Sax wanted additional collateral in the form of the personal signatures of my wife and myself to guarantee the government's 100 percent guarantee. I sincerely believe that Sax thought he was being benevolent or he would not have ended his letter in the following manner: "May I also say that it is a pleasure to do business with people like yourself."

Sax's offer to do business was one that I could afford to refuse.

In the 1960s, people like me were probably considered to be excellent candidates for the funny farm when we appeared at a major bank asking for a $500,000 line of credit. I will never forget how I had to verbally wrestle with Norman M. Alperin, the chairman of Drexel National Bank at 3401 South Martin Luther King Drive, to get a $60,000 line of credit. That hassle should not have been necessary because my family had banked at Drexel since 1900, and I, personally, had banked there since the late 1930s. Finally, on a cold

January morning in 1962, Alperin, with his board's approval, agreed to extend Sivart Mortgage a $100,000 line of credit. The condescending tone of Alperin's voice when he made the credit offer offended me so deeply that I stormed out of the bank empty-handed, never to return except to close out my accounts.

The cost of maintaining black pride and personal dignity can be extremely high.

For three months I walked the streets of downtown Chicago daily in search of a bank that would extend a line of credit to Sivart Corporation. One afternoon while sitting in my office at 414 East 47th Street with both hands clutched about my head, G.H. Wang, a friend and former Chinese ambassador, walked in. With a startled look on his face he said, "Mr. Travis, what is hurting you?"

I reluctantly told him the Exchange and Drexel Bank stories. He shook his head and said, "I want you to meet my friend Mr. Humphrey, chairman of the Central National Bank of Chicago."

On March 21, 1962, I met Humphrey and he, in turn, arranged for G.H. Wang and me to meet with the senior officers of the bank. Within eight days the bank had approved a line of credit for $200,000 with the understanding that we would transfer all bank balances controlled by the Sivart Mortgage Corporation to the Central National Bank. The working relationship was excellent. Before the end of the 1960s, our line of credit had been extended to three million dollars at Central National Bank.

I succeeded in opening the banking doors, with the help of a friend, before I could unglue the passage to educational preparedness in the field of mortgage banking. It was not until the fall of 1962 that a school sponsored by the Chicago Mortgage Bankers was opened at Central YMCA Junior College at 119 South LaSalle Street that actually allowed black enrollment. Charles A. Tatum, my executive assistant, and I jumped at the opportunity to enroll. We became the first graduates of the Central YMCA Mortgage Banking School on June 17, 1963. The educational opportunity for blacks was so unique at Central "Y" that Marion Jordan, an UMBA member, commuted to Chicago weekly by plane from Kansas City, Missouri, to attend two Monday evening classes in mortgage banking.

Prior to my enrollment at Central "Y" my only educational exposure to mortgage banking had been derived from reading newspapers and real estate

trade magazines. It was my need to fill an educational void that prompted me
to write President Johnson and request that he intercede on my behalf to gain
membership in the Mortgage Bankers of America. President Johnson assigned
his White House counsel to investigate my allegation. After an exchange of
letters and calls between the White House and the MBA, I subsequently received a MBA membership application in the fall of 1965.

Now what I needed were two active members as signatories. I visited a
dozen mortgage banking offices and each one offered some senseless reason
for not being willing to put his name on the line for a black applicant. Finally,
I asked the president of the largest and most respected name in the mortgage
banking industry to sign. I told him that the president of the United States
was interested in seeing my application processed. He blurted out, "To hell
with the president." I left his LaSalle Street office and walked slowly down that
canyon-like street wondering if the whole world were anti-black.

I was ready to give up when I remembered having met Harry Gottlieb, a
mortgage banker, at some social function. I went directly to Harry's office in
the Inland Steel Building at Monroe and Clark and handed him the application. Harry looked at the application and said, "You are a red hot number,
Travis. However, if you were white I would sign this application. Therefore,
I am not going to let the fact that you are black change my behavior." Harry
suggested that since I banked at Central National Bank that Marvin Reynolds
should be the second signatory, and he was. I was finally admitted to the MBA
School of Mortgage Banking at Northwestern University in the summer of
1966 and graduated as the lone black mortgage banker in the class of '69 at
age forty-nine.

Never too late? I've never been much of a fan of that depressing cliché.

CHAPTER 18

The Contract Buyers League

IT IS POSSIBLE TO LOOK BACK ON THE 1960S AS A DECADE OF hope, especially after the Nixon administration cut off many of the avenues of opportunity in the early '70s. But it was also a time of gut-wrenching despair as the country was wracked again and again with blood-shed and rioting.

My own feelings of frustration and horror at some of the events during that critical time when America was finally trying to come to terms with its legacy of racial bigotry manifested themselves in painful episodes of psychoso-matic physical symptoms. Again and again, I would awaken at dawn, clutching my chest and screaming for relief from the excruciating pain that was throb-bing through my body. I was in the mouth of a devil with a thousand teeth, I recall telling my wife on one occasion when my scream of pain awakened her.

The first time I experienced these symptoms was on Friday, November 22, 1963. It is the curse of all my generation to remember exactly what we were doing on that day. I was driving south in Markham, Illinois, with Albert Brown, a real estate client and a classmate from DuSable High..

"John F. Kennedy, the thirty-fifth president of the United States, has been shot," a voice on the radio said. And then, only moments later, the voice said, "The president is dead."

I pulled the car over to the curb.

"Man, I feel sick. My body is throbbing with pain," I said. We sat for a few moments. "I'm sorry. I just don't feel like showing any houses."

Brown nodded. I made a U-turn and drove back into Chicago. I dropped Brown off and went directly home.

"You're home early," Moselynne said. I was too agonized to answer. I walked into the bedroom and sat down in a chair in the corner. I began to weep uncontrollably. Moselynne came in and stared at me in wonder. She hadn't heard the news. She didn't understand what was wrong with me until I finally managed to gasp, "Why did the young president have to die such a violent and senseless death?"

Kennedy's murder foreshadowed a decade that was to be filled with years of fears, tears, and grief. The weeping Memorial Statue of Abraham Lincoln drawn by Pulitizer Prize cartoonist Bill Mauldin captured most Americans' mood. It wasn't only black Americans who were thrown into paralysis, but we had a special cause for bitterness. John Kennedy had been our "white" hope. In him, for the first time, we had seen the possibility of an America not plagued with racial inequities.

These hopes were devastated and travestied through the decade in the successive assassinations of Malcolm X, Medgar Evers, Dr. Martin Luther King, Jr., Robert Kennedy, Fred Hampton, Mark Clark, and hundreds of others who died in the struggle for black liberation.

The last time I saw Dr. Martin Luther King, Jr., alive, was in August of 1967, in San Francisco.

I was in town for a NAREB convention when Q.V. Williamson, who was president of the association, asked five directors to go with him to the airport to meet Dr. King's plane. We stood waiting as he walked off the plane, accompanied only by a fellow minister. Here was the acknowledged leader of Black America, a Nobel Prize winner, hated and reviled as much as he was loved, a fearless center of controversy for years—and he walked in alone, with not a single security guard. My heart almost stopped beating. We must all have had the same feeling, because the six of us immediately encircled Dr. King and briskly walked him through the crowded airport.

I think each one of us was thinking during those moments that we were eight walking targets.

That evening, I talked for the last time with Dr. King. He laid out his plans for the Southern Christian Leadership Conference's Poor People's Campaign for the following summer. It would be directed, he said, at establishing a base for economic development, with emphasis on jobs, housing, education, and the medical needs of the poor. All this was to be accomplished through direct subsidies from the federal government. It was an ambitious plan, and some were urging him to move more slowly. But I think most of us had the feeling then that we had to move while the country was still listening to black people. We knew how difficult it is to get your message across when nobody is listening.

At 7:30 p.m. on Thursday, April 4, 1968, I was sitting in my office at 840 East 87th Street. Again, I had the radio on. A voice broke into the programming: Dr. Martin Luther King, Jr. had been killed in Memphis, Tennessee. It was less than eight months after our meeting in San Francisco. Dr. King had become an unguarded target in the gunsights of James Earl Ray.

In the 24 hours after Dr. King's death, rioting erupted in 125 American cities. Nationally, 69,000 troops were called out to suppress the predictable violent reactions to his death. The riots caused 46 deaths, 2,600 serious injuries, and 22,000 arrests. The recordable property losses exceeded $100 million.

In Chicago, acting Gov. Samuel H. Shapiro called 6,000 National Guardsmen to active duty. Areas of the West Side went up in flames.

As I stood in my office at 87th Street, I could see the sky redden as fires swept through the West Side. The spectacle of a grieving, frustrated people turning its anger and horror on itself was enough to make you weep. There was fear, too, of course: the fear that the violence would go on and reach into every area of the city.

The schools let their students out at before noon that day, and as I sat in my office, I could hear the sound of shattering glass as they went down the commercial street breaking windows. Only a small door in our building was kicked in: apparently the word was quickly passed that this was a black business.

Though black middle class areas escaped the worst of the violence, the riots only further divided the city. Mayor Richard J. Daley proved that Chicago was seething with racial hate when he issued his famous order to his police to "shoot to kill or maim" any looters. Black organizations vocally protested that obviously racist order.

The damage the rioting did to the black community in Chicago—and elsewhere—is inestimable. White businessmen, including large chain operations as well as small Jewish merchants, never rebuilt in areas that had gone up in the riots. In the other black areas relatively untouched by the violence, fear of the future made them move out. The closing of commercial establishments, many of which have never been fully rebuilt by black merchants, spurred the redirection of black shopping out to all-white suburban areas.

Without Dr. King, and with the memory of the racist horror that had
stilled his voice, black leaders floundered. There were many voices, articu-
late voices with strong ideas of what needed to be done, but it was difficult
to regain a unified sense of purpose. Still, the work went on, and more and
more blacks were talking about the economic issues that had always been my
concern. Today, the Arab-owned businesses are a primary source of question
marks among the black community.

And tomorrow?

A National Black Economic Development Conference was called in the
month of the first anniversary after Dr. King's death on April 25, 1969, by the
Interreligious Foundation for Community Organization (IFCO). I delivered
a paper on housing at the conference, which was held in Detroit. It was subsequently published in the April 1970 edition of *The Black Scholar* as, "The
1970 Homestead Act." It has since been republished in a book entitled, *Contemporary Black Thought: The Best From The Black Scholar, 1973*, and again
in a Department of Housing and Urban Development funded edition of *The
Black Scholar* released in December 1979. The following are brief excerpts
from the article:

> *Historically, because of our position of servitude, we were nev-
> er permitted to be counted among the landed gentry. When
> land in America, during the late 18th century, was selling for
> 8 and 9 cents an acre, most black people in this country were
> in shackles and chains or prohibited, by law, from becoming
> landowners. In those few instances where we were permitted
> to buy, the absence of security was always present because of
> the fear of being dispossessed by an angry white individual or
> mob. Many instances are recorded in history where blacks had
> to leave land, home, and personal effects in the middle of the
> night, simply to escape with their lives.*
>
> *The 1785 Ordinance of the Continental Congress set the
> price of land at a dollar per acre, plus expenses. It was usually
> sold in sections of 640 acres each and larger quantities were
> sold, by negotiations with the Congress, at a few cents per acre.
> Such cities as Cleveland, Cincinnati, and Marietta were de-
> veloped by The Ohio Company, which purchased 114 million*

acres at a price of 8 to 9 cents per acre in 1787. If we compare the price The Ohio Company paid for its land with the current prices of from $500 to $800 per acre for raw farmland, and $2,500 to $3,000 an acre for land adjacent to metropolitan areas, I think we can readily see that some new economic innovations will have to be applied if the black man is ever to participate in the mainstream of our capital development.

Regrettably, our founding fathers and their successors never saw the need of a land reform act that would include the black brother. Even though blacks fought in every battle, including the American Revolution, when land grants were given to soldiers in lieu of pay, the historians have yet to find any recorded documentation showing that black soldiers participated in the 1776 G.I. Bill.

Julian Bond, the very young Georgia state representative, delivered a brilliant paper on politics. Fannie Lou Hamer, the Mississippi civil rights leader, gave a fiery and passionate address on voter registration.

An unexpected main event took place in the early evening on April 26, 1969. By the time I arrived at the hall with my tape recorder, all the seats had been filled by the 500 community leaders who represented every major city and civil rights organization in the country. I opted to sit on the floor near the lectern, as opposed to standing in the rear of the auditorium. After about a half hour's wait, a tall muscular young man stepped up to the lectern dressed in a faded-blue denim overall. He had a head covered with a voluminous shock of black curly hair, and reddish brown skin that gave him an Indian appearance. The man was James Forman, director of international affairs for Student Non-Violent Coordinating Committee (SNCC), and a fellow Roosevelt University graduate.

Forman electrified the hall with a gusty delivery of his Black Manifesto, which demanded restitution from both the Christian churches and the Jewish synagogues. His speech was constantly interrupted with applause, foot stamping, and emotional shouts of "right on, brother" and "power to the people." This was the first time I had ever become emotionally part of an audience that had been lifted into a mental state that bordered on mass hysteria.

Here is part of what Forman said:

We, the black people assembled in Detroit, Michigan, for the National Black Economic Development Conference, are fully aware that we have been forced to come together because racist White America has exploited our resources, our minds, our bodies, our labor. For centuries we have been forced to live as colonized people inside the United States, victimized by the most vicious, racist system in the world. We have helped to build the most industrial country in the world.

We are, therefore, demanding of the white Christian churches and Jewish synagogues which are part and parcel of the system of capitalism, that they begin to pay reparations to black people in this country. We are demanding $500,000,000 from Christian white churches and the Jewish synagogues. This total comes to 15 dollars per nigger. This is a low estimate, for we maintain there are probably more than 30,000,000 black people in this country. Fifteen dollars a nigger is not a large sum of money and we know that the churches and synagogues have a tremendous wealth and its membership, White America, has profited and still exploits black people. We are also not unaware that the exploitation of colored people around the world is aided and abetted by the white Christian churches and synagogues.

This demand for $500,000,000 is not an idle resolution or empty words. Fifteen dollars for every black brother and sister in the United States is only a beginning of the reparations due us as people who have been exploited and degraded, brutalized, killed, and persecuted. Underneath all this exploitation, the racism of this country has produced a psychological effect upon us that we are beginning to shake off. We are no longer afraid to demand our full rights as a people in this decadent society.

I came back to Chicago with my brain reeling. Reparations for past inequities was not a new idea in America, but this was the first time that any black had demanded financial restitution from religious institutions. The boldness of Forman's message sent us all away on an emotional high.

But back in Chicago, things had to be fought out on a much grittier level.

I had been concerned ever since I started in the real estate business over the way whites exploited blacks by selling them houses on contract, without a mortgage. I knew that such contracts were often terribly inflated, with legal provisions that meant the buyer—so desperate to get out of the black ghetto that he often failed to fully understand what he was getting into—could lose all interest in a home he had been paying on for years by missing a single payment. The heartbreak that such a situation could cause was graphically demonstrated just a few blocks from my office in 1970.

Some thousand families in this situation had banded together to fight the injustice by withholding their payments and putting them in escrow to try to force renegotiation of contracts that were clearly unjust. For example, one man had signed a forty-one-year contract in 1960 for a South Side home at the price of $31,950, with a down payment of $3,500 and monthly payments of $227. An appraisal valued the house at only $25,000, and the Contract Buyers League figured he eventually would have paid around $85,000 for it. By 1970, when the man joined with about 430 other families in withholding his payments, he had paid more than $20,000 in taxes, principal and interest. If the League did not succeed in challenging the contracts in court on the grounds that they violated an 1866 Illinois statute barring racial discrimination in the sale of property and exploitation on the basis of race, he stood to lose every penny of that investment.

I read about the Contract Buyers League's efforts with a mixture of admiration and apprehension. These people were protesting a terrible evil, but they were doing it at the risk of devastating retribution. Poor families who had been exploited all their lives, they stood to lose an investment of half a lifetime's work in many cases. I had no reason to believe that the courts would sort this thing out and rectify the injustice.

That was why on the day it was announced the Cook County Sheriff would begin evicting those families from their homes, I drove over to South Eggleston Avenue and stood in a crowd watching the spectacle of twelve families' belongings being carried out and set in the mud. The sidewalk and streets became filled with rocking horses, beheaded dolls, baby carnages, rolled-up bedding, dining room tables, refrigerators, sofas, and television sets. There were also paintings of Dr. Martin Luther King, Jr. and John and Robert Kennedy heaped up in the mud and unseasonable snow of April 1970. The watching crowd, kept back by burly police officers, added their tears to those of the ex-homeowners.

I didn't sleep more than two hours the night following the evictions. Every time I closed my eyes I saw the expressions of the weeping women and children. Standing helplessly by their sides were their men, wet-eyed with anger, watching their life savings and dreams being boarded up and plastered over with "keep out" signs.

The following day the Rev. Jesse Jackson called and asked me to attend a Saturday morning Operation Breadbasket meeting. There he introduced me to Sidney Clark, South Side chairman of the CBL, and I also met Louis Diamond, president of Midstate Homes, Inc., the contract seller of more than one hundred homes on the South Side. Universal Builders, holders of more than five hundred contracts on South Side homes, was not represented at the Breadbasket meeting. Contract buyers had been evicted from seventy of the Universal homes, and some of those homes had been fire-bombed and dynamited. The contract buyers and the sellers were in a stalemate that seemed to offer no way out but violence.

To avoid further bloodshed, I began to meet with Louis Diamond to try to find a way out. He had displayed to me some sensitivity to the plight of the contract buyer families. We met for several hours, just the two of us, for nine consecutive days, and finally we thought we had a solution: Diamond agreed to reduce the contract principal on the unpaid balance by 14 percent, providing the contract buyers agreed to pay their delinquencies, and only if I was able to find mortgages with a below-market interest rate with no discount cost to either buyer or seller. The agreement was designed to save an average of five thousand dollars for each participating contract buyer.

I had pledged to do the impossible. I had promised to obtain 7 percent mortgages in a tight money market where the prevailing interest rate was 8.5 percent.

I knew that the economics of my proposition would not make sense to any business institution, and therefore I packaged it as the social issue it was. I made calls to two black-owned banks and two black-controlled insurance companies in addition to four white lending institutions, and asked each to commit one hundred thousand dollars in mortgage money to the Contract Buyers League families. Within forty-eight hours George S. Harris, president of Chicago Metropolitan Mutual Assurance Co., had committed one hundred thousand dollars; as had Al Boute, president of Independence Bank; Earl B. Dickerson, president of the Supreme Liberty Life Insurance Company; and Harold Algar, president of the Seaway National Bank.

The instant response of the four black institutions delighted me. It was different with the white institutions. They showed no sense of social obligation to the contract buyers. They saw no reason to make 7 percent loans, and that was that. One Loop banker, though, indicated he would participate at an 8.5 percent rate plus a 5 percent discount! Having gained the backing of the black lending institutions, I was able to negotiate an additional $3.5 million mortgage commitment with Oakley Hunter, president of the Federal National Mortgage Association in Washington, D.C.

CHAPTER 19

Reading the Obits

MY FATHER HAD NEVER MANAGED TO HAVE BREAKFAST with Mama and me since he usually left the house shortly after five a.m., except on Sunday. One particular Sunday he had his face buried in the funny papers while my mother and I were gabbing away. I must have been about nine years old.

"I dreamed last night that I was going to be rich and Daddy wouldn't have to work anymore," I said.

My mother smiled at me—the kind of smile a mother gives in response to a childhood fantasy.

My father folded his paper abruptly and looked at me.

"Everybody wants to be rich, boy," he said. "You concentrate on getting that food into your mouth and then worry about how you're going to get through this day without getting a spanking."

"That was a true dream," I said. "That dream was as clear as the day is long, Daddy. I figure it's just a matter of working hard."

My father snorted. "Your mother and I and your uncles don't know nothing but hard work."

I took a few bites of an apple. "I understand that," I said. "It's just—well, if a person really sets out to be rich, you know, and plans and works at it, well, it might happen outside of a dream. Mr. Charles Murray across the street is rich. Why not me?"

My father smiled, shook his head, and picked up his paper again. "Okay, millionaire, it sounds easy as pie," he said. He then rubbed me on the head and said, "Maybe your dream might come true."

My father's attitude toward my business plans turned out to be a common one. Years later, when I was scouring around the city in search of new opportunities, I often got that funny little headshake from people. They thought I was crazy. Didn't I know a black man's chances of making it were razor slim?

No, I didn't know that. Once I began to see how the business world worked, I couldn't get the idea out of my head that black-controlled businesses could bring more and more blacks into mainstream America. As I got more formal education about America's history and the workings of commerce, it only seemed like a more reasonable proposition, not less.

I couldn't see any conflict in blacks riding on the wagon of commerce that they once pulled.

At first, of course, I got into business to provide a comfortable living for my family. But the millionaire lifestyle that many successful businessmen adopt has always seemed alien to me.

I think one reason for that is that my success has been a double satisfaction. Not only was I making enough money to support my family in comfort, but I was proving wrong all those prognosticators who predicted I would never make it. I'm afraid a black person in America is going to be able to get that double satisfaction for a long time to come.

In the 1960s, when a lot of privileged whites were taking notice of blacks for the first time, it became obvious that there was a basic misunderstanding. White college kids by the thousands were suddenly breaking with their parents' establishment and turning their back on the Mercedes cars and the Caribbean cruises and all the other trappings of success. They expected to turn around and find in the black man a humble, simple, non-materialistic person upon whom to model their new lives.

They were shocked, then, when they found out that that's not what we blacks were all about at all. It's very well to give up your Mercedes and your mink coat when you know you can have them if you just reach out your hand. But we had never had that. We had lived poor, and we knew what it was like: it was rotten. We wanted to experience the good things. Maybe not forever— but just once!

It was thinking about that kind of thing that made me realize my attitude toward material success would always be bound up with my feelings about the situation of blacks in America. Very early in my career—when my success was still pretty shaky—I got myself involved with social projects that didn't seem to have a lot of potential for contributing to my personal economic gain. But I found that a person who goes out of his way to empathize with others and make opportunities to show social concern—and still survives the first five years in business—will build a solid foundation for a very successful enterprise. That's because the enterprise will then be important to a lot more people than just yourself.

It may be that some will interpret your empathy as weakness and your social concern as naïveté. But you can count on your God-given barracuda instincts to balance the scale.

Some time in the late 1950s, I remember sitting in the Chicago Title & Trust offices with Circuit Court Judge Kenneth Wilson. Wilson turned to me with a smile and said, "You know, Chicago is fortunate."

"Why is that?"

"Because a guy with your talents could have decided to be a con man instead of an honest businessman. And you know what? I think you could sell the Golden Gate Bridge."

I laughed. "You've got something there," I said. "You know, I could talk a fellow out of his shoes if I wanted to. Sometimes I've had to restrain myself."

Joking aside, Wilson had a point. A lot of black youngsters grow up with the wheeler-dealer, the drug pusher, and the pimp as the only models of economic success that they know. And that's very unfortunate.

Business success requires single-mindedness. You can't permit yourself to be distracted by any scheme that will conflict with your objective. The commercial goal must be in the front of your mind constantly. This requires a discipline that costs more in personal sacrifice than most people are either willing or able to make. The aura of success is sweet, but the price is never cheap.

The successful men I know and have read about were all clock-watchers. The pure sociologist seldom survives in business because of his unwillingness to watch the clock of commerce. Social experiments can go on forever, whereas a viable business plan had better be finite. Time is a tool that must be used carefully, because there is no lay-away plan for holding its hands.

I used to try to convince my marketing staff of this principle. At the beginning of each sales meeting, I would designate someone to read aloud the obituaries of some recently deceased prominent citizens. I wanted to cure my salesmen of the disease of procrastination, which they all suffered from to a degree. Since I know that disease is contagious, I still read the obituary column daily as a reminder that my own time clock is finite.

I try to invest my time the same way I invest my money. I spend very little on small talk or small thoughts. I want to make it yield intellectual or monetary benefits. On lucky days, it yields both.

Time must be made to adapt to the work to be completed. I never let myself sit at a desk with four hours of work to be completed in an eight-hour time frame. I either fill the extra four hours with a new task or leave the office in search of a new business opportunity.

Those kinds of things are true for anyone, black or white. But blacks face some special hurdles if they want success. One is plain fear, and I don't discount it. There are still plenty of things to be afraid about in our lives. But I think too often we give in to that fear without really knowing what we're afraid of. We opt for security before we really know what we can do.

The one thing my mother and my wife always agreed on was that after I got through with junior college, I should go into the post office and get a nice secure job, with a nice, secure paycheck. They had my best interests at heart, and they weren't discounting my abilities. They just thought the world was going to prove too much for me. Even so, I still wanted to take a few risks. If I'd taken their advice, I'd probably be the best letter sorter the post office ever had—but I sure would have missed out on a lot of fun.

Many young blacks see that they're in a trap, and they get so angry and frustrated that they become paralyzed. I'm not saying they're wrong about that trap. It still exists.

I recognized that trap very early in my life. I decided the idea was not to step on the spring so it would close on you. That's a kind of sixth sense you develop that I can't quite explain. At Camp Shenango, I stepped on the spring. I was in the wrong place at the wrong time. But it hasn't happened since.

I know about the rage many blacks feel about their situation. I recognize that, too. But I never let it overwhelm me. If I let that kind of rage build in me, then I'm dying. I can't sit back and make a program of hating whites. I've got other things to do.

Reading, combined with an ongoing educational program, is a top prerequisite for operating a successful business. During my first twenty years in real estate I always carried at least ten academic hours in evening courses each year at schools like Roosevelt University, Central YMCA Junior College, the

Illinois Institute of Technology, Chicago Kent College of Law, and North-western University. I always read ten newspapers daily, including the Chicago papers plus the *Wall Street Journal, American Banker*, the *Washington Post*, the *New York Times,* and the *Christian Science Monitor*. I still fit in at least five newspapers daily, two books a month, and a dozen trade journals, as well as at least two five-day educational seminars a year.

Academic training, combined with experience, taught me how to look at an almost devastated piece of real estate and see a gold mine instead of a disas-ter. The first lesson I learned was never to buy other people's paint. I've saved as much as 300 percent by fixing a wreck myself instead of paying a much higher price for a painted doll.

I'm an early riser and always have been. I found this one common thread among all the successful men I've known or read about: they're not sleepers. I've always had a high energy level, and a long time ago I decided I wasn't going to worry about standing out or being different. When people tell me to slow down—and for some reason, somebody is always telling me that—I tell them to speed up.

President Johnson asked me to participate in the White House Confer-ence, "To Fulfill These Rights," in 1966. President Nixon asked me to join his Housing Task Force in writing the 1970 Housing Bill. President Gerald Ford brought me into both his energy and inflation think tanks. Vice President Nelson Rockefeller presented me with the first Black Enterprise Award in finance at the White House in 1975, and President Jimmy Carter asked me to a White House briefing and luncheon in 1979.

I've met and shared the dais with then-Presidential candidate Ronald Reagan at the Executive Club of Chicago. I remember that everybody was saying he'd never get to be president. He was just an out-of-work actor, and he was too old, they said. And now Reagan is sitting in the White House getting ready to cut his seventy-first birthday cake.

Blacks spend so much of their energy fighting nightmares that very little is left to spend on following their dreams. I know that looking at our situa-tion can be downright sickening at times. But there's another side of it that we ought to look at sometimes, too. With all our handicaps, we've increased our income from $50 billion annually in 1960 to $127 billion in 1980. There were more than one million blacks attending college in 1980, as compared to a quarter of a million in 1966. We have a multitude of black elected public

officials throughout the land, and mayors in a number of major cities like Atlanta, New Orleans, Detroit, Los Angeles, and Washington, D.C.

The first black president of the United States has already been born and
will be elected before the year 2000, providing the rest of us build on the legal
victories of the forties and fifties, the civil rights struggle of the sixties, and the
political victories of the seventies.

I remember that when I was thirty-eight, a lot of my friends thought I
had reached the high point of my life with my election to a second term as
president of the Dearborn Real Estate Board. They knew how important that
was to me, and I guess they expected that from then on I'd be taking things a
little easier.

One of those friends was the late Wilbur Slaughter, a fellow realtist. He
was a copper-colored, quaint-faced man. One late afternoon before a Dearborn Real Estate Board meeting, he glared at me with his piercing, intelligent
eyes and said, "Boy, are you lucky! This has got to be the zenith of your real
estate career."

I only smiled at Slaughter's remark. But inwardly, I was saying to myself,
"Man, are you wrong. This is nice, sure. But there is going to be a lot more to
my life than this."

And there was.

And there will be more.

Acknowledgments

I DESPAIR OF CALLING THE ROLE OF ALL THE PERSONS WHO assisted and encouraged me through every stage of the manuscript for this book, but I am confident that I shall be forgiven if I name only those whom I pressed hardest to be critical of my work. My mother, Mrs. Mittie Travis, who is eighty-four years old, was a major contributor to my writing this book. She was the fountainhead for all of the early family history. Her life-long habit of saving family pictures (over two thousand) and letters enabled me to document what would have otherwise been naked oral history. Much of the dialogue in the beginning chapters of this book is a byproduct of her excellent memory.

The late Lois Dubin was one of my most avid readers and a very construc-tive critic. Ripley Binga Mead Jr., cousin of the late Jesse Binga, the pioneering banker, was a constant resource in that he made aged members of his family available to me to discuss old Chicago as it was for blacks before the turn of the century. In addition, Mr. Mead gifted me with hundreds of unpublished photographs of old Chicagoans. I am also deeply indebted to Anthony Over-ton, III, grandson of Anthony Overton, the banker, industrialist, insurance pioneer, and Spingard Medal winner. The use of the Overton files and papers was an invaluable ingredient in my research. Attorney Oscar Hill, another Overton grandson, was very helpful in arranging several interviews with his late father, Richard Hill, the President of the Douglas National Bank. In sub-sequent interviews with Oscar Hill, I was able to gain a great deal of insight into the elder Overton. Attorney Hill and Overton resided in the same house for over thirty years.

Dr. Donald Joyce and his staff at the Carter G. Woodson Public Library literally opened the doors for me to Chicago's historical past through the use of their excellent Vivian Harsh Afro-American collection. A special appreciation to Archie Motley of the Chicago Historical Society for the use of the Claude A. Barnett files. Innumerable thanks are due Mary F. Grady, Regional Coordinator of Community Services, United States Department of Commerce, Bureau of the Census. Thanks, too, to Nina Tabb, Vice President of *Dollars & Sense* magazine, for making their historical library available to me.

My high school civics teacher, Mary J. Herrick, who is a young eighty-four year old, gave me a great deal of encouragement and advice. In addition, she presented me with an invaluable series of DuSable High School senior class books dating from the first class that graduated in 1936 through 1976. The series was used extensively in the writing of this book. She also made me the recipient of a box filled with more than three hundred personal letters to her from DuSable G.I.'s who were serving all over the globe during World War II. Several of the letters were used in that chapter of the book concentrating upon the war years.

Letters in support of my writing efforts from both Dr. Sterling Stuckey, Professor of History, Northwestern University, and Dr. William M. Tuttle, Jr., Professor of History at the University of Kansas, gave me the necessary buoyancy to stay afloat in Chicago literary waters.

I owe more than I can say to Donald C. Walker, Editor and Publisher of the *Dollars & Sense* magazine, who published in his distinguished periodical many of the articles which proved to be the genesis of this book.

Thanks to my administrative assistant, Robert Warner, Jr., for his unlimited patience in deciphering and making sense of my script. I also owe a special thanks to my senior researcher, Ruby Davis, for doubling in brass at a critical hour and transcribing in long hand the last eight taped interviews for this book. I was also very fortunate to have been encouraged, some years ago, by Barbara Reynolds, Vice President and Editorial Director of *Dollars & Sense* magazine; Joy Darrow, Managing Editor of the *Chicago Daily Defender*, and Louis Martin, former President of the *Chicago Daily Defender*, to exercise what they perceived as writing talents. My only hope is that I lived up to their expectations.

CHICAGO, ILLINOIS
NOVEMBER 11, 1981

Notes and Documentation

PROLOGUE

BOOKS

Anderson, Jervis. *A. Philip Randolph: A Biographic Portrait*. Harcourt, Brace, Jovanovich, Inc., New York, 1972.

Angle, Paul M. *The Chicago Historical Society: 1856–1956, An Unconventional Chronicle*. Rand McNally & Company, Chicago, 1956.

Andreas, A.T. *History of Chicago, Vol. 1*. A.T. Andreas Company, 1885.

Car Service Rules of Pullman's Palace Car Company. W.R. Pottinger, Printer, Chicago, 1893.

Dubin, Arthur D. *Some Classic Trains*. Kalmbach Publication, Milwaukee, Wisconsin, 1964.

Historic City: The Settlement of Chicago. City of Chicago, Department of Development and Planning, 1976.

Instruction Manual for Employees on Cars of the Pullman Company. The Pullman Company, Chicago, 1897.

Lowe, David. *Lost Chicago*. Houghton Mifflin Company, Boston, Massachusetts, 1975.

Mayer, Harold M. and Richard C. Wade. *Chicago: Growth of a Metropolis*. The University of Chicago Press, 1969.

Pierce, Bessie Louise. *The History of Chicago: 1673–1848*. Alfred A. Knopf, New York, 1937.

Ransom, Reverdy C. *The Negro*. Ruth Hill, Publisher, Boston, Massachusetts, 1935.

Ransom, Reverdy C. *The Pilgrimage of Harriett Ransom's Son*. A.M.E. Sunday School Union, Nashville, Tennessee, 1946.

Sinclair, Upton. *The Jungle*. Upton Sinclair, Publisher, 1905.

Work, Monroe Nathan. *Negro Real Estate Holders of Chicago.* Unpublished M.A. Thesis, University of Chicago, 1903.

OFFICIAL STATISTICS

Census Data for the City of Chicago, 1900.

Illinois Central Train Schedule, 1900.

DIRECTORIES AND REFERENCES

Chicago City Directory for years 1860–61 and 1870–71.

Tillotson's Pocket Map and Street Guide of Chicago and Suburbs, 1904.

PERIODICALS

"A 100-Year Odyssey On Black Housing: Chicago, 1900–2000," *Dollars & Sense* magazine, 3rd Quarter, 1977.

CHAPTER ONE

BOOKS

Angle, Paul M. *The Chicago Historical Society: 1856–1956, An Unconventional Chronicle.* Rand McNally & Company, Chicago, 1956.

Duster, Alfreda M., ed. *Crusade for Justice: The Autobiography of Ida B. Wells.* University of Chicago Press, 1970.

Gosnell, Harold F. *Negro Politicians: The Rise of Negro Politics in Chicago.* University of Chicago Press, 1935.

Hammurabis, F.H. *The Negro in Chicago: 1779 to 1929, Vol. 1 & 2.* Washington Intercollegiate Club of Chicago, Inc., 1929.

Historic City: The Settlement of Chicago. City of Chicago, Department of Development & Planning, 1976.

Lowe, David. *Lost Chicago.* Houghton Mifflin Company, Boston, Massachusetts, 1975.

Mayer, Harold M. and Richard C. Wade. *Chicago: Growth of a Metropolis.* The University of Chicago Press, Chicago, 1969.

Ransom, Reverdy C. *The Negro.* Ruth Hill, Publisher, Boston, Massachusetts, 1935.

Work, Monroe Nathan. *Negro Real Estate Holders of Chicago.* Unpublished M.A. Thesis, University of Chicago, 1903.

PERIODICALS

"The South Loop Legacy," *Chicago Magazine*, September, 1978.

DIRECTORIES AND REFERENCES

The Colored Men's Professional and Business Directory of Chicago. I.C. Harris, Publisher, Chicago, 1885.

CHAPTER TWO

BOOKS

Ashbaugh, Carolyn. *Lucy Parsons: American Revolutionary.* Charles H. Kerr Publishing Company, Chicago, 1976.

Cayton, Horace R. and George S. Mitchell. *Black Workers and the New Unions.* Negro University Press, Westport, Connecticut, 1970 (Reprint).

DuBois, W.E.B. *Black Reconstruction.* Albert Saifer, Publisher, Philadelphia, 1935 (Reprint).

Duster, Alfreda M., ed. *Crusade for Justice: The Autobiography of Ida B. Wells.* University of Chicago Press, 1970.

Gosnell, Harold F. *Negro Politicians: The Rise of Negro Politics in Chicago.* University of Chicago Press, 1935.

Hammurabis, F.H. *The Negro in Chicago: 1779 to 1929, Vol. 1 & 2.* Washington Intercollegiate Club of Chicago, Inc., 1929.

Hanna, Hilton E. and Joseph Belsky. *The 'Pat' Garman Story: Picket and the Pen.* American Institute of Social Science, Inc., Yonkers, New York, 1960.

Harlan, Louis R. *Booker T. Washington: The Making of a Black Leader, 1856–1901.* Oxford University Press, New York, 1972.

Historic City: The Settlement of Chicago. City of Chicago, Department of Development & Planning, 1976.

Holli, Melvin G. and Peter Jones, ed. *The Ethnic Frontier.* William B. Eerdmans Publishing Company, 1977.

Hoyt, Hommer. *One Hundred Years of Land Values in Chicago: 1830–1933.* The University of Chicago Press, Chicago, 1933.

Lewis, Lloyd and Henry Justin Smith. *Chicago: The History of Its Reputation.* Harcourt, Brace & Company, New York, 1929.

Lowe, David. *Lost Chicago.* Houghton Mifflin Company, Boston, Massachusetts, 1975.

Mayer, Harold M. & Richard C. Wade. *Chicago: Growth of a Metropolis.* The University of Chicago Press, Chicago, 1969.

Ottley, Roi. *The Lonely Warrior: The Life and Times of Robert S. Abbott.* Henry Regnery & Company, 1955.

Pecks, Edward. *The Long Struggle for Black Power*. Charles Scribner Sons, New York, 1971.

Sandburg, Carl. *The Chicago Race Riots*. Harcourt, Brace & Howe, 1919.

Scott, Emmet J. *Negro Migration During the War*. Arno Press and the New York Times, New York, 1969.

Spears, Allan H. *Black Chicago: 1900–1920*. The University of Chicago Press, 1967.

Stuart, M.S. *An Economic Detour: A History of Insurance in the Lives of American Negroes*. Wendell Mallett and Company, New York, 1940.

Strickland, Arvah E. *History of the Chicago Urban League*. University of Illinois Press, Urbana and London, 1966.

Taitt, John, ed. *The Souvenir of Negro Progress: Chicago, 1779–1925*. The De Saible Association, 1925.

The Negro in Chicago. The Chicago Commission on Race Relations. The University of Chicago Press, 1922.

Tuttle, William M., Jr. *Race Riot*. Athenaeum Press, New York, 1977.

Washington, Booker T. *Up from Slavery*. Double Day Press, New York, 1901.

Washington, Booker T., W.E.B. DuBois, et al. *The Negro Problem*. Arno Press, New York, 1969.

Woodson, Carter G. *The Rural Negro*. The Association for the Study of Negro Life and History, Inc., Washington, D.C., 1930.

PERIODICALS

"Some Chicagoans of Note," *The Crisis,* November, 1915.

"Race Riots and The Press," *The Half-Century Magazine,* August, 1919.

"Negro Life in Chicago," *The Half-Century Magazine,* May, 1919.

NEWSPAPERS

Chicago Defender. "Binga-Johnson Wedding The Most Brilliant Ever Held In Chicago," Feburary 24, 1912.

Chicago Defender. "Welcome To Our Carnival Delegates And Friends," August 17, 1912.

Chicago Defender. "Miss Hattie Holliday Crowned Queen of State Street Carnival," August 31, 1912.

Chicago Defender. "Mrs. J.C. Binga Hostess," August 2, 1913.

The Chicago Daily News. "One Chicago Bank Is Entirely 'Colored'," December 14, 1916.

The Chicago Tribune. "The Coliseum: Historically, An Incredible Hulk," March 27, 1980.

OFFICIAL STATISTICS

Census Data for the City of Chicago, 1900.

LETTERS

Letter from Oneida Daniels Woodard, dated August 12, 1977, which states that Roy Frence, Sr., and his family moved into a two-flat building next to her family in the 4000 block of Winthrop Avenue in 1908. She also discussed another black family by the name of Frinches who opened an integrated fashionable restaurant that same year called "Frinches Pantry" on Evanston Avenue, which was later renamed Broadway. The "Pantry" was located on Broadway near Lawrence.

CHAPTER THREE

BOOKS

Bruder, Stanley. *Pullman: An Experiment in Industrial Order and Community Planning.* Oxford University Press, New York, 1967.

Cayton, Horace R. and George S. Mitchell. *Black Workers and the New Unions.* Negro University Press, Westport, Conn., 1970 (Reprint).

Duster, Alfreda M., ed. *Crusade for Justice: The Autobiography of Ida B. Wells.* University of Chicago Press, 1970.

Gosnell, Harold F. *Negro Politicians: The Rise of Negro Politics in Chicago.* University of Chicago Press, 1935.

Hanna, Hilton E. and Joseph Belsky. *The 'Pat' Gorman Story: Picket and the Pen.* American Institute of Social Science, Inc., Yonkers, New York, 1960.

Herrick, Mary J. *The Chicago Schools: A Social and Political History.* Sage Publications, Beverly Hills/London, 1971.

Historic City: The Settlement of Chicago. City of Chicago, Department of Development and Planning, 1976.

Hoyt, Hommer. *One Hundred Years of Land Values in Chicago: 1830–1933.* University of Chicago Press, 1933.

Lewis, Lloyd and Henry Justin Smith. *Chicago: The History of Its Reputation.* Harcourt, Brace and Company, New York, 1929.

Lowe, David. *Lost Chicago.* Houghton Mifflin Company, Boston, Massachusetts, 1975.

Mayer, Harold M. and Richard G. Wade. *Chicago: Growth of a Metropolis.* The University of Chicago Press, Chicago, 1969.

Ottley, Roi. *The Lonely Warrior: The Life and Times of Robert S. Abbott.* Henry Regnery and Company, Chicago, 1955.

Sandburg, Carl. *The Chicago Race Riots.* Harcourt, Brace & Howe, 1919.

Scott, Emmett J. *Negro Migration During the War.* Arno Press and the New York Times, New York, 1969.

Spears, Allan H. *Black Chicago: 1900–1920.* The University of Chicago Press, 1967.

Strickland, Arvah E. *History of the Chicago Urban League.* University of Illinois Press, Urbana and London, 1966.

Stuart, M.S. *An Economic Detour: A History of Insurance in the Lives of American Negroes.* Wendell Mallett and Company, New York, 1940.

Taitt, John, ed. *The Souvenir of Negro Progress: 1779–1925.* The De Saible Association, 1925.

The Negro in Chicago. The Chicago Commission on Race Relations. University of Chicago Press, 1922.

Tuttle, William M., Jr. *Race Riot.* Athenaeum Press, New York, 1977.

Woodson, Carter G. *The Rural Negro.* The Association for the Study of Negro Life and History, Inc., Washington, D.C. 1930.

CHAPTER FOUR

BOOKS

Gosnell, Harold F. *Negro Politicians; The Rise of Negro Politics in Chicago.* University of Chicago Press, 1935.

Hammurabis, F.H. *The Negro in Chicago: 1779 to 1929, Vol. 1 & 2.* Washington Intercollegiate Club of Chicago, Inc., 1929.

Harris, Abrams L. *The Negro as Capitalist: A Study of Banking and Business Among American Negroes.* The American Academy of Political and Social Science, Philadelphia, 1936.

Hickok, Lorena. *One Third of a Nation.* University of Illinois Press, Chicago, 1981.

Historic City; The Settlement of Chicago. City of Chicago, Department of Development and Planning, 1976.

Lowe, David. *Lost Chicago.* Houghton Mifflin Company, Boston, Massachusetts, 1975.

Mayer, Harold M. and Richard C. Wade. *Chicago: Growth of a Metropolis.* University of Chicago Press, 1969.

Myrdal, Gunnar. *An American Dilemma.* Harper and Brothers, New York, 1944.

Pells, Richard H. *Radical Visions and American Dreams.* Harper & Row, 1973.

Quarles, Benjamin. *The Negro in the Making of America.* Collier-MacMillan Ltd., London, 1970.

The Fabulous Century: 1930–1940. The Editors of Time–Life Books, Time Inc., New York, 1969.

Stuart, M.S. *An Economic Detour: A History of Insurance in the Lives of American Negroes.* Wendell Mallett and Company, New York, 1940.

PERIODICALS

"Jesse Binga," *The Crisis,* December, 1927.

"A Poignant, Relevant Backward Look at Artists of the Great Depression," *Smithsonian,* October, 1979.

NEWSPAPERS

Chicago Daily Defender. "Saga Of Two Banks Brings Up An Old Tune," July 17, 1979.

Chicago Daily Defender. "South Park National Bank Will Soon Open," January 7, 1930.

Chicago Daily Defender. "To Re-Open," March 7, 1930.

Chicago Daily Defender. "Banks Closed Temporarily,"

Chicago Daily Defender. "MT. Glenwood Plans Loans For Victims Of Bank Crisis," August 9, 1930.

Chicago Daily Defender. "Given Plans Whereby Institution Can Open," September 6, 1930.

Chicago Daily Defender. "Jesse Binga's Wife Asks That Estate Be Conserved," October 11, 1930.

Chicago Daily Defender. "To Open Binga Bank," February 14, 1931.

Chicago Daily Defender. "Binga Arrested," March 7, 1931.

Chicago Daily Defender. "Binga Still In Jail On Soup Diet," March 14, 1931.

Chicago Daily Defender. "J. Binga Is Released From Jail On Bond," April 18, 1931.

Chicago Daily Defender. "Binga Bank To Pay Some Money Soon," May 16, 1931.

Chicago Daily Defender. "High Cost of Settling Bank's Affairs Is Under Court Probe," November 7, 1931.

Chicago Tribune. "State Street Yesterday And Today," October 28, 1979.

DIRECTORIES AND REFERENCES

Black Who's Who in Chicago, 1927, from F. H. Hammurabis, *The Negro in Chicago: 1779 to 1929, Vol. 1.* Washington Intercollegiate Club of Chicago, Inc., 1929.

Simms' Blue Book and National Negro Business and Professional Directory, James M. Simms, Publisher, Chicago, 1923.

CHAPTER FIVE

BOOKS

Brashler, William. *The Don: The Life and Death of Sam Giancana.* Harper & Row Publishers, New York, 1977.

Calloway, Cab. *Of Minnie the Moocher and Me.* Thomas Y. Crowdly, 1976.

Cronon, Edmund David. *Black Moses: The Story of Marcus Garvey and the Universal Negro Improvement Association.* The University of Wisconsin Press, Madison, 1955.

Dance, Stanley. *The World of Earl Hines.* Thomas Y. Crowdly & Company, New York, 1977.

Drake, St. Clair and Horace Cayton. *Black Metropolis: A Study of Life in a Northern City, Vol. 1 & 2.* Harper & Row Publishers, New York, 1945.

Garvey, Amy Jacques. *Philosophy and Opinion of Marcus Garvey.* Frank Cass & Company, Ltd., London, 1967.

Gilmore, Al-Tony. *Bad Nigger!: The National Impact of Jack Johnson.* Kennikat Press, Port Washington, New York, 1975.

Gottfried, Alex. *Boss Cermak of Chicago.* University of Washington Press, Seattle, 1962.

Hammurabis, F.H. *The Negro in Chicago: 1779 to 1929, Vol. 1 & 2.* Washington Intercollegiate Club of Chicago, Inc., 1929.

Henderson, Bancroft Edwin. *The Negro in Sports.* The Associated Publishers, Inc., Washington, D.C., 1949.

Holt, Glen E. and Dominic Pacyga. *Chicago: A Historical Guide to the Neighborhoods—The Loop and Southside.* Chicago Historical Foundation, 1979.

Hoyt, Hommer. *One Hundred Years of Land Values in Chicago: 1830–1933.* University of Chicago Press, Chicago, 1933.

Johnson, Jack. *Jack Johnson is a Dandy: An Autobiography.* The New American Library, New York, 1969.

Kobler, John. *Capone.* G.P. Putnam's Sons, New York, 1971.

Lait, Jack and Lee Mortimer. *Chicago Confidential.* Crown Press, New York, 1950.

Lomay, Allan. *Mister Jelly Roll.* University of California Press, Berkeley, 1950.

Lucas, Robert. *Black Gladiator.* Dell Publishing Company, Inc., New York, 1970.

Mayer, Harold M. and Richard C. Wade. *Chicago: Growth of A Metropolis.* University of Chicago Press, 1969.

Myrdal, Gunnar. *An American Dilemma.* Harper and Brothers, New York, 1944.

Ottley, Roi. *The Lonely Warrior: The Life and Times of Robert S. Abbott.* Henry Regnery & Company, Chicago, 1955.

Philpott, Thomas Lee. *The Slum and The Ghetto: Chicago 1880–1930*. Oxford Press, New York, 1978.

Twombly, Robert C. *Blacks In White America Since 1865*. David McKay Company, Inc., New York, 1971.

NEWSPAPERS

Chicago Daily Defender. "Johnson In The Lime Light," February 12, 1910.

Chicago Daily Defender. "We Have Them All To Beat," February 5, 1910.

Chicago Daily Defender. "Champions Take Long Road Jog," April 6, 1910.

Chicago Daily Defender. "Champion Jack Johnson: The Undefeated Hero," April 23, 1910.

Chicago Daily Defender. "Champion Jack Johnson In Town Tomorrow," March 12, 1910.

Chicago Daily Defender. "Jack Johnson And James Jeffries," July 2, 1910.

Chicago Daily Defender. "$1,000.00 Punch Bowl To Champion Jack Johnson," August 6, 1910.

Chicago Daily Defender. "Johnson Is After $60,000 Property," December 3, 1910.

Chicago Daily Defender. "Jack Johnson In London," June 17, 1911.

Chicago Daily Defender. "Jack Johnson Forms Land Co. In Mexico City, Mexico," June 7, 1919.

Chicago Daily Defender. "Johnson Refused Service, Druggist License Revoked In Mexico City, Mexico," June 12, 1919.

DIRECTORIES AND REFERENCES

Black Who's Who in Chicago, 1927 from F.H. Hammurabis, *The Negro in Chicago: 1779 to 1929, Vol. 1*. Washington Intercollegiate Club of Chicago, Inc., 1929.

CHAPTER SIX

BOOKS

Cronon, Edmund David. *Black Moses: The Story of Marcus Garvey and the Universal Negro Improvement Association*. University of Wisconsin Press, Madison, Wisconsin, 1955.

Garvey, Amy Jacques. *Philosophy and Opinion of Marcus Garvey*. Frank Cass & Company, Ltd., London, 1967.

Hammurabis, F.H. *The Negro in Chicago: 1779 to 1929, Vol. 1 & 2*. Washington Intercollegiate Club of Chicago, 1929.

Herrick, Mary J. *The Chicago Schools: A Social and Political History*. Sage Publications, Beverly Hills/London, 1971.

Hoyt, Hommer. *One Hundred Years of Land Values in Chicago: 1830–1933*. University of
     Chicago Press, 1933.

Kobler, John. *Capone*. G. P. Putnam's Sons, New York, 1971.

Lucas, Robert. *Black Gladiator*. Dell Publishing Company, Inc., New York, 1970.

Travis, Dempsey J. *Don't Stop Me Now*. Children's Press, 1970.

NEWSPAPERS

Chicago Daily News. "The Bloody Reign of Tony Capone," January 4, 1976.

CHAPTER SEVEN

BOOKS

Allen, Jack and John L. Betts. *History: U.S.A.* American Book Company, New York, 1969.

Barnett, Ida Wells. *On Lynching*. Arno Press and New York Times, 1969.

Beldon, F.E. *Christ in Song*. Review & Herald Publishing Association. Washington, D.C.,
     1908.

Carter, Dan T. *A Tragedy of the American South*. Louisiana State University Press, 1960.

Drake, St. Clair and Horace Cayton. *Black Metropolis: A Study of Life in a Northern City,
     Vol. 1 & 2*. Harper & Row Publishers, New York, 1945.

Franklin, John Hope. *From Slavery to Freedom*. Alfred A. Knopf, New York, 1947.

Haskell, S.N. *Bible Handbook*. Review & Herald Publishing Association, Washington, D.C.,
     1919.

Myrdal, Gunnar. *An American Dilemma*. Harper and Brothers, New York, 1944.

Patterson, Haywood and Earl Conrad. *Scottsboro Boy*. Double Day, New York, 1950.

Strickland, Arvah E. *History of the Chicago Urban League*. University of Illinois Press, Ur-
     bana and London, 1966.

The Fabulous Century: 1930–1940. The Editors of Time–Life Books, Time Inc., New York,
     1969.

White, Walter. *Rope and Fagot*. Arno Press and the New York Times, 1969.

Wright, Richard. *Black Boy*. Harper & Brothers Publishers, New York, 1937.

NEWSPAPERS

Chicago Daily News. "Welcome to the '30's," March 10, 1975.

Chicago Daily News. "Chicago Flocked to Big 1933 Fair," December 6–7, 1975.

CHAPTER EIGHT

BOOKS

Allen, Jack and John L. Betts. *History: U.S.A.* American Book Company, New York, 1969.

Barnum, Donald T. *The Negro in the Bituminous Coal Mining Industry.* The Wharton School of Finance & Commerce, Department of Industry, Industrial Research Unit, 1970.

Bennett, Lerone, Jr. *Before the Mayflower.* Johnson Publishing Company, Chicago, 1964.

Cayton, Horace R. and George S. Mitchell. *Black Workers and the New Unions.* Negro University Press, Westport, Connecticut, 1970 (Reprint).

Dubin, Arthur D. *Some Classic Trains.* Kalmbach Publication, Milwaukee, Wisconsin, 1964.

Haggard, Howard W. *The Science of Health and Disease.* Harper and Brothers Publishers, New York, 1938.

Kardiner, Abram. *The Mark of Oppression.* The World Publishing Company, 1962.

King, Martin Luther, Jr. *Stride Toward Freedom.* Harper & Brothers Publishers, 1958.

McKissick, Floyd. *3/5 of a Man.* The MacMillan Company, London, 1969.

Mays, Benjamin E. *Born to Rebel.* Charles Scribner's Sons, New York, 1971.

Myrdal, Gunnar. *An American Dilemma.* Harper and Brothers, New York, 1944.

Scheener, Allen, ed. *Harlem on My Mind: 1900–1968.* Random House, New York, 1968.

Woodson, Carter G. and Lorenzo Greene. *The Negro Wage Earner.* The Association for the Study of Negro Life and History, Inc., Washington, D.C., 1930.

Woodward, C. Vann. *The Strange Career of Jim Crow.* Oxford University Press, 1957.

PAMPHLETS

The Power of Coal. National Coal Association, Division of Education, Washington, D.C.

PERIODICALS

The Message. "Soul Food and Survival," November–December, 1978.

NOTES FROM INTERVIEWS

Notes from interviews with Dr. Robert L. Kimbrough of Chicago, an ex-Alabama coal miner; my cousin, Joseph Story, of Cleveland, Ohio, an ex-Kentucky coal miner; and my cousin, Strickland Davis, of Newark, New Jersey, an ex-Pennsylvania coal miner. Both first cousins were present at our grandmother's funeral.

CHAPTER NINE

BOOKS

Bogle, Donald. *Toms, Coons, Mulattoes, Mammies and Bucks.* Viking Press, New York, 1973.

Chilton, John. *Who's Who of Jazz. Storyville to Swing Street.* Time–Life Records, Special Edition, New York, 1978.

Drake, St. Clair and Horace Cayton. *Black Metropolis: A Study of Life in a Northern City, Vol. 1 & 2.* Harper & Row Publishers, New York, 1945.

Dykeman, William and James Stokely. *Neither Black nor White.* Rhinehart & Company, Inc., 1957.

Frazier, E. Franklin. *Black Bourgeoisie: The Rise of a New Middle Class in the United States.* The Free Press, Glencoe, Illinois, 1957.

Garvey, Amy Jacques. *Philosophy and Opinion of Marcus Garvey.* Frank Cass & Company, Ltd., London, 1967.

Grier, William H. and Price M. Cobbs. *Black Rage.* Basic Books, Inc. New York, 1968.

Hammonds, John with Irving Townsend. *John Hammond on Record.* Ridge Press, New York, 1977.

Herrick, Mary J. *The Chicago Schools: A Social and Political History.* Sage Publications, Beverly Hills/London, 1971.

Louis, Joe with Edna and Art Rust, Jr. *Joe Louis: My Life.* Harcourt, Brace, Jovanovich, Inc. New York, 1978.

Major, Gerri and Doris E. Saunders. *Black Society.* Johnson Publishing Company, Inc., Chicago, 1976.

McCarthy, Albert. *Big Band Jazz.* Berkley Publishing Corp., New York, 1977.

Patterson, Lindsay, ed. *The Negro in Music and Art.* Publishers Company, Inc., New York, 1967.

NEWSPAPERS

Chicago Daily News. "Blacks Distrust Leaders," May 15, 1968.

Chicago Sun Times. "Black Singles Mingle But Not In Loneliness—Industry Activity," November 28, 1972.

Chicago Sun Times/Parade. "Black Is Beautiful But Not In South Africa," April 8, 1973.

Chicago Tribune Magazine. "In Defense Of Being Black And Successful," August 18, 1974.

New York Times Magazine. "The Negro Is Prejudiced Against Himself." November 29, 1964.

New York Times Magazine. "The Negro's Self Image—The Reader React," December 13, 1964.

New York Times Magazine. "The Negro's Middle-Class," October 24, 1964.

PAMPHLETS

Goodman, Benny. *Giants of Jazz*. Time–Life Books Inc., 1979.

DIRECTORIES & REFERENCES

DuSable High School's First Four June Class Year Book, 1935–39, Chicago, Illinois.

Reviewed both the 1933 and revised 1961 blue prints and plot plans for DuSable High School.

Music Master. Official monthly Journal of the American Federation of Musicians, local 208, Chicago, Illinois, March, 1941.

Savoy Chatterbox. November 28, 1938, Chicago, Illinois. Music contract between Jack Travis and Club Deluxe, dated November 1, 1939.

LETTERS

Letter dated August 15, 1939 from Colored Associated Orchestras to Jack Travis confirming date at Warwick Hall on September 1, 1939.

Letter dated August 6, 1938 from Musician Protection Union Local #208, A.F. & M., Inc. to Jack Travis giving official notice that my band was to appear at the Musicians Annual Picnic, August 8, 1938, Birutes Grove, 79th at Archer, at 2 p.m.

Letter dated September 23, 1941 from Madelle B. Boosfield, Principal of Phillips High School, and C.C. Willard, Principal of DuSable High School, inviting me to be their guest at a luncheon to be given on October 2, 1941, at Morris' Eat Shop, 410 East 47th Street, Chicago, Illinois.

CHAPTER TEN

BOOKS

Allen, Jack & John L. Betts. *History: U.S.A.* American Book Company, New York, 1969.

Anderson, Jervis. *A. Philip Randolph: A Biographic Portrait*. Harcourt, Brace, Jovanovich, Inc., New York, 1972.

Brooks, Gwendolyn. *A Street in Bronzeville*. Harper & Brothers Publishers, New York, 1945.

Dobson, Andrew. *Uncle Joe's Journal*. Minsip Publishing Company, Indianapolis, Indiana, 1937.

Drake, St. Clair and Horace Cayton. *Black Metropolis: A Study of Life in a Northern City, Vol. 1 & 2*. Harper & Row Publishers, New York, 1945.

Franklin, John Hope. *From Slavery to Freedom*. Alfred A. Knopf, New York, 1947.

Herrick, Mary J. *The Chicago Schools: A Social and Political History*. Sage Publications, Beverly Hills/London, 1971.

Hickok, Lorena. *One-Third of a Nation*. University of Illinois Press, Chicago, Illinois, 1981.

Myrdal, Gunnar. *An American Dilemma*. Harper and Brothers, New York, 1944.

Pells, Richard H. *Radical Visions and American Dreams*. Harper & Row, 1973.

Strickland, Arvah E. *History of the Chicago Urban League*. University of Illinois Press, Urbana & London, 1966.

LETTERS

Letters dated from September 1939, through December 1941, to Mrs. Mary Herrick from DuSable graduates who were unsuccessful in finding employment.

NEWSPAPERS

Chicago Defender. "Satchumo Armstrong Opens At State-Lake Theatre," July 1, 1939.

Chicago Defender. "Another Delay For Speedy Erection Of Ida B. Wells, Low-Cost Housing Project," July 29, 1939.

Chicago Defender. "Bunny Berigan Opens At Savoy August 12," August 5, 1939.

Chicago Defender. "Preliminary Ground Work on $8,000,000 Ida B. Wells Began Wednesday," August 5, 1939.

Chicago Defender. "W.P.A. To Drop 2 Million From Rolls By August," July 22, 1939.

Chicago Defender. "Family's Window Stoned At Jane Addams Homes," August 12, 1939.

Chicago Defender. "Pay Binga Depositor $55,536.96," August 19, 1939.

Chicago Defender. "New Scale Boosts W.P.A. Salaries $60,000,000," August 19, 1939.

Chicago Defender. "78,750 People In Chicago Will Be Affected By W.P.A. Shut Down," September 2, 1939.

Chicago Defender. "Committee Asked To Act In Delay Of Ida B. Wells Homes; Seek U.S. Probe," September 30, 1939.

Chicago Defender. "Women Cry And Laugh As Joe Louis Wins," September 30, 1939.

Chicago Defender. "Hansberry Loses In A Restrictive Covenants Case," October 21, 1939.

Chicago Defender. "1,000 To Get Jobs On Ida B. Wells Homes Within 3 Weeks," October 28, 1939.

Chicago Defender. "Reliefers To Be Given W.P.A. Jobs," November 11, 1939.

Chicago Defender. "Freedom for Scottsboro Boys in Sight," November 18, 1939.

CHAPTER ELEVEN

BOOKS

Allen, Jack and John L. Betts. *History: U.S.A.* American Book Company, New York, 1969.

Brooks, Gwendolyn. *A Street in Bronzeville.* Harper and Brothers Publishers, New York, 1945.

Burrell, Berkley. *Getting It Together.* Harcourt, Brace and Jovanovich, New York, 1971.

Chilton, John. *Who's Who of Jazz: Storyville to Swing Street.* Time–Life Records (Special Edition), New York, 1978.

Drake, St. Clair and Horace Cayton. *Black Metropolis: A Study of Life in a Northern City, Vol. 1 & 2.* Harper & Row Publishers, New York, 1945.

Killens, John Oliver. *And Then We Heard the Thunder.* Alfred A. Knopf, Inc., New York, 1963.

Lee, Ulysses. *United States Army in World War II—Special Studies: The Employment of Negro Troops.* Office of the Chief of Military History, United States Army, Washington, D.C., 1966.

McCarthy, Albert. *Big Band Jazz.* Berkley Publishing Corporation, New York, 1977.

Motley, Mary P., ed. *The Invisible Soldier: The Experience of the Black Soldier in World War II.* Wayne State University Press, Detroit, Michigan, 1975.

Quarles, Benjamin. *The Negro in the Making of America.* Collier-Macmillan Ltd., London, 1970.

Schoefeld, Seymour J. *The Negro in the Armed Forces: His Values and Status Past, Presently, and Potential.* The Associated Publisher, Washington, D.C., 1945.

Stuckey, Elma. *The Big Gate.* Precedent Publishing, Inc., Chicago

This Fabulous Century: 1940–1950. Editors of Time–Life Books, Time, Inc., New York, 1967.

Travis, Dempsey J. *Don't Stop Me Now.* Children's Press, 1970.

PERIODICALS

"Black Chicago: Three Score Plus One, Part VII," by Dempsey J. Travis, *Dollars & Sense* magazine, June/July, 1980.

"This Is The Army," *Negro Digest,* February, 1944.

NEWSPAPERS

The Chicago Defender. "Mourn City Victim of Georgia MP," December 12, 1942.

The Chicago Defender. "War Workers Rallying As Good Fellows," December 12, 1942.

The Chicago Defender. "Chicago Given Status Of Acting Civilian Aide By Stimson," February 13, 1943.

The Chicago Defender. "Library Life Assets Show Gain of $400,000," April 3, 1943.

The Chicago Defender. "Negro Sailors At Great Lakes Lead Bond Sales," April 3, 1943.

The Chicago Defender. "To Fight 'Jim Crow' In Local Bar Association," May 29, 1943.

The Chicago Defender. "Kill M.P. In Race Clash At Ga. Camp," June 12, 1943,

The Chicago Defender. "Weaver Heads Mayor Kelly's Race Committee," January 8, 1944.

The Chicago Defender. "Mayor Seeks Data On Employment Of War Veterans," January 29, 1944.

The Chicago Defender. "Protest Slum Project Site On Southside," February 19,1944.

The Chicago Defender. "Shoe Stamp 18 Not Good After April 30," April 8, 1944.

The Chicago Defender. "Covenant Suit Would Evict 1000 Families," February 5,1944.

The Chicago Defender. "Randolph Maps Plan For Nation Wide Conference," May 13, 1944.

The Chicago Defender. "Keep Hands Off West Chesterfield Project–NAACP," April 8, 1944.

The Chicago Defender. "FDR Names 3-Man Board In FEP-Railroad Dispute," January 8, 1944.

The Chicago Defender. "Housing Has Not Failed, Declares CHA Chairman," January 8, 1944.

The Chicago Defender. "Spur Bond Drive For S.S. Robert S. Abbott," March 18, 1944.

The Chicago Defender. "OPA Starts Big South Side Drive On High Rentals," March 18, 1944.

The Chicago Defender. "Overcrowding Tenants More Serious Than Ever," March 18, 1944.

The Chicago Defender. "Service Guild To Aid Abbott Ship Bond Drive," April 22, 1944.

CHAPTER TWELVE

BOOKS

Burrell, Berkley. *Getting It Together: Black Businessmen in America.* Harcourt, Brace and Jovanovich, Inc., New York, 1971.

Jones, Henry Williams. *The Housing of Negroes in Washington, D.C.* Howard University Press, Washington, D.C., 1929.

Killens, John Oliver. *And Then We Heard the Thunder.* Alfred A. Knopf, New York, 1962.

Lee, Ulysses. *United States Army in World War II—Special Studies: The Employment of Negro Troops.* Office of the Chief of Military History, United States Army, Washington, D.C, 1966.

Motley, Mary P. *The Invisible Soldier: The Experience of the Black Soldier in World War II.* Wayne State University Press, Detroit, Michigan, 1975.

Schoenfeld, Seymour J. *The Negro in the Armed Forces: His Value and Status Past, Presently, and Potential.* The Associated Publishers, Washington, D.C., 1945.

Travis, Dempsey J. *Don't Stop Me Now.* Children's Press, 1970.

PERIODICALS

"Black Chicago: Three Score Plus One, Part VIII," by Dempsey J. Travis, *Dollars & Sense* magazine, August/September, 1980.

"White Folks Do The Funniest Things," by Langston Hughes, *Common Ground,* Winter, 1944.

"For Germans Only," by Donald Jones, *Common Sense*, December, 1943.

"These Are Our Heroes," by Louis E. Burnham, *Spotlight,* December, 1943.

NEWSPAPERS

Chicago Daily Defender. "Blast Detroit Mayor In Cop Whitewash," July 17, 1943.

Chicago Daily Defender. "Van Dorn Soldiers Keep Arms," July 17, 1943.

Chicago Daily Defender. "Riots At A Glance," June 26, 1943.

Chicago Daily Defender. "Blame Prejudice Police For Detroit Fatalities," June 26, 1943.

Chicago Daily Defender. "Riots In Los Angeles," June 26, 1943.

Chicago Daily Defender. "Segregation Rules WAAC Race Volunteers Lag," by Enoch P. Waters, Jr., January 16, 1943.

Chicago Daily Defender. "Savoy Ballroom Closed; Mixed Dancers Seen Cause," by Alfred Duckett, May 1, 1943.

Chicago Daily Defender. "Covenant Ban Loses Test In Legislature," June 12, 1943.

Chicago Daily Defender. "Seven Die, 150 Hurt In Ten Outbreaks," June 19, 1943.

Chicago Daily Defender. "Pennsylvania Railroad Ends Jim Crow Trains In State of Illinois," January 16, 1943.

Chicago Daily Defender. "Reign of Terror Against Black Soldiers In Valle Jo, California," January 2, 1943.

Chicago Daily Defender. "Ask Street Car Jobs For Negroes," January 16, 1943.

The New York Age. "Dancer Joins Negro USO Camp Shows Unit," June 3, 1944.

The New York Age. "Negro And White Wainwright WAC's Separated In Iowa, Paper Charges," November, 1944.

The New York Age. "President Roosevelt Declares For Permanent FEPC; Wants Post-War Period Free From Discrimination," November 4, 1944.

The New York Age. "President Roosevelt Approves Navy's Plan To Enlist Negro Women As Waves and SPARS," October 28, 1944.

The New York Age. "57 Negro Soldiers Jailed In Arizona When They Strike Against Prolonged K.P. Duty," September 23, 1944.

The New York Age. "War Department Order Forbidding Discrimination At Army Posts Is Protested by Governor of Alabama," September 21, 1944.

The New York Age. "Philadelphia Strike Ended; Four Strike Leaders Arrested, Fired From Jobs; Army Still On The Job," August 12, 1944.

The New York Age. "Philadelphia Scene Of Riot In Protest Against Negro Motormen," August 5, 1944.

Afro-American. "D. C. Rooms Advertised For 'Light Colored' Tenants," August 15, 1944.

Afro-American. "General Davis Denies Saying Army Free of Bias," by J. Robert Smith, April 15, 1944.

Afro-American. "Dr. Charles Drew Wins 29th Spingarn Medal," April 1, 1944.

Afro-American. "30 Get Wings At Tuskegee," May 27, 1944.

Afro-American. "CIAA Hits Army, Navy For Ignoring Colored Athletes," April 29, 1944.

Afro-American. "Hitler Preaches Ghetto System, U.S. Practices It," April 29, 1944.

Afro-American. "Robeson Weeps As 8,000 Cheer At Birthday Party," April 22, 1944.

Afro-American. "Increased Racial Tension Looms In San Francisco," April 15, 1944.

Afro-American. "Ask Volunteers For Ethiopia," April 15, 1944.

Afro-American. "Racial Progress Cited At Tuskegee," April 15, 1944.

CHAPTER THIRTEEN

BOOKS

Abrams, Charles. *The City Is the Frontier*. Harper & Row Publishers, New York, 1965.

Clark, Dennis. *The Ghetto Game: Conflicts in the City*. Sheed and Ward, New York, 1962.

Ebony Pictorial History of Black America, Vol. 2. Editors of Ebony Magazine, Johnson Publishing Company, Chicago, 1970.

Glazer, Nathan and Davis McEntire. *Housing and Minority Groups*. University of California Press, Berkeley, 1960.

Myerson, Martin and Edward C. Banfield. *Politics, Planning and the Public Interest*. The Free Press, New York, 1955.

Myerson, Martin, Barbara Terrett, and William L. C. Wheaton. *Housing, People, and Cities*. McGraw-Hill Book Company, Inc., New York, 1962.

McEntire, Davis. *Residence and Race*. University of California Press, 1960.

Rapkin, Chester and William G. Grigsby. *The Demand for Housing in Racially Mixed Areas*. University of California Press, Berkeley, 1960.

Steiner, Oscar H. *Our Housing Jungle and Your Pocketbook*. University Publishers, Inc., New York, 1960.

Weaver, Robert C. *The Negro Ghetto*. Harcourt, Brace and Company, New York, 1948.

NEWSPAPERS

Chicago Daily Defender. "Loop Hotels Ban: Won't Serve Both Races Together," January 26, 1946.

Chicago Daily Defender. "Crack Down On Jim Crow Rink At White City," January 26, 1946.

Chicago Daily Defender. "Pressure On Congress Key To More Homes, Expert Say," by Robert Lucas, June 8, 1946.

Chicago Daily Defender. "U.S. Supreme Court Aids Race Restrictive Pacts, NBA Charges," May 4, 1946.

Chicago Daily Defender. "New Dormitories 'For White Only,'" by Richard E. Goldsberry, April 27, 1946.

Chicago Daily Defender. "Northwestern Gets O.K. On Jim Crow Dorm," May 4, 1946.

Chicago Daily Defender. "Hunt White Vandals Who Bomb Negroes," February 2, 1946.

Chicago Daily Defender. "NAACP Brings Columbia Riot Victims To Chicago," April 27, 1946.

Chicago Daily Defender. (Advertisement) "Anna Lucasta," a play by Philip Yordan with original New York cast.

Chicago Daily Defender. "Open Fire On Jim Crow In U. Of C. Hospitals," February 9, 1946.

Chicago Daily Defender. "Ask Probe of Bus Finn's Anti-Negro Policy," February 2, 1946.

Chicago Daily Defender. "Police Arrest 10 Pickets In Strike At Stockyards," January 12, 1946.

Chicago Daily Defender. "Restrictions On Labor Are No Path To Progress," June 8, 1946.

Chicago Daily Defender. "Says Return To Africa Negroes' Only Salvation," June 1, 1946.

Chicago Daily Defender. "Huge Housing Meet Sunday: OPA, Low-Rent Chief Topics," April 27, 1946.

Chicago Daily Defender. "A Glimpse Of Beauty," by W. E. B. DuBois, April 27, 1946.

Chicago Daily Defender. "Americans Set Roots Of Racism In Panama," by U. G. Dailey, M.D., May 4, 1946.

Chicago Daily Defender. "Widows Fight Over Body of Marcus Garvey," by George Padmore, London Correspondent, 1946.

Chicago Daily Defender. "Rip White City Roller Rink," February 2, 1946.

Chicago Daily Defender. "Tenants To File Feb. 1 For Wentworth Gardens," January 26, 1946.

Chicago Daily Defender. "Clear Officer In Loading Of Negro Troops," by Venice Spraggs, January 7, 1946.

Chicago Daily Defender. "Judges Refuses To Drop Jim Crow Covenant Case," January, 1947.

Chicago Daily Defender. "Evanston Veterans Sue City For Housing Equality," January 11, 1947.

Chicago Daily Defender. "The Need For Interracial Solidarity In Unions," January, 1947.

Chicago Daily Defender. "Educator Tells U.S., End Bias," January, 1947.

Chicago Daily Defender. "American Race Prejudice Must Be Destroyed," by Robert Abbott, April 5, 1947.

Chicago Daily Defender. "Probe Attack By Whites In Tension Area," January, 1947.

Chicago Daily Defender. "Jackie Robinson Signs To Play For Brooklyn," January, 1947.

Chicago Daily Defender. "1946 Lynching Record," January, 1947.

Chicago Daily Defender. "Survey Shows White Only Ads Gain Job Market," April, 1947.

Chicago Daily Defender. "Governors Rename Racist To Own Vacancy," January, 1947.

Chicago Daily Defender. "4 Testify To Jim Crow On I.C. Crack Train," March 13, 1948.

Chicago Daily Defender. "Thousands Vow To Keep Park Manor White," by Stephan Lewis, March 6, 1948.

Chicago Daily Defender. "Bar GI's From Nurse Training," by Charles A. Davis, March 13, 1948.

Chicago Daily Defender. "Negroes Play Big Role In Meat Strike," March 13, 1948.

Chicago Daily Defender. "Fear Mounts At Rumor Anti-Slum Program Means Negro Clearance," March 13, 1948.

Chicago Daily Defender. "Railway Workers Win Injunction To Halt Replacement By Whites," February 14, 1948.

Chicago Daily Defender. "Charges Mail Order House With Job Bias," January 31, 1948.

Chicago Daily Defender. "Order Ends Segregated National Guard," February 14, 1948.

Chicago Daily Defender. "Neisner Dime Store, Hit By Job Bias Charge, Closes Its Door," March 6, 1948.

Chicago Daily Defender. "Vets Appeal Cab Bias Verdict of U.S. Court," March 13, 1948.

Chicago Daily Defender. "Randolph Asks Civil Disobedience Unless Military Forces End Bias," April 13, 1948.

Chicago Daily Defender. "Ask Anti-Trust Probe Of Bias In Home Loans," April 3, 1948.

Chicago Daily Defender. "Buttons To Boost War On Segregated Army," April 24, 1948.

Chicago Daily Defender. "Neisner Bros. Tells Service To Community," April 24, 1948.

Chicago Daily Defender. "Hurl Stones, Lawsuit At Woodlawn, Residents," April 24, 1948.

Chicago Daily Defender. "25 Families Escape Ouster From Englewood," by Charles A. Davis, April 24, 1948.

Chicago Daily Defender. "Hoodlums Mob Man On Street," January 3, 1948.

Chicago Daily Defender. "Prejudice Blocks Nurse Training," by Lillian Scott, January 24, 1948.

Chicago Daily Defender. "White Mother Charges New Son-In-Law Has Negro Blood," 1948.

Chicago Daily Defender. "Train Bypasses Jim Crow Fans," by Lillian Scott, July 3, 1948.

Chicago Daily Defender. "New VA Chief Pledges Equality Of All Vets," January 10, 1948.

Chicago Daily Defender. "Segregated Travel Law Under Fire; High Court To Study Biased Policy," by Venice Spraggs, October 15, 1949.

Chicago Daily Defender. "Truman Pat on Ending Army Bias," October 8, 1949.

Chicago Daily Defender. "No Civil Rights Compromise—Truman," January, 1949.

Chicago Daily Defender. "Segregtion In County Jail Ends," by R. B. Goldsberry, 1949.

Chicago Daily Defender. "Action on FEPC Slated Next Week," 1949.

Chicago Daily Defender. "Green, AFL Chief, Warns Congress: Wants Action On Civil Rights Bill," by Louis Martin, 1949.

Chicago Daily Defender. "Seeks Missouri Law To Oust Railroad Porters From Jobs," 1949.

Chicago Daily Defender. "Negro Wins Plea To Enter Kentucky U.," April, 1949.

Chicago Daily Defender. "Convenant Leaders State Opposition At City Council Hearing," by Richard Goldsberry, February 5, 1949.

Chicago Daily Defender. "Hospital Bias Bill Again In Legislature," 1949.

Chicago Daily Defender. "NAACP Youth Gets Offer Of Compromise In Theatre Row," 1949.

Chicago Daily Defender. "Brokers Charge FHA, VA Deny Mortgage Insurance To Negroes," by Chuck Davis, 1949.

Chicago Daily Defender. "Truman Stands Firm On Rights, Demands A 'Square Deal' For All," 1949.

Chicago Daily Defender. "Hoodlums Try Again To Burn Park Manor Home," April, 1949.

CHAPTER FOURTEEN

BOOKS

Anderson, Martin. *The Federal Bulldozer: A Critical Analysis of Urban Renewal, 1949–1962.* The M.I.T. Press, Cambridge, Massachusetts, 1964.

Banfield, Edward C. and Morton Grodzins. *Government and Housing.* McGraw-Hill Book Company, Inc., New York, 1958.

Bowly, Devereux Jr. *The Poorhouse Subsidized Housing in Chicago: 1895–1976.* Southern Illinois University Press, Carbondale, Illinois, 1978.

Brown, Frank London. *Trumbull Park.* Regnery, Chicago, 1959.

Haar, Charles M. *Federal Credit and Private Housing.* McGraw-Hill Book Company, Inc., New York, 1960.

Mayer, Harold M. and Richard C. Wade. *Chicago: Growth of a Metropolis.* University of Chicago Press, 1969.

Meyerson, Martin and Edward C. Banfield. *Politics, Planning and the Public Interest.* The Free Press, New York, 1955.

Ross, Peter H. and Robert A, Dentler. *The Politics of Urban Renewal.* The Fress Press, Glencoe, Illinois, 1961.

Weaver, Robert C. *The Negro Ghetto.* Harcourt, Brace & Company, New York, 1948.

Wilson, James Q., Editor. *Urban Renewal: The Record and The Controversy.* The M.I.T. Press, Cambridge, Massachusetts,1966.

Wolman, Harold. *Politics of Federal Housing.* Dodd, Mead & Company, New York, 1971.

OFFICIAL DOCUMENTS

Housing Hearings Before the United States Commission on Civil Rights: May 5 and 6, 1959. U. S. Government Printing Office, Washington, D.C., 1959.

NEWSPAPERS

Chicago Daily Defender. "Dr. Julian Raps Housing Farce," January, 1950.

Chicago Daily Defender. "Rap Judge, Prosecutor In Chicago Riot Trials," January, 1950.

Chicago Daily Defender. "Police Lift Ban On 'No Way Out' Film," January, 1950.

Chicago Daily Defender, "Puts O.K. On Jim Crow Travel," February 25, 1950.

Chicago Daily Defender. "Governor Acts As Cicero Cops Flop," July 14, 1951.

Chicago Sun Times. "Frank London Brown, Labor Teacher, Dead At 34," 1962.

CHAPTER FIFTEEN

BOOKS

Bogle, Donald. *Toms, Coons, Mulattoes, and Bucks.* Viking Press, New York, 1973.

Conant, James B. *Slums and Suburbs: A Commentary in Schools in Metropolitan Areas.* McGraw-Hill Book Company, New York, 1961.

Cripps, Thomas. *Slow Fade to Black: The Negro in American Film, 1900–1942.* Oxford University Press, London, 1971.

Doob, Leonard W. *Public Opinion and Propaganda.* Archon Books, Hamden, Connecticut, 1966.

Griffith, Richard and Arthur Mayer. *The Movies.* Simon and Schuster, New York, 1957,

Hughes, Langston and Arna Bontemps, ed. *The Poetry of the Negro: 1746–1949.* Double Day and Company, Inc., New York, 1951.

King, Martin Luther, Jr. *Strides Toward Freedom.* Harper and Brothers, 1958.

Wilson, James Q. *Negro Politics: The Search for Leadership.* The Free Press, Glencoe, Illinois, 1960.

OFFICIAL DOCUMENTS

Housing Hearings Before the United States Commission on Civil Rights: May 5 and 6, 1959. U.S. Government Printing Office, Washington, D.C.

LETTERS

Letter from Enoc P. Waters, Jr., Executive Editor, The Chicago Daily Defender, to Jack Travis, dated July 21, 1953.

Letter from Edward J. Sparling, President, Roosevelt University to Dempsey J. Travis, dated March 30, 1955.

PERIODICALS

Ebony. "The Till Case People One Year Later: Tragedy Alter Lives of Whites, Witnesses."

Ebony. "Land of the Till Murder: the Delta Is Blazing Today with Fierce Racial Tensions," by Clotye Murdock.

The Crisis, "Mississippi Barbarism," October, 1955.

The Crisis. "Fate of the World," October, 1955.

Parade. "Americans Who Can't Speak Their Own Language," by Lloyd Shearer, June 11, 1967.

NEWSPAPERS

Chicago Daily Defender. "Urges Halt To South Side Minority Ghetto," April 3, 1954.

Chicago Daily Defender. "Mob Victim Faces Trial April 27," April 17, 1954.

Chicago Daily Defender. "Howard Hits City, Leaves Trumbull," May 8, 1954.

Chicago Daily Defender. "Marshall Receives Abbott Award; Says Jim Crow Will End By 1963," by Lee Blackwell, May 15, 1954.

Chicago Daily Defender. "Sees Danger Of Bias In 'Private' High School Proposal For Kenwood," January 9, 1954.

Chicago Daily Defender. "Interracial Schools Works In Atlanta: University System Shows It Can Be Done In Dixie," January 9, 1954.

Chicago Daily Defender. "Five Held In Trumbull Disturbance," January 9, 1954.

Chicago Daily Defender. "CHA Reaffirms Anti-Bias Policy, Asks Panel To Help Work It Out," January 16, 1954.

Chicago Daily Defender. "Ban School Jim Crow On Army Post," February 6, 1954.

Chicago Daily Defender. "Business League Studies Proposal To Drop 'Negro' From Its Name," October 23, 1954.

Chicago Daily Defender. "Racist Attacks Hit Englewood," May 1, 1954.

Chicago Daily Defender. "Violence Shocks W. Chesterfield," April 24, 1954.

Chicago Daily Defender. "Housing Industry Takes Wait, See Attitude On President's Proposal," January 30, 1954.

Chicago Daily Defender. "UNCF Hails School Decision As Major Step To Racist Equality," May 22, 1954.

Chicago Daily Defender. "10,000 Jam Till Mass Meet Here," by Robert L. Birchman.

Chicago Daily Defender. "Defender Puts Up $5,000 Reward For Till Killers," November 5, 1955.

Chicago Daily Defender. "U.S. Gets 3,000 Till Letters, But Can't Act," November 26, 1955.

Chicago Daily Defender. "World Awaits Verdict Of Till Kidnap Jury," by Lee Blackwell.

Chicago Daily Defender. "Senate May Hear Till Lynch Story," October 29, 1955.

Chicago Tribune. "Poitier's Legacy To His Family Breathes Life Into The Past," May 28, 1980.

Chicago Tribune, "School Count Shows Racial Picture and Class Size," by Clay Gowran, November 3, 1963.

Chicago Tribune. "Principals Bare Problems, Needs of City Schools," by Casey Banas, July 26, 1964.

Chicago Sun Times. "Conant Reverses Stand, Backs Integrated Schools," by Terry Ferrer, November 15, 1964.

Chicago Tribune. "Suburb School Pay Is Higher: Teachers Start Better, Gain Faster," by Casey Banas, October 25, 1964,

Chicago Daily News. "Slum Pupils: Accent On the Positive," by Lois Wille, November 4, 1964.

Chicago Daily News. "Study Reveals Some Shocking School Flaws," by Sylvia Porter, April 15, 1965.

Chicago Sun Times. "Blame Schools For Few Negroes In Medicine," by Frank Sullivan, October 5, 1965.

Chicago Sun Times. "Academic Lag Indicated At Negro High Schools," by Christopher Chandler, June 8, 1966.

Chicago Sun Times. "List Most-Crowded High Schools," by Christopher Chandler, March 15, 1966.

Chicago Sun Times. "What Hurts DuSable Pupils," October 22, 1966.

The New York Times. "Substitutes for Ph. D.," June 26, 1966.

The New York Times. "Noe 'Educational Parks,'" June 26, 1966.

Chicago Sun Times. "Increased Segregation Reported In City's Public Schools," September 27, 1966.

Chicago Daily Defender. "Charges HEW Is Abetting 'New Kind' of Racial Bias," March 6, 1972.

CHAPTER SIXTEEN

BOOKS

Anderson, Jervis. *A. Philip Randolph: A Biographic Portrait.* Harcourt, Brace, Jovanovich, Inc., New York, 1972.

Brown, Frank London. *Trumbull Park.* Regnery, Chicago, 1959.

McEntire, Davis. *Residence and Race.* University of California Press, 1960.

Rapkin, Chester and William G. Grigsby. *The Demand for Housing in Racially Mixed Areas.* University of California Press, Berkeley, 1960.

Reddick, L.D. *Crusader Without Violence: Biography of Martin Luther King Jr.* Harper & Bros., New York, 1959.

Robeson, Paul. *Here I Stand.* Beacon Press, Boston, Mass., 1958.

Wilson, James Q. *Negro Politics: The Search for Leadership.* The Free Press, Glencoe, Illinois, 1960.

Wilson, James Q., ed. *Urban Renewal: The Record and the Controversy.* The M.I.T. Press, Cambridge, Massachusetts, 1966.

NEWSPAPERS

Chicago Sun Times. "Catholic Weekly Hits Martin Luther King Ban," February 16, 1957.

Chicago Sun Times. "Desegregation Strife Boosts NAACP Fund Over $1 Million," January 8, 1957.

Chicago Sun Times. "WGN-TV Keeps Martin Luther King Film Ban," January 9, 1957.

Chicago Sun Times. "Warn Of A Trend To Negro 'Ghetto,'" by Ruth Moore, January 24, 1957.

Chicago Defender. "General Gruenther Says 'No' To Restrictive Covenant," by Ruth Montgomery, February 3, 1957.

Chicago Defender. "Ark. Guards Show Mettle Enforcing Integration," by Shelby Scates, October 3, 1957.

Chicago Defender. "Suspend 3 At Central High After Kicking Incident," October 5, 1957.

Chicago Defender. "All Quiet, Guards Gunless At Little Rock School," by John Barrow, October 22, 1957.

Chicago Defender. "Nab Adult Coed; Pupils Hang Effigy," by Shelby Scates, October 5, 1957.

Chicago Defender. "Travel Bias Foe Runs Into Some," October 5, 1957.

Chicago Defender. "Says U.C. Aim: Thin Out Negroes," January 19, 1957.

Chicago Defender. "N.Y. Ask AAA to Oust Chicago Auto Club For Bias," February 23, 1957.

Chicago Defender. "New Book Probes Status of Chicago's Negro Life," April 13, 1957.

Chicago Defender. "Housing Integration Issue Splits Hyde Park," by Mansfield Peters, January 26, 1957.

Chicago Defender. "Reveal Move To Segregate Vets," April 13, 1957.

Chicago Defender. "State Troops Guard 9 Pupils," October 1, 1957.

Chicago Defender. "Fear Exclusion Scheme In Rebuilding Of Hyde Park," October 19, 1957.

Chicago Defender. "Real Estate Insurance Good Career To Follow: Ability To Mix Plus Training Equals Goal," by Dempsey J. Travis, December 14, 1957.

Chicago American. "NAACP Sees Ike, Hits School Ruling," June 23, 1958.

Chicago American. "Negro Student Says They Want To Go Back," June 23, 1958.

Chicago American. "NAACP's 9-Point Rights Plan," June 23, 1958.

Chicago American. "Nations Eyes On Hyde Park Plan. Protests May Reshape Big Housing Program," June 24, 1958.

Chicago American. "NAACP Objects," June 24, 1958.

Chicago American. "Smooth Integration," June 24, 1958.

Chicago American. "College Integration 8 to 25 Years Away," June 19, 1958.

Chicago American. "U.S. Judge Puts Off Action For 21/2 Years," June 21, 1958.

Chicago American. "Negro Hits Race Bias In Chicago," by Les Brownlee, June 12, 1958.

Chicago American. "Minorities Urged To Unite," by Wesley South, June 19, 1958.

Chicago American. "More Fire Insurance For S. Side Urged," April 17, 1958.

Chicago Defender. "Threaten To Bomb Home Of Englewood Clergyman," October 21, 1958.

Chicago Daily Tribune. "Refuse to O.K. Insurance In Disputed Area," March 1, 1958.

Chicago Defender. "Friend's Suggestion Paid Off For Travis," February 22, 1958.

New Crusader. "Realtist Back Mayor's Slum Drive," February 22, 1958.

Chicago Defender, "Push Plan To Get Fire Insurance," July 26, 1958.

Chicago Defender. "Civic Leaders Seek Daley's Aid In Fight On Arsonists," July 30, 1958.

Chicago Defender. "Group Of Officers From Chicago Insurance Brokers Association Calls On Illinois Insurance Director Joseph S. Gerber," February 8, 1958.

Daily Defender. "Dearborn Real Estate Board Members Meeting With State Insurance Director Joseph S. Gerber," April 23, 1958.

Daily Defender. "Install Travis As Realty Head," February 22, 1958.

Chicago American. "South Side Plans Slum War Huddle," By Les Brownlee, February 7, 1958.

Chicago Defender. "Mass Meeting On Bias In Englewood," February 22, 1958.

Chicago American. "Mayor Daley Seeks Aid in War On Firetrap," January 31, 1958.

Chicago American. "Find Dixie-Style Terror In Englewood," May 23, 1958.

The New Crusader. "Dearborn Real Estate Board Refutes Charge," October 31, 1959.

Chicago Daily News. "Charges Race Bias In Fire Insurance," by Henry Hanson, March 25, 1959.

Chicago Defender. "In Chicago Racism Does Follow You To The Grave," by R. C. Keller, May 16, 1959.

Chicago Defender. "Insurance Conspiracy Against Negro Bared," by Simeon Osby, March 30, 1959.

Chicago Sun Times. "Sivart Corp. Become The First Negro-Owned Mortgage Comp," Real Estate News, June 30, 1961.

Chicago Daily News. "Realtist To Hear Author Frank London Brown," May 21, 1959. Real Estate News, May 15, 1959.

OFFICIAL DOCUMENTS

Statement of Dempsey J. Travis, President of the Dearborn Real Estate Board, Inc., before the President's Commission On Civil Rights, May 1959.

LETTERS

Letter From: A.L. Foster, Executive Director, Cosmopolitan Chamber of Commerce, To: Dempsey J. Travis, February 24, 1957.

Letter From: Edward J. Sparling, President, Roosevelt University, To: Dempsey J. Travis, February 25, 1957.

Letter From: Richard J. Daley To Dempsey J. Travis, May 1, 1957.

Letter From: Joseph L. O'Neal, President, Adams Oakley Property Improvement Association. To: Dempsey J. Travis—July 25, 1958 Re: Mass Meeting.

Letter From: Charles L. Warden, Secretary, National Society of Real Estate Appraiser's, Inc. To: Dempsey J. Travis July 25, 1958—Re: "Very Important Meeting"

Letter From: Dempsey J. Travis To: Richard J. Daley, July 26, 1958.—Re: Black Displacement as a Result of Highway Programs.

Letter From: Fred J. Smith, State Senator 11th District, General Assembly To: Dempsey J. Travis, March 25, 1959.

Letter To: Dempsey J. Travis, From: Commission on Civil Rights, Washington D.C., April 21, 1959.

Letter To: Dempsey J. Travis, From: James Q. Wilson, Instructor, The University of Chicago, September 24, 1959.

Telegram To Dempsey J. Travis From: Roy Wilkins, NAACP Executive Secretary, December 20, 1959.

CHAPTER SEVENTEEN

BOOKS

Bowly, Devereux, Jr. *The Poorhouse: Subsidized Housing in Chicago, 1895–1976*. Southern Illinois University Press, Carbondale, Illinois, 1978.

Handlin, Oscar. *Race and Nationality in American Life*. Little, Brown & Company, Toronto, 1957.

Lowe, Jeanne R. *Cities in a Race with Time*. Random House, New York, 1967.

McKay, David H. *Housing and Race in Industrial Society*. Croom Helm, London, 1977.

Meyerson, Martin and Edward C. Banfield. *Politics, Planning and the Public Interest*. The Free Press, New York, 1955.

Steiner, Oscar H. *Our Housing Jungle and Your Pocketbook*. University Publishers, Inc., New York, 1960.

Tebbel, Robert. *The Slum Makers*. The Dial Press, New York, 1963.

Young, Whitney M., Jr. *Beyond Racism*. McGraw-Hill Book Company, New York, 1969.

JOURNALS

"The Urban-Suburban Investment-Disinvestment Process: Consequences for Older Neighborhoods," by Calvin P. Bradford and Leonard S. Rubinowitz. *The Annals of the American Academy of Political and Social Sciences*, Vol. 422, (November, 1975), 77–96.

NEWSPAPERS

Chicago Sun Times. "Group To Fight Negroes Going To Park Forest," January 21, 1960.

Chicago Defender. "Pledges Fight For 'Fair Shake,'" April 9, 1960.

Chicago Defender. "Housing Authors NAACP Speakers," April 16, 1960.

Chicago Defender. "Delegates of The National Association of Real Estate Brokers Met With Norman P. Mason, United States Housing Administrator," April 30, 1960.

Chicago Defender. "Defy Racists At Park Swim Pool," July 30, 1960.

Chicago Defender. "Negro Family First In U.S.A. To Get New FHA Help," August 27, 1960.

Chicago Defender. "Dempsey Travis Out To Win 'Rights' Gain," July 23, 1960.

Chicago Daily News. "Mortgage Credit Refusals Squeeze Minorities Here: Loan Practices Force Them To Buy Homes On Contract," by Nicholas Shuman, June 25, 1961.

Chicago Daily News. "Negroes First Graduates of Mortgage Banking Class," June 17, 1963.

Chicago Daily News. "Negro Mortgage Firm Here Gets Eastern Funds," by Ralph Gray, August 26, 1963.

Atlanta Daily World. "Mortgage Bankers Get $40 Million For Housing," March 31, 1963.

Chicago Sun Times. "Banker Urges More Home Mortgage Loans To Negroes," August 27, 1963.

Chicago Defender. "Southside Realty Firm In $3 Million 'First,'" July 15, 1963.

Chicago Courier. "Integration 200 Years Away Without An Open Occupancy Law: Travis," August 10, 1963.

Chicago Sun Times. "Negroes Move Into 'Wealthiest' Suburb," by Ronald Berquist, December 7, 1963.

NEWS RELEASES

WBEE *Citizen Salute* to Dempsey J. Travis, dated April 11, 1963, re: remortgage funds available to Negro home buyers.

OFFICIAL DOCUMENTS

Housing Hearings Before The United States Commission On Civil Rights: May 5 and 6, 1959. U.S. Government Printing Office, Washington, D.C., 1959.

LETTERS/TELEGRAMS

Letter from E. J. Dee, Assistant Commissioner, Field Operations, Federal Housing Administration to Dempsey J. Travis, President, The Sivart Corporation.

Letter from Donald S. Prey of the United Citizens' Committee For Freedom of Residence In Illinois to Dempsey J. Travis, dated May 3, 1960, re: NAACP Conference.

Letter from Rogers, Rogers, Strayhorn & Harth, Attorneys at Law to Dempsey J. Travis, re: discriminatory practices of the 50th On The Lake Motel and The Thunderbird Motel.

Letter from (Rev.) Theodore M. Hesburgh, C.S.C., President, University of Notre Dame to Dempsey J. Travis, dated March 10, 1960, re: NAACP Installation.

Telegram from Roy Wilkins to Dempsey J. Travis dated February 5, 1960, re: lobby for passage of civil rights legislation.

Telegram from President Richard M. Nixon to Dempsey J. Travis dated March 2, 1960, re: 1960 Freedom Fund Dinner.

Telegram from Roy Wilkins to Dempsey J. Travis dated April 28, 1960, re: State Conference Presidents and key NAACP leaders.

Letter from Mayor Richard J. Daley to Dempsey J. Travis dated February 29, 1960, re: Nonpartisan police board.

Letter from Jerome M. Sax, Executive Vice President, The Exchange National Bank of Chicago to Dempsey J. Travis dated July 14, 1960, re: Sivart Mortgage Corporation.

CHAPTER EIGHTEEN

BOOKS

Allen, Robert L. *Black Awakening in Capitalist America.* Doubleday & Co., Garden City, New York, 1969.

Chrisman, Robert and Nathan Hare. *Contemporary Black Thought: The Best from the Black Scholar.* The Bobbs-Merrill Company, Inc., New York, 1973.

Haddad, William F. and G. Douglas Pugh, Editors. *Black Economic Development.* Prentice-Hall, Inc., Englewood Cliffs, New Jersey, 1969.

Lecky, Robert S. and H. Elliott Wright, Editors. *Black Manifesto: Religion, Racism, and Reparations.* Sheed and Ward, New York, 1969.

Ofari, Earl. *The Myth of Black Capitalism.* Monthly Review Press, New York, 1970.

Reynolds, Barbara A. *Jesse Jackson: The Man, The Movement, The Myth*. Nelson-Hall, Chicago, 1975.

Sternbieb, George and James W. Hughes. *America's Housing Prospects and Problems*. Rutgers University Center for Urban Policy Research, New Brunswick, New Jersey, 1980.

DIRECTORIES AND REFERENCES

Ebony Pictorial History of Black America, Vol. 3. Editors of Ebony, Johnson Publishing Company, Chicago, 1970.

NEWSPAPERS

Chicago Sun Times. "Rights Groups Build Up To Massive Action," by Basil Talbott, Jr., July 10, 1966.

Chicago Sun Times. "King, Daley to Meet Monday, Discuss Rights Demands," by Basil Talbott, Jr., July 9, 1966.

Chicago Sun Times. "Cicero Leaders Hail Guard Call-Up," by Cecil Neth, August 25, 1966.

Chicago Sun Times. "W. Side Erupts In New Violence," July 15, 1966.

Chicago Sun Times. "Human Relations Unit Begins Probe of Realty Companies," by Robert S. Kleckner, August 5, 1966.

Chicago Sun Times. "37 Hurt As Mob Attacks Gage Park Rights Marchers," August 1, 1966.

Chicago Sun Times. "Experts Predicts No Early End To Negro Ghettos," by Ruth Moore, August 21, 1966.

Chicago Sun Times. "Open Housing Proposals Ready," by Basil Talbott, Jr., August 26, 1966.

Chicago Sun Times. "Court Acts Against Tavern Refusing To Service Negro G.I.," August 19, 1966.

Chicago Sun Times. "Sue 10 Maywood Aides In Sale of Home To Negroes," July 9, 1966.

Chicago Sun Times. "King Schedules March Into South Deering Today," by Art Petacque, August 21, 1966.

Chicago Sun Times. "President Signs Bill; Fair Housing Law Of The Land," by Tom Littlewood, April 12, 1968.

Chicago Sun Times. "$100,000 In Mortgage Funds Available To Contract Buyers," June 19, 1970.

Chicago Defender. "Dempsey Travis And C.B.L. Officers Discuss Victory On 'For Blacks Only'," July 11–17, 1970.

Chicago Defender. "Travis to D.C.: C.B.L. Okays Mortgage Plan," April 14, 1970.

Chicago Tribune. "Story of One Man's Fight to Aid Contract Buyers," by Arthur Siddon, August 16, 1970.

Chicago Daily News. "$100,000 Relief: CBL Getting Second Break In Two Weeks," by Betty Washington, June 19, 1970.

Chatham Citizen. "Travis Seeks U.S. Mortgage Aid: New Plan May Save CBL From Questionable Pact," by Gus Savage, Week of April 15, 1970.

Sun Times. "Daley Tells Terms of Pact To End CBL Evictions," by Thomas M. Gray, April 11, 1970.

Sun Times. "Urge Blacks: Learn Finance Expertise," October 9, 1970.

American Banker. "Black Mortgage Banker Voices Pessimism About Institutionalized Racism," by William Zimmerman, July 21, 1970.

Chicago Defender. "Blacks Trapped In Housing Fight," by Robert McClory, March 7, 1972.

Chicago Defender. "Denounce Racism In HUD, FHA," February 16, 1972.

New York Times. "HUD Criticized On Housing Curbs In Minority Areas of Cities," by John Herbers, April 18, 1972.

Sun Times. "Black Urges 'Urban Homestead Act'," by Grayson Mitchell, April 8, 1972.

Boston Evening Globe. "Black Caucus At Harvard: Suburban Housing Not Answer," by John Abbott, April 7, 1972.

New York Times. "Black Mortgage Bankers Discuss Problems," by Robert D. Hershey, Jr., February 11, 1972.

Sun Times. "Site Rules Hit In Housing Poor," by Philip Greer, February 11, 1972.

Chicago Tribune. "HUD Site Criteria Assailed," by Joseph Egelhof, February 11, 1972.

Chicago Tribune. "Between the Lines of HUD's New Plan," by Vernon Jarrett, February 6, 1972.

American Banker. "HUD's New Site Selection Criteria Attacked by Leading Black Banker," by Harry F. Wille, February 18, 1972.

The Washington Post. "Subsidized Housing Rules Hit," by Philip Greer, February 13, 1972.

PERIODICALS

Jet. "New HUD Regulations Hurt Urban Blacks," March 2, 1972.

LETTERS

Letter from Dempsey J. Travis, President, United Mortgage Bankers of America, to Senator Charles H. Percy dated September 6, 1967, re: mortgage capital gap in the central cities.

Letter from Senator Charles H. Percy to Dempsey J. Travis dated September 1, 1967 re: proposals to advance the opportunities for home ownership.

CHAPTER NINETEEN

BOOKS

Allen, Robert L. *Black Awakening in Capitalist America: An Analytic History*. Doubleday & Company, Inc., New York, 1969.

Baily, J. Edward III. *Living Legends in Black*. Baily Publishing Company, Detroit, 1976.

Brink, William and Louis Harris. *The Negro Revolution in America*. Simon and Schuster, New York, 1964.

Burrell, Berkley. *Getting It Together*. Harcourt, Brace and Jovanovich, New York, 1971.

Gloster, Jesse E. *Economics Of Minority Groups*. Premier Printing Company, Houston, Texas, 1973.

A Summary Report of the Forum—What Our National Priorities Should Be, April 5, 6, 7, 1972. Harvard University, Cambridge, Massachusetts, 1972.

Travis, Dempsey, J. *Don't Stop Me Now*. Children's Press, 1970.

DIRECTORIES AND REFERENCES

Rather, Ernest R., ed. *Chicago Negro Almanac and Reference Book*. Chicago Negro Almanac Publishing Company, Inc., Chicago, 1972.

The Ebony Success Library, Vol. 1: 1,000 Successful Blacks. Editors of Ebony Magazine, Johnson Publishing Company, Inc., Chicago, 1973.

The Ebony Success Library, Vol. 2: Famous Blacks Give Secrets of Success. Editors of Ebony Magazine, Johnson Publishing Company, Inc., Chicago, 1973.

PERIODICALS

Chicago Reporter. "Black Enterprise List Reveals Chicago Top Black Business Gross Up $5.47 Million," August, 1976.

Dollars & Sense. "Black Chicago: Three Score Plus One," Twelve consecutive installments, June, 1979–May, 1981.

The Bankers Magazine. "Banks, Business, and the Black Community," by Dempsey J. Travis, Spring, 1969.

Real Estate Review. "An Autopsy Of The Ghetto," by Dempsey J. Travis, Winter, 1972.

Savings Bank Journal. "Opportunity Or Detour," by Dempsey J. Travis, May, 1972.

Risk Management Magazine. "Ghetto Investment: A Good Investment," by Dempsey J. Travis, June–July, 1972.

The Black Scholar. "Black Businesses: Obstacles To Their Success," by Dempsey J. Travis, 1973.

The Black Scholar. "Barrier To Black Power In The American Economy," by Dempsey J. Travis, October, 1971.

The Black Scholar. "The 1980 Homestead Act," by Dempsey J. Travis, November–December, 1979.

Jet. "Need Not Be 'Tom' To Be Accepted, Says Realtor, April 7, 1966.

Business Week. "Negro Business Feels Stresses of Success," April 9, 1966.

Ebony. "Negro Pioneers In Mortgage Banking," July, 1967.

Ebony. "Don't Buy Other Peoples Paint," February, 1976.

NEWSPAPERS

Chicago Sun Times. "Why Two Rich Blacks Prefer South Side Life," by Quid a Lindsey, May 15, 1977.

The Atlanta Constitution. "Chicago: U.S. Black Business Mecca," April 9, 1980.

Chicago Daily News. "Union to Lend $7.6 Million for Low-Cost Negro Homes," by Robert M. Lewin, July 30, 1965.

The New York Times. "Union allots aid for Negro homes: $7.6 Million being lent by garment workers here," July 30, 1965.

Chicago Defender. "Travis Realty to Sell 70 Markham Homes," Week of August 28–September 3, 1965.

The Courier. "Exclusive Sales Agency Awarded to Travis Realty," August 28, 1965.

LETTERS

Letter from Gaylord A. Freeman, Jr. Vice Chairman of the Board, The First National Bank of Chicago to Dempsey J. Travis dated May 21, 1964. Re: Invitation to join Chicago Urban League Business Advisory Council.

Letter from Otto Kerner, Governor of Illinois to Dempsey J. Travis dated November 2, 1964. Re: Thank you for support.

Letter from Jacqueline Kennedy to Dempsey Travis dated September 4, 1964. Re: Contribution to John F. Kennedy Library.